A DEED SO ACCURSED

THE AMERICAN SOUTH SERIES

Elizabeth R. Varon, Editor

A Deed So Accursed

LYNCHING
IN MISSISSIPPI AND
SOUTH CAROLINA,
1881–1940

Terence Finnegan

UNIVERSITY OF VIRGINIA PRESS | CHARLOTTESVILLE AND LONDON

University of Virginia Press

Printed in the United States of America on acid-free paper

First published 2013

1 3 5 7 9 8 6 4 2

Library of Congress Cataloging-in-Publication Data
Finnegan, Terence, 1961–
A deed so accursed : lynching in Mississippi and South Carolina, 1881–1940 / Terence Finnegan.
p. cm.—(The American South series)
Includes bibliographical references and index.
ISBN 978-0-8139-3384-9 (cloth : alk. paper)
ISBN 978-0-8139-3385-6 (e-book)
1. Lynching—South Carolina—History—19th century.
2. Lynching—South Carolina—History—20th century.
3. Lynching—Mississippi—History—19th century. 4. Lynching—Mississippi—History—20th century. I. Title.
HV6465.S6F56 2013
364.1'34—dc23 2012029593

To Lori Jeanne

CONTENTS

ACKNOWLEDGMENTS

I could not have completed this work without the expert advice and assistance of many archivists and librarians who are too numerous to name individually. I benefited greatly from the assistance of the archival staff at the National Archives, College Park, Maryland; the Mississippi Department of Archives and History, Jackson; and the South Carolina Department of Archives and History, Columbia. Librarians at the University of Illinois Library, Urbana; the Cheng Library at William Paterson University, Wayne, New Jersey; and the Skillman Library at Lafayette College, Easton, Pennsylvania, were especially helpful in locating both primary and secondary source materials. Professor Orville Vernon Burton, who was my mentor at the University of Illinois, helped me persevere and was a continual source of inspiration and assistance. Richard Holway, my editor at the University of Virginia Press, demonstrated remarkable patience and provided perceptive suggestions to improve the manuscript. I wish to express my thanks and gratitude for the innumerable insightful criticisms that I received from historians and scholars who understand the past far better than I do. During the early stages of this research, I received a generous dissertation grant from the Harry Frank Guggenheim Foundation, without which I never would have begun the many years of work that it took to complete this book.

My parents, John and Charmaine Finnegan, inspired in me a love for history and for truth that motivated me to write this book. It could not have been written, however, without the love and support of Clare, James, Mary, John, Lucille, Margaret, Joseph, Thomas, and Hanora, and, most of all, Lori Jeanne, to whom it is dedicated.

PORTIONS OF chapters 2 and 4 were published previously as "Lynching in the Outer Coastal Plain Region of South Carolina and the Origins of African American Collective Action, 1901–1910" in *Toward the Meeting of the Waters: Currents in the Civil Rights Movement of South Carolina During the Twentieth Century,* ed. Winfred B. Moore and Orville Vernon Burton (Columbia: University of South Carolina Press, 2008), 41–49; "The Equal of Some White Men and the Superior of Others" in *Men and Violence: Gender, Honor, and Rituals in Modern Europe and America,* ed. Pieter Spierenburg (Columbus: Ohio State University Press, 1998), 240–54; and "Who Were the Victims of Lynching?: Evidence from Mississippi and South Carolina" in *Varieties of Southern History: New Essays on a Region and its People,* ed. Bruce Clayton and John Salmond (Westport, Ct.: Greenwood Press, 1996), 79–95.

CHAPTER 3 was published in an earlier version as "Lynching and Political Power in Mississippi and South Carolina" in *Under Sentence of Death: Essays on Lynching in the South,* ed. W. Fitzhugh Brundage (Chapel Hill: University of North Carolina Press, 1997), 189–218, and is republished with permission.

A DEED SO ACCURSED

Introduction

> The distressing circumstances in this revival of lynch law in different parts of the South is, that it shows that prejudice and hatred have increased in bitterness with the increasing interval between the time of slavery and now. I have been frequently asked to explain this phase of our national problem. . . . The resistance met by the negro is to me evidence that he is making progress. . . . The negro meets no resistance when on a downward course. It is only when he rises in wealth, intelligence, and manly character that he brings upon himself the heavy hand of persecution.
>
> FREDERICK DOUGLASS

> There is little difference between the Ante-bellum South and the New South. Her white citizens are wedded to any method however revolting, any measure however extreme, for the subjugation of the young manhood of the race. They have cheated him out of his ballot, deprived him of civil rights or redress therefor in the civil courts, robbed him of the fruits of his labor, and are still murdering, burning, and lynching him.
>
> IDA B. WELLS-BARNETT

At Gettysburg, Abraham Lincoln expressed hope that the unprecedented bloodshed of the Civil War would result in a "new birth of freedom" for the American nation, but in the aftermath of the war, white and black southerners engaged in a relentless cycle of violence over whether or not African Americans would be accorded the full benefits of citizenship. Reactionary whites violently ended the experiment of Reconstruction in order to restore their political and social hegemony, but racial conflict intensified, and the abomination of lynching became so widespread that prescient African American reformers wondered if southern society could endure much longer. Frederick Douglass attributed the vicious rise in lynching to the material and social progress that African Americans had made since the end of the war. Similarly, Ida B. Wells-Barnett regarded lynching as a form of terrorism that southern whites inflicted on the "peoplehood," humanity, and economic security of African Americans.[1] Wells-Barnett traced the origins of lynching directly to emancipation, which she claimed had engendered countless "acts of conscienceless outlawry" among whites. During slavery, the economic value of an enslaved person had, according to Wells-Barnett, constrained the violent tendencies of whites who merely scourged rather than killed their bondsmen, but emancipation had unleashed "a new system of intimidation" that allowed whites to kill African Americans with "absolute impunity."[2]

After the end of the Civil War, many whites considered the expectations of African Americans for social equality as a "crime against nature" and regarded male-headed African American households as a threat to both their "sense of order" and "their rightful control of property."[3] When Reconstruction ended, whites attempted to obliterate the desire of African Americans for civil equality and economic independence through concerted violence directed primarily against African American males. Whites who resorted to extralegal violence did so because it abrogated the legitimacy of the law that had conferred political and civil rights on freedmen and because they hoped to elicit communal sanction for the violent repudiation of the rights of African Americans.

During Reconstruction, the Ku Klux Klan had attempted to characterize some of its murderous activities as lynching, which most whites at that time regarded as the "apolitical punishment of crime." But with the exception of the South Carolina backcountry, the Klan never convinced a broad spectrum of the white community that terroristic violence was a legitimate expression of communal values.[4] After the end of Reconstruction, however, elements of the white community, especially landowners, embraced lynching as a legitimate means to thwart the continued quest of African Americans for political and civil rights.[5] Only after African Americans had been expelled from the polity and whites had solidified into a racial bloc, however, did it become possible for some whites to justify widespread lynching as the will of the community. The stereotype of the fearsome "black beast rapist" emerged after the dissonant voices of African Americans had been purged from the political process, which enabled whites to justify the gratuitous violence of lynching as an evil necessary to combat a crime that ostensibly was too horrible to endure.[6] Many whites could not conceive of a social order that tolerated African American independence and autonomy, and lynching enabled whites to dispel their anxieties and fears in a cauldron of bloodshed that they hoped would restore order and security to southern society.[7]

But African Americans never relented in their quest for equality and autonomy. Lynching did not result in a racial rapprochement that was predicated upon African American "inferiority" because African Americans refused to accept the terms.[8] Lynching could eliminate individual opposition to white dominance, but it could never resolve the fundamental contradiction between African American freedom and racial subordination. Indeed, many whites recognized that the "law could never be made oppressive enough to effectively control African Americans," which was why some elements of the white community embraced extralegal violence.[9] The vitriol with which some southern whites practiced and defended lynching was barbaric and depraved, but it was consonant with white intransigence toward the civil and political rights of African Americans. The bloody spectacle of lynching inspired many whites to embrace a culture of whiteness that was predicated upon the violent repudiation of black equality.[10]

Although lynching emanated from the economic and social advances that African Americans made after the Civil War, the violent manifestations of the doctrine of white supremacy occurred unevenly throughout the South.[11] Southern whites resorted to racial violence in an attempt to eviscerate the desire of African Americans for social and political equality, but the communal and economic tensions that incited racial conflict were more apparent in some regions of the South than in others, which is why lynching ebbed and flowed over time and place.[12]

In some respects, Mississippi and South Carolina were quite similar during the lynching era, but the two states had dramatically different experiences of interracial violence. Both states lay within the Deep South cotton belt, which was dominated by black tenant agriculture, and both states had roughly the same proportion of African American population. From 1880 to 1940, Mississippi had a mean percentage of black population of 55.1, while the corresponding figure for South Carolina was 53.4. White residents from both states, moreover, enthusiastically supported racial demagogues for statewide political offices. James Kimble Vardaman and Theodore Bilbo from Mississippi and Benjamin Ryan Tillman and Coleman Blease from South Carolina were all virulent racists who served as state governors and United States senators.[13]

In terms of lynching, however, Mississippi and South Carolina were almost at opposite ends of the southern spectrum. From 1881 to 1940, Mississippi had more lynching incidents, 572, than any other state, while South Carolina ranked eighth of eleven former Confederate states with 178 lynching incidents.[14] The lynching necrology upon which this study is based was constructed from extant lynching inventories, such as those compiled by the *Chicago Tribune,* the National Association for the Advancement of Colored People (NAACP), and the Tuskegee Institute.[15] Although some antilynching activists and organizations went to great lengths to confirm the veracity of a reputed lynching incident, the actual number of lynching victims from any given region or state will never be known with certainty. In some parts of the South, lynching occurred so frequently and elicited so little interest from taciturn local officials that the fate of some victims was known only to the mobs who killed them. Although southern newspapers showed no reticence when reporting on lynching, reporters and editors certainly did not receive information about every lynching or perhaps overlooked lynchings that occurred in remote areas and garnered little or no attention from authorities or the local population. Nevertheless, most scholars have assumed that extant necrologies compiled from public sources, such as newspapers and coroner's records, are indicative of the overall level of lynching activity over time.[16]

The respective lynching records of Mississippi and South Carolina are summarized in figures 1 and 2, which show that although the temporal pattern of lynching was similar in the two states, the level of lynching activity was much greater in Mississippi than in South Carolina. From

FIGURE 1. Lynching incidents and executions in Mississippi, 1881–1940 (five-year moving average)

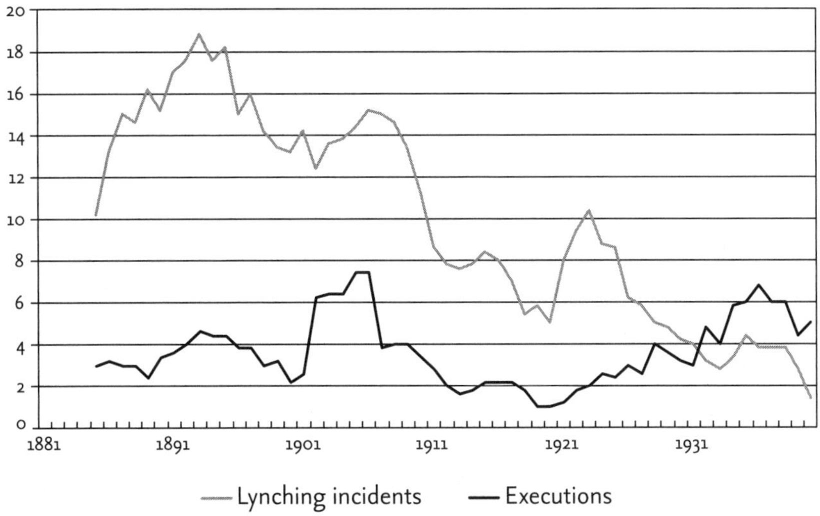

FIGURE 2. Lynching incidents and executions in South Carolina, 1881–1940 (five-year moving average)

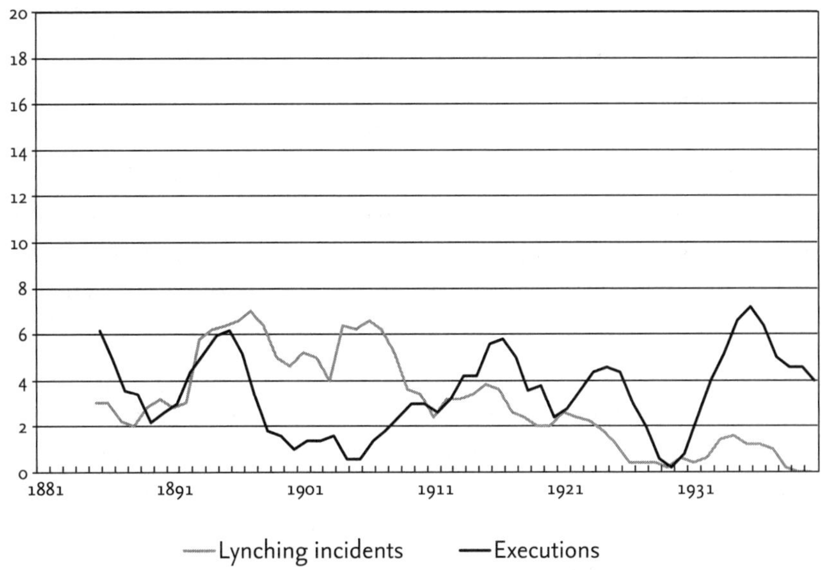

1881 to 1940, the black population of South Carolina was approximately 90 percent of that of Mississippi, but Mississippi endured more than three times as many lynching incidents as did South Carolina. Even after adjusting for differences in African American population, Mississippi had 270 percent more lynchings than did South Carolina.[17]

In both states, lynching apparently was worst in the 1890s (at least in terms of the number of lynching incidents) and declined continuously thereafter. The main difference was that Mississippi experienced more of its lynching incidents after 1920 than did South Carolina (16.1 percent in Mississippi compared to only 8.4 percent in South Carolina). Most historians consider the 1890s as the nadir of southern race relations because during this decade lynching reached epidemic proportions.[18] But the typical explanations concerning the causes of lynching—such as the exploitive nature of the cotton economy; the weakness of southern public institutions; the backward, boring, and repressive aspects of southern agrarian life; the devastating impact of the depression of the 1890s; the fear among whites of black sexual crime; the desire among lower-class whites to preserve their superior caste position in regard to African Americans; and the need to protect and preserve traditional white male values and conventions—do not explain why lynching occurred so much more frequently in Mississippi than in South Carolina.[19]

The lynching plague in South Carolina was neither as intense nor as protracted as in Mississippi.[20] In South Carolina, lynching incidents equaled or exceeded ten per year only three times during the sixty-year period; Mississippi, in contrast, had twenty-seven years with ten or more lynching incidents (see figs. 1 and 2). The worst lynching years in South Carolina stretched from the late 1880s to approximately 1905, an eighteen-year period during which lynching incidents averaged nearly six per year. In Mississippi, intense lynching activity began in the early 1880s and lasted until 1908, spanning more than a quarter century in which lynching incidents averaged fifteen per year. South Carolina experienced a brief resurgence of lynching activity during the Blease years, from 1911 to 1915, and then again after World War I, from 1919 to 1921. Thereafter the state was free from lynching for fourteen of the next nineteen years, with no lynching at all after 1934. Mississippi, on the other hand, had two secondary lynching periods. The first began in 1912 and lasted until 1923, during which time lynching incidents averaged around eight per year. A second, less bloody era spanned the years 1924 to 1938, when Mississippi experienced almost four lynching incidents per year.

The baneful lynching record of Mississippi stemmed from the dense concentrations of African Americans in some regions of the state and the exploitive nature of the postbellum economy, which fomented racial acrimony between black and white males. The material desires of peripatetic African Americans conflicted with those of white landlords and employers, which made some regions of Mississippi mordant cauldrons of racial antagonism. In parts of Mississippi, a pervasive fear of black violence and resistance existed among whites that infected other regions and made lynching a more lethal contagion in Mississippi than in South Carolina.

Although whites in South Carolina deemed "subordination in all things as the natural condition of the negro," demographic, economic, and political conditions in South Carolina insulated some African Americans from racial conflict and attenuated the desire of whites to resort to the rope and faggot.[21] Whites in South Carolina utilized judicial proceedings more often than lynching to deter blacks from resorting to violence against whites. The militant actions of African Americans in South Carolina, moreover, were an impediment to extralegal violence, especially in the lowcountry regions, which had large black majorities.[22] South Carolina blacks, through their collective action, political organization, and out-migration, dampened the fervor of whites for lynching.

Scholars have established a close correlation between the social and economic realities associated with cotton-based tenant agriculture and lynching activity. In Georgia, for instance, according to William Fitzhugh Brundage, lynching was most common in "those regions where plantation agriculture and the racial line separating white landlords and black laborers were most pronounced."[23] In Louisiana, Michael Pfeifer finds, mob killing was concentrated in northern cotton-belt regions and grew out of racial tensions that "underlay exploitative arrangements in the rural cotton economy, domestic service, and the credit-based mercantile system."[24] In most of the South, Stewart Tolnay and E. M. Beck claim, "black lynching victims were almost twice as likely to be from cotton-dominated areas than those less dedicated to cotton production."[25] And in the Deep South, in particular, J. William Harris asserts, the Mississippi Delta "was a far more dangerous place for blacks than the Sea Island region, with the eastern Piedmont in between."[26]

Lynching was most intense in regions such as the Yazoo Delta in Mississippi and the Western Piedmont in South Carolina, where cotton production was the center of economic activity and where black tenancy rates were high.[27] Much of Mississippi, however, was developed after the Civil War, which fostered social conditions more fluid than those in South Carolina. The relatively unsettled nature of race relations in Mississippi, in combination with the dense concentrations of African Americans who lived in some regions of the state, produced an onslaught of lynching that did not occur in South Carolina.

Lynching was worst in regions of Mississippi and South Carolina where African Americans frequently challenged the racial hegemony of white landlords or employers. If a region had a dynamic and fluid African American population that was not amenable to traditional methods of racial control, then lynching was more evident. Lynching happened less frequently in regions where whites utilized more "civilized" methods of social control, such as legal execution, to subjugate blacks. South Carolina had a more benign lynching record than did Mississippi in part because whites in South Carolina legally executed more African Americans than whites did in Mississippi. The legal system in Mississippi was more antagonistic to the due process rights of African Americans than in South Carolina, and consequently, lynching occurred more frequently in Mississippi than in South Carolina.[28]

Lynching in predominantly African American regions was directly related to the incessant conflict between white landlords and black tenants. Where this conflict was most intense, white males were often the "victims" of alleged crimes that precipitated a lynching. Where the personal security of white males was more at risk, lynching was more common. The Yazoo Delta of Mississippi, for example, became the worst lynching region in the United States largely because the economic and social aspirations of black tenants conflicted with the labor requirements of white cotton planters. As the economic predicament of African American tenants in the Delta grew worse, however, the nature of lynching changed. Lynching became less frequent and more stereotypical, and lynching in retaliation for alleged rape took on greater prominence in the Delta. The catalyst for most lynchings in predominantly black regions, however, was the desire of African Americans to maintain a modicum of freedom and autonomy even as they resisted the daily indignities of white racism.

Changes in social organization also had a discernible impact on lynching. In the Old Natchez region of Mississippi, for example, the transition from sharecropping to a fixed-rent tenant system precipitated a dramatic increase in lynching. Cash or fixed-rent tenants had more freedom from white supervision than did sharecroppers, and whites reacted violently to this development. In the Upper Piedmont of South Carolina, on the other hand, the segregated nature of the textile industry removed black and white laborers from direct competition with one another, which lessened the need for lynching.

Lynching also had a political dimension that did not end with Reconstruction. The level of lynching activity in regions of Mississippi and South Carolina was related to the strength or weakness of African American political organizations, especially the Republican Party. The psychological, social, economic, and political elements of white racism merged in lynching, which dehumanized African American males so that whites could justify disfranchisement. Consequently, whites lynched African Americans more frequently for alleged sexual crimes before disfranchisement than afterward. Widespread paranoia among whites concerning black sexual predators developed alongside disfranchisement and apparently inverted the racial fears that spawned from lynching.

Although lynching victims came from all segments of society, certain types of people suffered more than others. In the predominantly rural states of Mississippi and South Carolina, racial conflict was most prevalent in the landlord-tenant relationship; hence the majority of black lynching victims were agricultural workers. In fact, most lynchings stemmed from interpersonal conflicts between people who knew and worked with one another. In cotton-producing regions, for example, lynching had a distinctive seasonal component that ebbed and flowed with the labor demands of cotton cultivation. When a black worker got the better of a dispute with his white employer, whites sometimes responded with lynching in the hope of eliminating future affronts to white dominance.

Racial stereotypes were also an important determinant of lynching behavior. The isolated and unsavory working conditions of many itinerant African American laborers, for example, invoked suspicion and fear among the white population. Consequently, whites lynched African Americans who were not farmworkers for alleged sexual crimes more frequently than they lynched agricultural laborers. African Americans who achieved success in southern society were also the target of lynch mobs. Landowners and professionals were lynched for maintaining their dignity in spite of white harassment and violence or simply because the success of an African American affronted some whites. Occasionally, whites lynched black women, often with untamed brutality, to reinforce the notion that the entire African American community could be held accountable for any black person who resisted racial oppression.

Not all lynching, however, was directly attributable to communal notions of white supremacy. Many mobs lynched more for private than communal motives, which explains why mobs varied greatly in size, organization, behavior, and purpose. Lynching in retaliation for alleged murder and attempted murder or alleged sexual assault garnered the most community support and therefore the largest mobs. Private, secretive mobs, on the other hand, tended to lynch in retaliation for less serious crimes, such as assault, theft, or arson. The size of mobs varied not only with the alleged crime but also with the region. Where African Americans were more independent, better organized politically and socially, and more active in resistance to white aggression, lynch mobs were smaller. In cotton-producing regions, however, mobs were smaller primarily because planters were averse to involving the larger community in resolving labor conflict on plantations. Conversely, in the Piney Woods of Mississippi, the presence of itinerant black lumber workers encouraged the formation of larger mobs in response to phobias about

African American sexual predators. Larger mobs were common during the early twentieth century, when whites attempted to justify the imposition of racial segregation and used lynching to build communal solidarity around the concept of race. In general, where lynching was frequent, mobs were more daring, tenacious, and brutal.

In some places, however, lynching could divide whites more than it united them, and divisions within the white community affected mob size and function. Terroristic mobs of "whitecappers," for instance, operated in the southern regions of Mississippi and not only snuffed out the lives of black tenants, but also destroyed the property of white landlords. Whitecapping stemmed from competition between black and white farmers and from the frustration that disfranchisement engendered among lower-class whites. White businessmen and landlords actively opposed whitecappers, however, and these mobs usually were smaller than other lynch mobs that elicited more communal support.

The question remains as to why the river regions of Mississippi were so much more violent than the Piedmont regions of South Carolina. The larger African American population in the Mississippi River regions explains some of the difference, but even after adjusting for population, the Mississippi River regions were significantly more violent than the South Carolina Piedmont.[29] Part of the explanation is that white South Carolinians had so thoroughly terrorized the Piedmont during Reconstruction that race relations assumed a more compliant tone in the Piedmont than in the Delta. The Piedmont regions of South Carolina experienced widespread Reconstruction violence that had no parallel in a region like the Yazoo Delta, which remained largely unsettled until the 1880s. Much of this Reconstruction violence grew out of political and economic developments, especially grievances over land tenure, that only later came to the fore in a region such as the Yazoo Delta.[30] White South Carolinians, moreover, were more receptive than white Mississippians to using legal executions as a means of resolving real or imagined offenses against white sensibilities and order. This pattern began in antebellum times and continued throughout the late nineteenth and early twentieth centuries.[31]

Although South Carolina mobs could be as vicious as any in Mississippi, white Mississippians resorted to extralegal violence more often than white South Carolinians because race relations in Mississippi were more contentious than in South Carolina. The frontier-like conditions that existed in regions such as the Piney Woods or the Yazoo Delta required massive influxes of black laborers to clear land and harvest timber. To attract laborers, Delta planters promoted an idyllic vision of the Delta as a land of material prosperity and racial harmony. Initially, African Americans found this propaganda alluring, but they quickly realized that their desire for material prosperity and racial equanimity was incompatible with the requirements of large-scale plantation agriculture, which necessitated a subservient and quiescent caste of laborers.

Although whites attempted to forge a culture of whiteness out of the unremitting violence of lynching, African Americans never capitulated to the terror that whites inflicted. The opposition of African Americans to lynching was vigorous and sustained. African Americans responded to lynching with violence, work stoppages, economic boycotts, political gatherings, increased voter registration, criminal and civil court proceedings, and mass migration from regions that experienced frequent lynching. Most significantly, African Americans who lived through the terror of lynching never relinquished their quest for personal autonomy and freedom despite the continual efforts of some whites to suppress the desire of blacks for equality with violence. After Reconstruction, blacks in Mississippi and South Carolina vigorously contested the boundaries of freedom, which elicited an onslaught of brutality from whites in defense of white supremacy. From the wanton tragedy of lynching emerged the triumph of the modern civil rights movement, which emanated from the courage and perseverance of African Americans who dared to defy the violent depredations of whites.

1

"Strictly a White Man's Country, with a White Man's Civilization"

LYNCHING IN MISSISSIPPI

On the afternoon of 26 June 1919, several thousand Mississippians from around Ellisville in Jones County watched eagerly as a mob hanged John Hartfield from a tree near the same spot where Hartfield allegedly had raped a white telegraph operator a week and a half earlier. Although Hartfield had been mortally wounded during an intensive, ten-day manhunt, a mob hanged him and then inflicted further vengeance on his corpse, which was mutilated with gunshots and burned. After the ghoulish spectacle concluded, onlookers retrieved "souvenirs" from Hartfield's charred remains.[1] After the lynching, a story circulated among whites that Hartfield had been hanged from the same sycamore tree that Confederate troops had used to execute three insurgents in 1863.[2] During the Civil War, Ellisville had been part of the so-called "Free State of Jones," which had been a bastion of Confederate dissidents. Many whites from this section of Mississippi's Piney Woods had an ingrained fear of interracial contact and cooperation that was reminiscent of attitudes that had been common during Reconstruction, and some whites deftly utilized the "rhetoric of rape" to suppress both class and racial discord.[3]

John Hartfield, however, did not fit the stereotypical profile of a menacing rapist. Hartfield was a middle-aged porter who worked at a hotel in nearby Laurel. Whites claimed that Hartfield had raped eighteen-year-old Ruth Meeks after the two of them had disembarked from a trolley in Ellisville on Sunday evening, 15 June 1919. Some African Americans, however, claimed that Meeks was much older than whites acknowledged (in fact, she was in her mid-twenties) and that Hartfield and Meeks had been on intimate terms for years.[4] Whatever the truth of the matter, whites conceded that social changes that had coincided with World War I had heightened anxiety about the proper place of African Americans in southern society and had contributed to the lynching.

The Mississippi governor Theodore Bilbo, for instance, noted that "the attempt of the negro race to seek social and political equality" had increased after African American soldiers had returned from France, where Bilbo claimed that a "certain class of white women" had granted African American soldiers an inappropriate "social reception and familiarity." Although Bilbo claimed that whites deplored lynching, he insisted that racial tensions had been exacerbated by the opinions of northern African Americans, many of whom viewed intermarriage as "the only solution to the race problem." Bilbo declared bluntly that Mississippi was "strictly a white man's country, with a white man's civilization" and that the dreams of blacks "to share social and political equality will be shattered in the end." Lynching would cease, Bilbo claimed, when a "right conception of the proper relation that must exist between the races" was restored and when white and black southerners were "left alone . . . to solve their own problems." The *Jackson Clarion-Ledger* affirmed the governor's observations and claimed that lynching would remain a problem "so long as busy-bodies, who know nothing of conditions south of the Mason and Dixon line attempt to regulate our affairs and preach social equality to the negro."[5] Both Governor Bilbo and the *Clarion-Ledger* attempted to project blame for racial violence on outsiders who supposedly did not understand southern society. In reality, however, the prospect of equality between white and black Mississippians generated profound anxiety and discord in the local population that often manifested itself in violence and lynching.

White Mississippians had not always been so pessimistic about the prospects of race relations in their state. After the Civil War, whites had been eager to develop the fertile soils and abundant natural resources of the state and sought the assistance of African American farmers and laborers. The rich lands of the Yazoo Delta, for example, could not be utilized for cotton production until a reliable system of levees had been constructed for flood control, a process that took twenty or more years after the end of the Civil War.[6] In the latter part of the nineteenth century, newspapers routinely published stories about the mass exodus of African Americans from older regions of the South to parts of Mississippi, such as the Yazoo Delta, which white planters portrayed as a land of opportunity. In March 1890, for instance, stories circulated from New Orleans that Delta planters wanted to attract one hundred thousand African Americans and had "actually given homes to over thirty thousand within a year." The planters' "war cry" of "We want more niggers!" supposedly had put a "new face on the race question."[7]

Many Delta planters believed that the region had transcended the racial tensions that had plagued other parts of the South since the end of the Civil War. James S. Richardson, for instance, who was ostensibly the "largest planter in the world," depended heavily upon black tenants to cultivate 20,000 acres of cotton on his enormous 50,000-acre plantation. Richardson bragged that the huge influx of African Americans to the Delta resulted from a skillful publicity campaign engineered by Delta planters and agents of the Louisville, New Orleans, and Texas Railroad. When asked about race problems that had prompted blacks to flee to the Delta from other parts of the South, Richardson acknowledged that "anything which scares the negro from any other section of the country or will enable the agents to induce him to leave other States is a great help to us here."[8]

Richardson claimed that Delta planters had welcomed destitute African Americans from the worn-out lands of the South and had opened "to them a land of plenty." "We give them a whitewashed house with glass windows," Richardson boasted, "something they never had before, rent free; also wood, water and an acre of land. Most of them have their own cows, calves, mares and poultry." The economic opportunities in the Delta had already made the Carolinas "white states," Richardson claimed, and Delta planters still wanted more African American laborers. "We want an abundance of labor to make it dependent on the planter," Richardson said. Planters preferred blacks to whites because they could pay blacks less and blacks supposedly were more tractable than whites. White laborers, in Richardson's opinion, were "not adapted to the soil and we do not care for them." African American laborers, on the other hand, "when by themselves, make no trouble." Richardson boasted that blacks in the Delta were "healthy, prosperous, and contented." He claimed that Delta blacks had the "best schools" and that every plantation had one. Richardson confidently proclaimed that Delta planters would welcome African Americans laborers from any other state because "there is no race question where negroes have plenty to do, to eat and to wear."[9]

Richardson's hollow racial propaganda notwithstanding, it took more than slick publicity to attract tens of thousands of African Americans from other parts of the South to the Delta. In the late nineteenth century, the Delta offered some blacks the opportunity for genuine economic advancement. For a brief period in the late 1880s, for example, railroads eagerly sold uncleared land to African Americans at reasonable prices. The task of preparing land for cultivation was so enormous that many planters offered tenants three years' free use of any land that they cleared. The cash earned from timber sales allowed many African American tenants to purchase land, and as late as 1920, the majority of farm owners in the Delta were black. African Americans owned no plantations, but their farms averaged around 130 acres.

The increase in cotton prices after the turn of the century and the appearance of the boll weevil in 1908, however, severely limited economic opportunities for blacks. Higher cotton prices caused land values in the Delta to skyrocket, which effectively closed the door to landowning for many black farmers. The devastation of the boll weevil caused many landowners to lose their holdings and prompted black renters to opt for sharecropping in order to transfer more risk to landowners. By 1910, the majority of African American farmers in the Delta had become sharecroppers.[10]

Despite claims that the "race question" did not exist in the promised land of the Delta, the economic striving of African Americans resulted in racial tensions that often culminated in lynching. In the summer of 1889, for instance, trouble broke out on the 18,000-acre plantation of Captain

John Willis in Sharkey County when two discontented tenants murdered the plantation manager. A family of "mulattos" named Perkins, who had worked on the plantation for about two years, allegedly planned the murder of the plantation manager, A. B. Pitts, and assaulted his assistant named Rogers. Pitts, who belonged to a well-connected family from Alabama, had come to the Delta eight years earlier and had brought some two hundred blacks with him. On the day that Pitts was killed, he had supposedly tried to mediate a dispute between Rogers and two of the Perkins men, whom Rogers recently had forced to return to work on the plantation. A pervasive fear existed among Delta planters about tenant discontent and its potential negative economic consequences. "It is pretty well understood," claimed one observer, "that peace, at almost any price, is the motto on most large plantations where a disturbance is liable to cause the people to leave, to the great loss of the proprietors."

When violence did occur, however, planters could respond with fury, especially when African Americans committed an egregious transgression against white dominance. In the case of the murder of Pitts, not only did the black men kill the plantation manager with his own gun, but the black women continued to beat the manager's assistant long after the men had fled. Fifteen persons had supposedly participated in the attack, which prompted Captain Willis to organize a massive search for the perpetrators and to offer rewards ranging from $100 to $250. Search parties came from all over the rail line and teams of bloodhounds assisted. Less than two days later, two black men and two black women had reportedly been lynched. Those suspected of having actually committed the murder, however, apparently managed to escape into Arkansas. But whites refused to give up the chase and were still pursuing the suspects nearly three weeks after the murder of the plantation manager.[11]

A similar incident, which began when a black tenant violently attacked a white planter, resulted in one of the most heinous lynchings that ever occurred in the Delta or anywhere else. The trouble happened in February 1904 on the Eastland plantation near Doddsville, Sunflower County, when the longtime tenant Luther Holbert killed his employer, James Eastland. Holbert was not the archetypal "bad nigger" who inspired paranoia among whites who rationalized lynching. On the contrary, in 1852 Holbert had been born in slavery and had worked for the Eastland family for decades.[12] Holbert had come to Doddsville in 1888 to help the Eastlands clear the land that they had recently purchased for cotton farming.[13] Holbert had four children with his wife, Annie, whom he had married in 1884. Holbert also had a mistress, with whom he had at least one other child, and Eastland apparently decided to admonish Holbert about his lack of moral rectitude, which had angered another tenant. The twenty-one-year-old Eastland, however, did not handle the situation with sensitivity and brashly barged into a cabin where Holbert was visiting and ordered him to leave the plantation.[14] An argument then ensued in which Eastland killed a black tenant named Winters, and Holbert shot a bullet through Eastland's forehead (Holbert's neighbor, John Carr, was also killed in the fracas). Luther and Annie Holbert then fled the plantation for their lives. The couple was captured after a four-county chase in which two other blacks were shot because one of them resembled Holbert and refused to surrender when a posse ordered them to do so.

Upon their return to Doddsville, the Holberts were viciously tortured and then burned at the stake before approximately one thousand people.[15] Although Governor Vardaman reportedly dispatched troops to prevent the lynching, nothing could stop the mob, which chopped off the Holberts' ears and fingers and distributed them to onlookers. Luther Holbert was severely beaten, his skull fractured, and one of his eyes gouged out. Mob members also sadistically tortured the Holberts with a corkscrew. The descent into depravity occurred not in defense of white "womanhood" but because Holbert had resisted the violent intimidation of a white planter. The *Chicago Broadax* compared the lynching to a pogrom and said that it "reminds us of the Irishman who wanted to kill every black whiskered man he came in contact with for no other reason than he heard that several thousand years ago a Jew with black whiskers turned against his Jesus for 30 pieces of silver."[16] The anti-Vardaman *Vicksburg Herald* strongly condemned the heinous killing of the Holberts, and attributed the lynching to "savage degenerates" who had committed a "a deed so accursed of the laws of God and the instincts born in man, that every preacher in the land, every paper in the state, every one of its public bodies and officials should cry out upon the blood guilty men who have shamed them all."[17]

The Eastland case became a cause célèbre when Mississippi authorities brought a murder indictment against Woods Caperton Eastland, the brother of the deceased planter, who had unashamedly led the mob in its brutal work. For his defense, Eastland enlisted the aid of U.S. senator Anselm J. McLaurin, who endorsed lynching as "the only reasonable atonement for murders and assaults in the South." On the day that Eastland was acquitted, large crowds gathered outside the courthouse and cheered.[18] The memory of the Holbert lynching would reverberate for the next sixty years, and during the 1960s, civil rights activists who worked in Sunflower County feared for their safety after dark.[19]

The ever-present specter of planter-tenant discord often made it difficult for white authorities to resolve racial tensions through legal channels, especially when the court system appeared to grant procedural fairness to African Americans. In October 1925, for example, five black men were accused of robbing and mortally wounding Grover Nicholas, a plantation manager who was the adopted son of a prominent Delta planter named James Traynham. The five defendants included John Fischer, who reportedly had the mental capacity of a ten-year-old and was eventually executed for his part in the slaying; Raeford Leonard, whom Fischer claimed had struck the mortal blow and who received a life sentence for the murder; Smith Bunns, a teenager who was found dead in his cell with a broken neck that authorities blamed on an epileptic seizure; Albert Hobbs, a former preacher who turned state's evidence against the other defendants and was eventually released; and Lindsey Coleman, a tenant farmer who lived with Raeford Leonard and was lynched within thirty minutes of being acquitted of the murder of Nicholas.[20]

The trials of Coleman and the other defendants were racially charged from the outset. The lead defense attorney was Colonel Thomas S. Ward, a prominent lawyer from Canton, Mississippi, who was also the Grand Dragon of the Mississippi Ku Klux Klan. The presiding judge, William Alcorn, called a special term of court in order to try the accused in an expeditious manner and prevent a lynching. Alcorn told Ward that he was also willing to grant the defendants a change of venue and that he would ask the governor to call out the state militia if Ward thought that such measures were necessary to protect his clients. The defense planned to challenge the alleged confessions of Fischer and Leonard, claiming that the men had been tortured. Although the testimony of Hobbs undercut the defense, Coleman had several white witnesses who not only testified to his good character but also provided him with an alibi at the time of the murder. Although the case against Coleman was weak, few people expected an acquittal. When Coleman stood to hear Judge Alcorn read the verdict of the twelve white jury members, however, the judge incredulously declared Coleman "not guilty."

Immediately after Alcorn had read the verdict, the courtroom began to buzz with excitement. Ward feared for Coleman's safety and excitedly asked Alcorn for protection for his client. Before the judge could act on the request, however, Ward inexplicably fled from the courtroom with Coleman. As Ward and Coleman left the Coahoma County Courthouse in Clarksdale, two white men intervened and threw Coleman into a car with ten or fifteen men surrounding it. Although the Clarksdale sheriff witnessed the abduction, he did not pursue the lynchers. Later, Coleman's body was found on the outskirts of town with twenty-six bullet holes in it.

The audacious murder of Coleman was an affront even to the Mississippi criminal justice system, and four white men were eventually indicted for Coleman's murder, including James Traynham; Thomas Nicholas, who was the brother of the murdered plantation manager; Gold O. Cane, a coworker of Nicholas; and H. S. Blockley, a photographer from Clarksdale who was married to Nicholas's niece. The Clarksdale sheriff was also indicted for failing to perform his duty in connection with Coleman's lynching. In return for his testimony against the alleged lynchers, however, the sheriff was fined five hundred dollars for a lesser charge and the case against him was dropped.[21] The testimony of the sheriff notwithstanding, all of the accused were acquitted.

The loathsome lynching of Coleman, however, had unprecedented repercussions in the white community. Some whites blanched at the brutality of Coleman's murder and strongly condemned lynching. Mrs.

Minnie Brewer, who was president of the Coahoma County League of Women Voters and the wife of former Mississippi governor Earl Brewer, for example, characterized the lynching as "high-handed murder." Governor Henry Whitfield and numerous other state officials signed a pamphlet that denounced lynching.[22] The intense controversy surrounding the Coleman lynching took an emotional toll on Thomas Ward, who suffered a nervous breakdown and resigned his position as leader of the Mississippi Klan.[23]

The conflicting aspirations of white planters and black laborers coupled with white fear of black violence made lynching a dismal feature of Delta life well into the twentieth century. Not until the 1930s did lynching decline significantly in the Delta.[24] By then the African American percentage of the population in the region had fallen from an all-time high of nearly 84 percent in 1900 to slightly more than 73 percent in 1930. Although African Americans continued to migrate to the region, many only stayed temporarily, and instead chose to settle permanently in the more enticing and hospitable atmosphere of cities such as St. Louis, Chicago, and Detroit.[25]

As the economic prospects of African Americans in the Delta changed, so too did the nature of lynching. Before the turn of the twentieth century, the most common alleged cause of lynching was murder-related crimes that involved attacks on white men. After 1900, however, alleged crimes against women became a more frequent pretext for lynching, increasing from a low of approximately 12 percent during the 1890s to a high of approximately 29 percent during the 1930s. When the economic position of African Americans deteriorated, Delta whites lynched African Americans less frequently but for more stereotypical reasons. As tensions between planters and black laborers waned, the bogeyman of the black rapist apparently reaffirmed the continued need for lynching.[26]

The second-worst lynching region in Mississippi was the old cotton kingdom of the Natchez District in the southwest portion of the state (see map 1). Before the Civil War, the Old Natchez region had been the center of plantation agriculture in Mississippi. Consequently, the transition from slavery to a tenant-based agricultural system proved particularly unsettling. Desiring freedom in their daily lives, African Americans in the Old Natchez region rejected the wage labor system that planters preferred in favor of sharecropping. In the aftermath of the war, African Americans in the Natchez region challenged planters' attempts to control their labor and their lives by moving frequently, pilfering crops, and by setting their own work schedules or by not working at all. Although sharecropping left most African Americans impoverished and dependent upon landlords and merchants, it helped preserve the integrity and independence of black families, no small achievement in light of all the forces working against them.[27]

During the last two decades of the nineteenth century, the Old Natchez region experienced more lynching incidents than any other region in Mississippi. The worst decade for lynching in the Old Natchez region was the 1890s, when the transition from sharecropping to fixed-rent agriculture was in full swing. The decline in cotton prices at the end of the century encouraged merchants and landlords to switch to cash or fixed-rent tenants as a means of maximizing income. Black tenants had greater autonomy than did sharecroppers, although the debt that many tenants owed on tools and animals often lessened the difference.[28] Lynching activity peaked at a time when African Americans had become more independent of whites than in the past and when white landlords and merchants experienced prolonged economic distress.[29]

The decline of lynching activity in the Old Natchez region coincided with the arrival of the boll weevil in 1908. The devastating effect of the boll weevil on the cotton crop encouraged whites to diversify their crops, which lessened the need for African American labor. The boll-weevil infestation prompted a mass exodus of blacks from the region, many of whom migrated, at least temporarily, to the Yazoo Delta.[30] From 1910 to 1930, the African American population of the Old Natchez region declined nearly 10 percent. As blacks left the region with the approval of whites, racial tension decreased. In the thirty years after 1910, the Old Natchez region experienced only about 17 percent of its total lynching incidents, the smallest percentage of any region in the state.

The white region in Mississippi that had the most lynching incidents was the Red Hills, which occupied the east central portion of the state. The Red Hills was on the edge of the pine-lumber belt, and farmers from

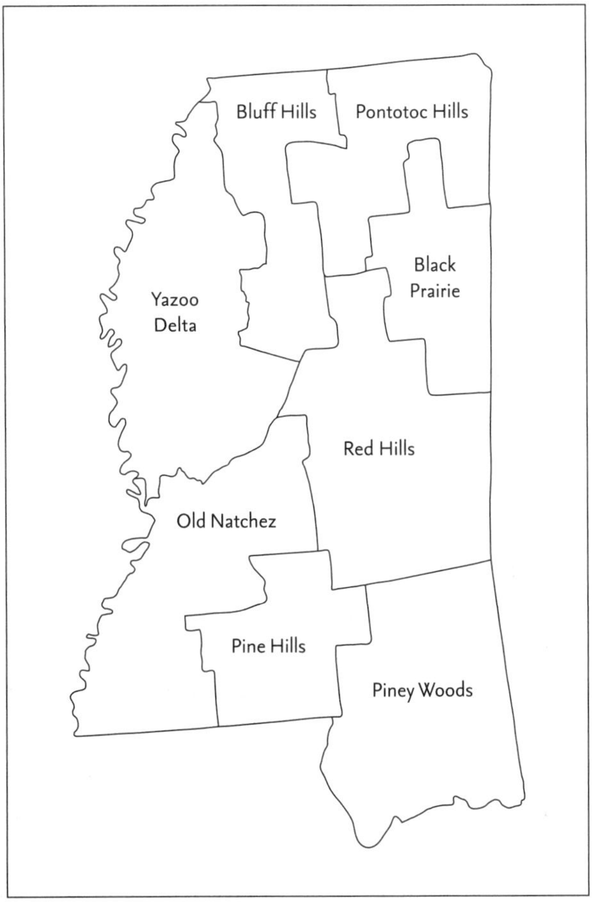

MAP 1. Mississippi regions

the Red Hills tended to be self-sufficient cotton growers who also harvested some forest products. During Reconstruction, the Red Hills had been a hotbed of Ku Klux Klan activity. Much of the violence during Reconstruction was centered on the Lauderdale County rail hub of Meridian, which eventually became known as "bloody Lauderdale." In March 1871, white supremacists broke up a Republican rally at Meridian, and two black Republican leaders were arrested for inciting mob violence. A riot broke out at the court hearing two days later, which prompted the Klan to bring in reinforcements from as far away as Alabama. Over the next several days, Klansmen terrorized the African American population, killing as many as thirty blacks. No one was ever indicted for the murders, although a white man from Alabama was convicted of raping a black woman during the riot.[31]

Lynching incidents in the Red Hills deviated from the pattern found in other predominantly white regions. Crimes against male victims as an alleged cause of lynching, for instance, exceeded crimes against female victims by 25 percent. Sexual and other alleged crimes against females were noticeably fewer in the Red Hills (24.4 percent) as compared to other white regions as a whole (33.1 percent). Assaults and property crimes, conversely, were more frequently cited as alleged causes of lynching in the Red Hills than in other white regions.

The Red Hills Reconstruction tradition of violence and lawlessness extended into the late nineteenth and early twentieth centuries and contributed to the region's unenviable lynching record.[32] Not all such violence was confined to African Americans, however, as the Red Hills claimed more than one-third of the white lynching victims in Mississippi.[33] Whites lynched F. M. B. Cook, for instance, who was a former white Republican candidate for Congress, after Cook made inflammatory statements about African American suffrage. Cook's lynching was not unexpected since his opinions had been so obnoxious that "white people for some time . . . [had] apprehended that trouble might follow."[34] Although the *Jackson Clarion-Ledger* regretted Cook's violent demise, the paper commented that "the people of Jasper are to be congratulated that they will not be further annoyed by Marsh Cook."[35]

Mobs from the Red Hills also lynched whites whose actions did not directly threaten perceived notions of white supremacy. In late November 1892, for example, a family of white outlaws named Tolbert wreaked havoc in Kemper County, which prompted a mob to lynch the father of the clan. After the other Tolberts had been either captured or killed, local sympathizers assassinated a white man who reportedly had revealed the hiding place of the outlaws.[36] About a decade later another "celebrated character," a suspected child murderer named William McAlpin, met his demise at the hands of mob from Smith County.[37]

Whites from the Red Hills apparently regarded lynching as the right of an "enraged populace" and refused to convict mob members who had been indicted for murder.[38] This permissive attitude sometimes led to wanton violence that no governmental authority could control. The Kemper County town of Wahalak, for instance, was a distribution center for black farmers in the region and had been the scene of repeated race riots since the Civil War. One riot that occurred in the early 1890s resulted in scores of African Americans being killed. About twelve years later, another riot resulted in a fire that destroyed much of Wahalak, which was afterward only partially rebuilt.[39]

In late December 1906, a racial conflict occurred on a train near Wahalak and resulted in at least six African Americans being lynched. A group of African Americans on a Mobile and Ohio passenger train allegedly attacked a white conductor, who retaliated and wounded a black man named Tom Simpson and killed an innocent bystander, who was also black. Although Tom Simpson fled the train for a friend's house, a local constable named O'Brien gave pursuit. When Constable O'Brien and another officer attempted to arrest Simpson, Simpson fired a shotgun blast at O'Brien that tore off the top of his head. The other officer tried to shoot Simpson, but when his gun misfired, Simpson escaped. A posse of whites captured Simpson and returned him to Wahalak, where blacks from the surrounding area had gathered for their traditional Christmas trading. Simpson somehow escaped again, perhaps with the help of some of the African Americans who had come to town. Whites then requested that Governor Vardaman dispatch the militia, which left from Meridian around 10:00 p.m. and upon arrival, found the situation calm.

On Christmas Day, however, violence broke out anew. At Crawford, which was one station north of Wahalak, rail workers stopped a troop train to check a "hot box" (an overheated axle). One of the conductors on the train was Robert Harrison, who a few days earlier had stabbed a black brakeman named Longstreet. While Harrison inspected the train, four of Longstreet's brothers appeared and shot Harrison. The Noxubee Rifles then opened fire and killed one of the Longstreet brothers, but the other three escaped. News of the white conductor's murder enraged local residents, who joined members of the militia in "nigger baiting."

Whites killed at least two other African Americans and burned the homes of several black families. The militia commander tried to quell the bloodshed by forbidding whites to ride in the woods, but more than a dozen African Americans probably were killed.

Meanwhile at Wahalak, whites singled out a prominent black family for persecution. A sheriff's posse invaded the house of Calvin Nicholson, one of the wealthiest African American farmers in the area, and shot Nicholson when he resisted. The deputy sheriff in charge at first protected Nicholson from further harm, but when three of the posse decided that Nicholson should be lynched, they overpowered the deputy, shot Nicholson, and then burned his corpse and his home. Nicholson's wife and ten children apparently escaped unharmed. The same day, whites from around Wahalak lynched Isham McNeis for an undetermined reason.

The day after Christmas, Governor Vardaman came to Scooba, which was about seven miles from Wahalak, to assume command of the militia. By this time, scores of African Americans had fled to Scooba and sought the protection of troops. Vardaman tried to calm the situation and offered a $250 reward for each of the three white men accused of killing Nicholson and a $350 reward for the capture of Tom Simpson (the black man accused of killing Constable O'Brien). Vardaman's actions drew criticism from the Scooba mayor, R. M. Quarles, however, who believed that the presence of troops had made the tension worse. Quarles claimed that the arrival of the militia precipitated a drinking binge among local whites, which exacerbated the racial antipathies. When Vardaman declared that it was "whiskey-soaked" and drug-addicted African Americans who needed to be controlled, Quarles countered that blacks in Scooba were law-abiding and that drunken whites had behaved despicably.[40]

Since Reconstruction, whites from the Red Hills had regularly resorted to collective violence in response to perceived threats from African Americans, and the desire to quash the aspirations of African Americans helped make the Red Hills the worst predominantly white region for lynching in Mississippi. Not surprisingly, the Red Hills experienced the state's last recorded lynching, the 1964 murders of civil-rights activists Andrew Goodman, Mickey Schwerner, and James Chaney, which resulted in the conviction of seven defendants on federal charges.[41]

To the north of the Red Hills were the fourth- and fifth-worst lynching regions in Mississippi, the Bluff Hills region (sixty lynching incidents) and the Black Prairie region (fifty-five lynching incidents). The Black Prairie region had been one of the state's richest cotton-producing areas, but after the arrival of the boll weevil in 1908, farmers diversified and supplemented cotton production with legumes and dairy farming.[42] The Bluff Hills, conversely, remained wedded to the cotton economy, but eventually soil erosion severely curtailed production. Both regions had majority black populations throughout the entire period. As late as 1910, the Black Prairie was still more than 60 percent black in population, but by 1940, African Americans constituted only a slight majority in the region (51.3 percent). In the Bluff Hills, the African American population declined less noticeably, from a high of about 64 percent in 1910 to a low of about 60 percent in 1940. The more diverse agricultural economy of the Black Prairie made its farmers better off than those in the Bluff Hills. From 1900 to 1940, an average of 15.3 percent of all African American farmers in the Black Prairie owned some land, while the corresponding figure for the Bluff Hills was only 12.6 percent.

Lynching in the Black Prairie remained at a more or less constant level, about twelve per decade, from the 1880s through the 1910s. After African Americans began leaving the region in droves, however, lynching declined precipitously, to about five per decade after 1920. In the Bluff Hills, the worst decade for lynching was the 1880s; thereafter lynching declined each decade until leveling off at about five per decade after 1910. The Bluff Hills had a few more lynching incidents than did the Black Prairie region, and not surprisingly, a greater percentage of alleged crime victims were male in the Bluff Hills than in the Black Prairie. These two regions were similar in many ways, however, especially in terms of demography and agricultural production, and so were their lynching records. In terms of lynching incidents and executions combined, the two regions had almost exactly similar experiences of racial repression (see table 1).

TABLE 1. Lynching incidents and executions in Mississippi by region, 1881–1940

Region	Lynching incidents	Executions	Mean percent black	Mean percentage of total Mississippi black population	Percentage of all Mississippi lynching incidents	Percentage of all Mississippi executions
Pontotoc Tennessee Hills	24	12	24.5	4.4	4.2	5.6
Piney Woods	54	15	29.3	4.2	9.4	7.0
Red Hills	76	21	38.9	10.5	13.3	9.8
Pine Hills	50	13	41.5	5.2	8.7	6.0
Black Prairie	55	21	61.5	12.4	9.6	9.8
Bluff Hills	60	17	62.0	12.1	10.5	7.9
Old Natchez	105	53	66.9	21.9	18.4	24.7
Yazoo Delta	148	63	80	29.2	25.9	29.3

Two predominantly white regions with similar lynching records were the Pine Hills and Piney Woods regions in the southern portion of the state. The Piney Woods had fifty-four lynching incidents from 1881 to 1940, while the Pine Hills had fifty. In terms of population, the Pine Hills had a larger percentage of African Americans, averaging 40 percent black over the period, while the Piney Woods averaged less than 30 percent African American. In per-capita terms, the Piney Woods and Pine Hills were the two worst lynching regions in Mississippi. Over the sixty-year period, the Piney Woods had 12 lynching incidents per 10,000 black population, while the Pine Hills had 9.2 lynching incidents per 10,000 black population. The violence that plagued these regions resulted mainly from the animosity that some whites felt toward independent African American farmers and the anxiety (especially in the Piney Woods) that itinerant African American laborers elicited in the minds of many whites.

The Pine Hills was one of the most diverse agricultural regions in Mississippi. In the late nineteenth century, prescient farmers realized that the thin topsoil in the Pine Hills was ideal for growing vegetables; hence even after the arrival of the boll weevil, many Pine Hills farmers continued to prosper.[43] Piney Woods farmers did not grow much cotton either, but instead focused on forest products, dairy production, and fruit or vegetable farming.

The poor soils found in both regions made them havens for African American landownership.[44] From 1900 to 1940, an average of 61 percent of all black farmers in the Piney Woods owned land; the corresponding figure for the Pine Hills was 40.2 percent. Although the Piney Woods was the only Mississippi region in which African American farm ownership exceeded half of all black farmers, the large number of black landowners in the Pine Hills made it the leading region in terms of the percentage of all farmers who were African American landowners (from 1900 to 1940, black landowners averaged 16 percent of all farmers in the Pine Hills and 10.9 percent of all farmers in the Piney Woods).

Forty-four percent of the lynching incidents in the Pine Hills occurred during the 1890s (the highest figure for any Mississippi region during any decade). The large number of African American farm owners in the Pine Hills caused an epidemic of "whitecapping."[45] Whitecappers usually were white farmers who were struggling economically and either killed or terrorized blacks in an attempt to force them from their lands. Competition from African American farmers coupled with resentment toward the disfranchising measures of the 1890 Mississippi constitution, which had affected not only blacks but also poor whites, made whitecapping the leading cause of lynching in the Pine Hills during the 1890s. After the state prosecuted some whitecappers, however, lynching declined significantly during the first decade of the twentieth century and practically had ceased by the late 1920s.

The worst decade for lynching in the Piney Woods was from 1901 through 1910, when a huge lumber boom began in earnest. The early 1890s saw unprecedented railroad expansion in the Piney Woods. With Hattiesburg as a focal point, railroads penetrated every part of the pine forest, bringing timber to the gulf ports of Pascagoula and Gulfport.[46] During the early years of the twentieth century, a severe labor shortage forced employers to adopt draconian measures to ensure a stable workforce. Taking a cue from agriculture, lumber firms often imposed a system of debt peonage upon employees that prevented workers from leaving. If a worker attempted to flee without paying a debt, "the hue and cry was out for him and he was returned regardless of the distance."[47]

While toiling in the lumber or turpentine camps of the Piney Woods, workers were at the mercy of their overseer, who could possess "the powers of life and death." Similar to Delta planters, most employers in the Piney Woods considered themselves accountable to no one in their meting out "justice" to black workers. Harsh discipline often resulted in the death of an African American worker, which often "went almost unnoticed" by the authorities. Some operators showed so little regard for the lives of black workers that the local African American population referred to some camps as "graveyards," and rumors were widespread that workers often "disappeared and were never seen again."[48]

Tensions between blacks and whites were high during the lumber period and often resulted in lynching. In the summer of 1921, for example, a white timber contractor attempted to assault a black girl, but a black turpentine worker named John Gray intervened. After Gray was arrested for wounding the contractor, a mob of enraged whites took Gray from the custody of law officers and shot him to death.[49] By the late 1920s, however, most of the accessible timber in the Piney Woods had been cut, and lumber mills moved their operations to other states. The end of widespread timber harvesting marked the end of widespread lynching in the Piney Woods.

The region with the fewest lynching incidents in Mississippi was the Pontotoc Tennessee Hills in the northeastern corner of the state. Only twenty-four lynching incidents occurred in the Pontotoc Tennessee Hills from 1880 to 1940, less than half the total of any other region in Mississippi. The Pontotoc Tennessee Hills had the highest percentage white population of any region in the state, averaging over 76 percent white during the sixty-year period. The relatively benign lynching record of the Pontotoc Tennessee Hills turns on its head the 1930s generalization about African Americans being "statistically safer" in black rather than white regions.[50]

Lynching in the Pontotoc Tennessee Hills frequently resulted from alleged attacks on white women. Only one lynching in the region resulted from an alleged property crime, which was unusual even for a white region. The paranoia surrounding the figure of the "black beast rapist" was perhaps strongest in a heavily white region like the Pontotoc Tennessee Hills, where racist stereotypes rather than personal experience informed many whites' perceptions of African Americans.

In the Pontotoc Tennessee Hills, the cry of rape had a power unparalleled in any other Mississippi region. In September 1925, for instance, whites accused a black timber cutter named L. Q. Ivy of raping the daughter of a white farmer named Bob Gaines. The circumstances surrounding Ivy's execution contained all the elements of an archetypal lynching. After the news of the alleged attack spread, bloodhounds were brought to the scene, and the dogs led the mob to a spot where some African American men had been cutting timber. After Ivy's arrest, officers took him to a New Albany hospital so that the victim could identify him. Although the young woman thought that Ivy looked like her attacker, she admitted that she was not sure if Ivy was the culprit.

Despite the woman's uncertainty, a mob was eager to lynch Ivy. U.S.

senator Hubert Stephens, a native of New Albany, tried to persuade the lynchers to disperse, but his pleas elicited contempt from the mob. "The boys didn't like for him to butt in," declared an irate mob member. "Go on home yourself," Stephens was told; "When we want your advice we'll ask for it." When officers took Ivy from New Albany to Aberdeen for safe-keeping, a mob informed Sheriff Johnny Roberts that he had would have to relinquish Ivy or face the consequences. Roberts told the mob that Ivy would be at the hospital in the morning where the young woman would again try to identify him. "If you let me get him in jail and locked up and then overpower me and get him," offered Roberts, "I can't help it."

When Roberts attempted to drive Ivy to New Albany, a car chase ensued. Mob members had barricaded all the roads outside of town, and Roberts claimed that the mob "forced" him to relinquish Ivy. The mob then took Ivy to a deserted barn in Rocky Ford, where they hanged him from a rafter and tortured him with fire and knives. Throughout the ordeal, Ivy continued to maintain his innocence. After the torture, a mob of some four hundred brought Ivy to the alleged crime scene and prepared to burn him. The lynching took place near a small sawmill, where the mob built a pyre while spectators stood on a huge pile of sawdust. Before Ivy was burned, he bowed his head and prayed. Ivy then confessed that he was the lone assailant, probably because he wanted to spare three other African American men who were being held in connection with the attack. As the flames engulfed him, Ivy made a last desperate plea for mercy and struggled to break loose from his chains. As the smell of burning flesh filled the air, Ivy finally succumbed. The crowd stood quietly for a while, mesmerized as the flames danced in the night. Soon the stench grew more powerful, however, and a dozen men piled more wood on the pyre to finish the grisly task. After the burning, many of the spectators walked nonchalantly away, and some mentioned that they would have to go New Albany to eat since the large crowd had bought all the available food in Rocky Ford.

After the ghastly lynching, rumors circulated that Governor Henry Whitefield might launch an investigation. When a mob member was asked if he was worried, he defiantly declared that "not an officer in Union

County or any of the neighbor counties will point out any member of the mob." Any officer who dared arrest a member of the mob faced dire consequences. "The best thing for him [the officer] to do," the lyncher warned, "would be to jump into an airplane headed for Germany." Most whites condoned the lynching of Ivy, and the unrepentant mob member bragged that even if the state arrested someone for the murder, "there'd be a million dollars ready in a few minutes to go his bond."[51] Throughout the sixty-year period under study, mobs in Mississippi acted with almost complete impunity, and only one out of twenty lynching incidents resulted in an arrest.

Uncomfortable with anything that suggested civil equality between the races, white Mississippians were reluctant to use the courts to resolve interracial conflicts, and every region in Mississippi had nearly double (or more) the number of lynchings as executions. In terms of the number of lynching incidents, lynching was worst in Mississippi's Yazoo Delta and the Old Natchez regions, both of which were heavily black, cotton plantation regions in the western part of the state. From a statistical vantage point, however, African Americans were "safest" in majority black regions and more vulnerable to mob vengeance in the three majority white regions in the southeastern part of the state (see table 1).[52] The daily tension that existed between black tenants and white landlords made lynching a frequent occurrence in majority African American regions in Mississippi. White males resorted to lynching not primarily to preserve and protect the virtue of their wives or daughters, but more frequently and more directly to defend the honor, property, and lives of white men. Race conflicts in which white males were the perceived victim were more acrimonious than those that involved white females, at least as far as lynching was concerned. Forty percent of all lynching in Mississippi resulted from alleged murders or attempted murders (see fig. 3), and more than 80 percent of the time the victim was male. Where the personal security of white males was at greater risk, lynching was more common.[53] Lynching in Mississippi, as the *Vicksburg Herald* admitted, stemmed from deep-seated "race antipathies" that inspired some whites to commit crimes that were "too monstrous for defense

FIGURE 3. Alleged crimes of black lynching victims in Mississippi (percent)

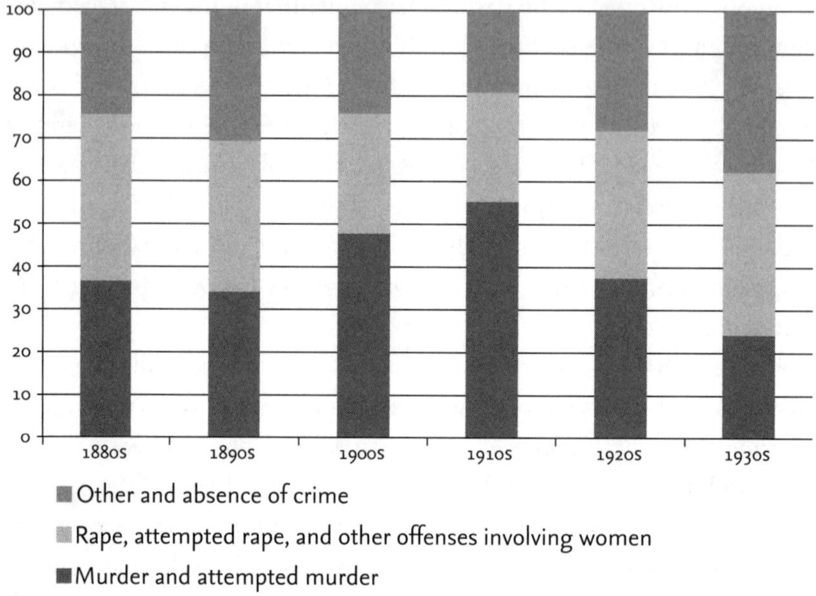

or palliation."[54] Some whites were acutely anxious about the efforts of African Americans to assert social or civil equality, especially where environmental and demographic conditions attenuated white hegemony, which resulted in widespread and intense lynching activity in many regions of Mississippi.

2

"To Hell with the Constitution"

LYNCHING IN SOUTH CAROLINA

At the 1912 meeting of the National Governors Association, South Carolina governor Coleman Blease stridently informed his esteemed colleagues that nothing could come between him and the "protection of the white women of South Carolina." "To h[ell] with the Constitution," Blease bellowed, "if it stands in the way of me and . . . the defence of the virtue of white women of my State." Blease's defiant defense of lynching did not stem from a concern about menacing black rapists, however, but arose from an exchange that Blease had with Wyoming governor Joseph Carey about state marriage laws and black heavyweight champion Jack Johnson, who was married to a white woman. The Governors Association was debating the desirability of states adopting uniform divorce laws when Blease declared that he was proud of South Carolina's ban on divorce and equally proud that "the boasted hero of the black race who claims to be the superior of the white man in the prize ring could not disgrace South Carolina by having himself united to a white woman within its borders, thank God, and if it did happen the law provides a punishment for him and a punishment for her, and the only reason that the law would be called in to protect them would be the location of the place in the State in which the crime might have been committed." Governor Carey then inquired if the Constitution and the laws of South Carolina had not afforded whites and blacks equal rights and equal protection under the law and if Blease had not taken an oath to uphold these principles. When the applause of the audience subsided, Blease uttered his notorious rejoinder.[1]

Blease's inflammatory remarks were intended to curry favor with conservative whites, whom Blease hoped would support him in a race against incumbent U.S. senator "Cotton Ed" Smith, but it was nevertheless significant that Blease's racist rhetoric was directed more against black equality than alleged black criminality. The rape rants that politicians like Blease delivered for political gain contravened southern practices that allowed African American defendants to have their day in court and appealed to segments of the southern populace who worried about legal changes that apparently guaranteed African Americans the same civil rights as whites.[2]

Although fear of the "black beast rapist" reached towering proportions among some supporters of Blease, many white southerners admitted that most lynching had little to do with protecting white women. In the mid-1890s, for instance, Governor John Gary Evans told the South Carolina General Assembly that the tacit approval of lynching for alleged sexual crimes had caused lynching to spread "like a loathsome contagious disease . . . over the entire category of crime."[3] Evans asserted correctly that lynching in retaliation for alleged sexual crimes had precipitated the lynching plague. During the 1880s, rape, combined with other offenses against women, ranked first among alleged causes of lynching in South Carolina (see fig. 4). After Benjamin Tillman and his allies fraudulently succeeded in excluding African Americans from political participation, however, alleged sexual crimes declined significantly as an ostensible cause of lynching.[4] Not surprisingly, in the ensuing decades lynching for minor offenses or for no apparent crime increased substantially over predisfranchisement levels.[5]

But white South Carolinians never took to the rope and faggot in the way that white Mississippians did. The most striking difference between South Carolina and Mississippi in regard to racial violence was the interplay between lynching and legal executions that existed in the two states. Every region in Mississippi had nearly twice (or more) the number of lynchings as compared to executions, but in South Carolina, every re-

FIGURE 4. Alleged crimes of black lynching victims in South Carolina (percent)

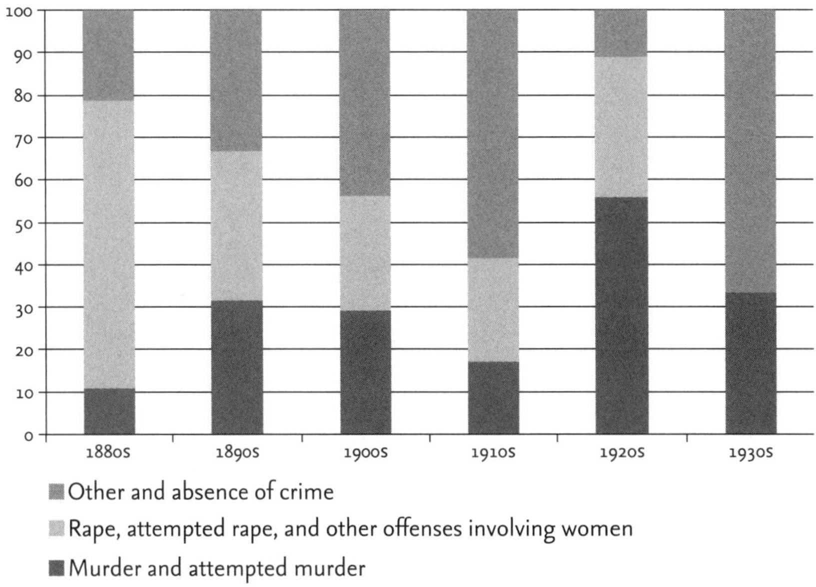

gion except the Western Piedmont had more executions than lynchings (see table 1, p. 28, and table 2).[6]

Whether or not lynching and legal execution were substitutable methods of racial oppression has been a perennial question for scholars of violence.[7] In the most comprehensive study of southern lynching, Tolnay and Beck claim that that "executions and lynchings were largely independent forms of social control in the South."[8] Other scholars, however, claim that lynching and legal executions increased in tandem with one another, especially during times of pronounced racial tension. More recently, Michael Pfeifer finds that "lynching came from the early modern death penalty, and the modern death penalty came from lynching."[9]

The evidence from Mississippi and South Carolina indicates that lynching and executions were substitute forms of social control. From 1881 to 1940, South Carolina performed 292 legal executions, 34 percent more than Mississippi's 218 legal executions during the same years.[10] Whereas Mississippi experienced 2.6 times as many lynching incidents

TABLE 2. Lynching incidents and executions in South Carolina by region, 1881-1940

Region	Lynching incidents	Executions	Mean percent black	Mean percentage of total South Carolina black population	Percentage of all South Carolina lynching incidents	Percentage of all South Carolina executions
Upper Piedmont	27	63	31.6	10.6	15.2	21.6
Northern Pee Dee	11	35	49.7	10.3	6.2	12.0
Midlands	19	37	50.3	7.8	10.7	12.7
Eastern Piedmont	21	33	57.3	13.4	11.8	11.3
Western Piedmont	46	27	58.9	15.5	25.8	9.2
Outer Coastal Plain	24	51	67.9	19.5	13.5	17.5
Inner Coastal Plain	19	20	68.1	10.2	10.7	6.8
Southern Pee Dee	11	26	70.3	12.6	6.2	8.9

as legal executions, South Carolina had 1.7 times as many legal executions as lynching incidents. State-sponsored executions in South Carolina put a damper on lynching activity, especially after 1910 (see fig. 2, p. 5). State executions in Mississippi, on the other hand, did not outnumber lynching incidents until the 1930s, when the lynching era finally had waned (see fig. 1, p. 5). Significantly, state-sanctioned executions in South Carolina surpassed lynching incidents a full decade earlier than on the national level, but the same situation did not occur in Mississippi until a decade after the national change.[11]

The execution records of the two states supports the notion that South Carolinians lived in a more settled, legalistic society than did residents of Mississippi. Why were white Mississippians more prone to lynching than white South Carolinians? Tradition explains some of the difference. As early as the 1830s, Mississippi was known as a place where "passion took precedence over the law." The Mississippi penal code, moreover, was so harsh that juries often refused to impose it, and planters were reluctant to relinquish their paternalistic prerogatives to the courts.[12] Popular attitudes toward the criminal justice system were also different in Mississippi than in South Carolina. In Mississippi, the de facto existence of so-called "Negro law," in which whites refused to judge and sentence blacks according to the same standards as whites, "turned the criminal justice system into a corrupt and capricious entity" that neither whites nor blacks respected. Consequently, arrest and conviction rates, especially in plantation regions of Mississippi, were low despite a high rate of violent crime.[13]

Although South Carolina whites shared the same assumptions about the innate inferiority of African Americans that existed among whites in Mississippi, South Carolinians relied more heavily on the courts as opposed to private agency to control crime. A higher percentage of state executions involved African Americans in South Carolina than in Mississippi, and by the turn of the twentieth century, South Carolina courts were trying blacks three times more frequently than whites. Black males who faced criminal indictment in South Carolina were convicted nearly 80 percent of the time, while the figure for white men was only 60 percent.[14] Even in terms of lynching, South Carolina authorities were over three times more likely to arrest mob members than were officials in Mississippi.[15]

Court etiquette in Mississippi, moreover, was more antagonistic toward African Americans than in South Carolina. Overt hostility from judges and law-enforcement officials toward African American attorneys in Mississippi courtrooms caused African Americans to prefer white instead of black attorneys. By the early 1910s, many communities in Mississippi had banned African American attorneys from practicing in court, and by the late 1930s, only a handful of black attorneys remained in the state.[16] South Carolina, on the other hand, had many prominent African American attorneys, including the intrepid Nathaniel Jerome Frederick, who in the late 1920s succeeded in obtaining a gubernatorial pardon for a black man who was convicted of raping a white woman.[17] A few years previously, Frederick had appealed the convictions of three African Americans to the South Carolina Supreme Court for murdering the sheriff of Aiken County. Although Frederick obtained a new trial for the defendants, local whites became so incensed over Frederick's efforts on behalf of the accused that a mob brutally lynched all three during a second trial.[18] Even in South Carolina, whites could tolerate only so much respect for the civil and legal rights of African Americans.

Lynching activity in South Carolina was concentrated mainly in the upland Piedmont counties of the state (see map 2). More than half of all the lynching incidents in South Carolina occurred in the three Piedmont regions. Although the South Carolina Piedmont was a cotton-producing region, it was also the most industrialized portion of the state. The Piedmont enjoyed an unprecedented era of industrial expansion in the thirty years following 1880 due in large part to the capital of a commercial class of shopkeepers, cotton merchants, and other entrepreneurs who thrived in the railroad towns of the Piedmont.[19] The relatively dense white population of some portions of the Piedmont made it an ideal place for the virtually all-white textile industry to expand.[20] The Upper Piedmont, for instance, was a heavily white region organized around the textile cities of Greenville, Spartanburg, and Anderson. The Eastern Piedmont, on the other hand, was a black majority region (until 1930) but also had significant textile operations in smaller towns and vil-

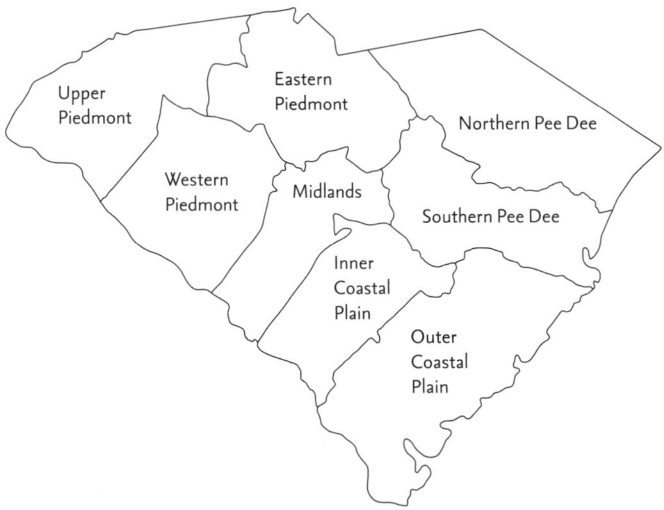

MAP 2. South Carolina regions

lages, such as Chester, Fairfield, Kershaw, Lancaster, Union, and York. The Western Piedmont contained the old upcountry black belt, which was centered around what had been the Edgefield District before the Civil War.[21] The Western Piedmont was the least industrialized portion of the Piedmont, and had the highest percentage of black population of any Piedmont region throughout the period.

In the 1880s, the Eastern Piedmont was South Carolina's worst lynching region. The Ku Klux Klan had been active in many of the counties in this region during Reconstruction.[22] Although seven of the ten lynching incidents that occurred in the Eastern Piedmont during the 1880s ostensibly resulted from rape or attempted rape, elements of Klan-style violence persisted. Signs or placards were often attached to a victim's body, warning African Americans that white men would use lethal violence to protect the virtue of their wives and daughters. The mobs involved in some of these lynchings often had well-conceived plans and carried them out with "military precision." Mob members, moreover, often were disguised with blackened faces, masks, or sheets.[23]

The worst lynching incident in the Eastern Piedmont, however, involved a mob of sixty undisguised men who broke into the jail at Yorkville in April 1887 and lynched five black "bandits" accused of brutally murdering a young white boy. The mob took the five men to a white oak tree, about a mile and a half from town, and hanged them. Although the court of General Sessions opened the morning after the lynching, many whites claimed that the mass murder was necessary to quash a clandestine black organization that was allegedly terrorizing the area.[24]

When a local paper condemned the lynching as "an outrage of the direst kind" that could "admit of no palliation or excuse," however, a local white teacher wrote to her betrothed that she was "disgusted" with the paper's denunciation of the "good law abiding citizens of York." The woman claimed that the lynching was entirely justified, especially since the white people of York could not be sure that the men would be convicted. The leader of the bandits was Giles Goode, who had been a member of the Republican militia that fought the Ku Klux Klan in the Chester County area during Reconstruction days.[25] The woman described Goode as a "desperate negro, half Indian but possessed of whole Indian characteristics shrewd, daring, and revengeful." Goode, the teacher claimed, had always managed to keep "some one between himself and the gallows." In this case, Goode had apparently convinced one of his underlings, who had turned state's evidence, to feign insanity, which cast doubt upon the outcome of the trial. In response, the "well ordered civilization and enduring good government" of York decided to lynch Goode and his allies as a warning to other African Americans that whites would stop at nothing to defend their property and their lives.[26] The white oak tree from which the men were hanged later became something of a shrine for white police officers, who for decades came regularly to Yorkville to cut "persuaders" from the branches of the tree.[27] White reactionaries used extralegal violence against African American leaders like Goode to ensure that "the promise to the Negroes of forty acres of land and a mule was never kept in our section."[28]

In the 1890s, lynching skyrocketed in the Western and Upper Piedmont. Both regions had more lynching incidents in the 1890s than in any other decade. Violence in the Western Piedmont, the bloodiest lynching region in South Carolina, had political connotations, reminiscent of the Ku Klux Klan political violence that had been so common in "bloody Edgefield" during Reconstruction.[29] In November 1898, for example, an election day riot in Phoenix, Greenwood County, precipitated an orgy of violence that ended ten days later with at least nine blacks lynched. Mobs of whites scoured the countryside for days "mad with the lust of blood, and killed the men [and one woman] whom they could kill with the least . . . risk to themselves."[30] The efforts of a wealthy family of white Republicans named Tolbert to challenge the provisions of the 1895 South Carolina constitution by encouraging black tenants to vote in the congressional election was an important precursor to the massacre. So too was the animosity that poor whites felt toward the Tolberts, who insisted on retaining black tenants even at a time of severe unemployment for many white farmers.[31] In the aftermath of the massacre, blacks fled the region by the hundreds for other parts of the state or for Georgia and Mississippi. It took some sections of the Western Piedmont years to overcome the subsequent loss of African American labor, which contributed to a sharp decline in lynching during the next decade.[32]

The pronounced difference in the number of lynching incidents among the three Piedmont regions was not a matter of coincidence. The animosity that existed between blacks and whites in the Western Piedmont resulted in part from the resentment that poor white tenants felt toward white landlords who preferred African American tenants. Equally significant were the violent conflicts that inevitably occurred between black tenants and their white employers. Racial antipathy was not evident to the same degree in the Upper and Eastern Piedmont regions, where the majority of whites lived in textile towns or villages. The lily-white nature of the textile industry limited the contact that many whites had with blacks, and consequently the conflicts that precipitated lynching. Also important were differences in the imposition of legal execution. The Western Piedmont had 1.8 times as many lynchings as the Upper Piedmont, for example, but the Upper Piedmont had 2.3 times as many legal executions as the Western Piedmont (the Eastern Piedmont also had more legal executions than the Western Piedmont). Apparently rural whites, who lived among large concentrations of African Americans, felt more inclined to seek immediate redress for perceived crimes and grievances than did their more urban counterparts, who lived in predominantly white towns and villages.[33]

Outside of the Piedmont, the worst lynching region in South Carolina was the Outer Coastal Plain, a heavily African American lowland region that was the only part of the state in which more than half of all black farmers were landowners. The lynching record of the Outer Coastal Plain presents an interesting comparison with that of its northern neighbor, the Inner Coastal Plain, which was a neoplantation region dominated by cotton production. The greater number of lynching incidents that occurred in the Outer Coastal Plain as compared to the Inner Coastal Plain contrasts with the lynching experience of coastal Georgia, where similar economic and social characteristics provided "a powerful brake on lynch mobs."[34]

By the late nineteenth century, commercial rice production in the lowlands, which once had been the mainstay of the Outer Coastal Plain, was in full decline and had all but vanished by 1910, in part because African Americans refused to work in rice gangs. With the exception of Charleston, much of this region was desperately poor. The prospect for significant industrial development, moreover, was hampered by environmental obstacles. Much of the region was swamp or pine barrens that possessed few mineral resources and little natural water power. The transition from rice production to truck farming and the harvesting of forest products paid few dividends, and by 1900, parts of the lowcountry had become some of the poorest areas of the entire country.[35]

The inability of lowcountry planters and merchants to rejuvenate the region's economy placed an additional strain on race relations, which made the opening decade of the twentieth century a period of prolonged brutality. From 1901 through 1910, the seven counties in the Outer Coastal Plain endured nearly 60 percent of the lynching that occurred in the region from 1881 to 1940, making this the worst decade for lynching (in percentage) for any region in the state's history. The tide of racial repression that covered South Carolina after the turn of the twentieth century prompted white leaders, especially the progressive governor Duncan C. Heyward, to vigorously denounce extralegal violence. African Americans also protested against lynching, and the collective efforts of African Americans had a tangible impact on whites and contributed to a precipitous decline in lynching during the 1910s and 1920s.

The first twentieth-century lynching that occurred in the Outer Coastal Plain region happened at Port Royal in Beaufort County and involved an African American sailor named William Cornish. Whites lynched Cornish for allegedly attempting to rape several white women, but the charges were unsubstantiated at best. Local African Americans reportedly launched an energetic search for Cornish's body, and rumors spread about a retaliation plot among African Americans.[36]

The next major lynching incident in the Outer Coastal Plain occurred in June 1902, when at least three black men (and possibly four) were lynched in Colleton County for allegedly killing a white woman during a robbery that occurred in late April of the same year. A mob took one of the lynching victims from police custody before tying the man to a pine tree and shooting him to death.[37] After the lynching, rumors of a race riot circulated, but the most dramatic consequence of the lynching was the resignation of George Koester, who was the founder of the *Columbia Record,* from his position as collector of internal revenue for South Carolina.

Koester's removal was largely the work of the African American activist Edmund Deas, also known as the "Duke of Darlington," who was chairman of the South Carolina Republican Party. Deas was a fearless spokesman for the rights of African Americans, and his advocacy had once elicited the ire of supporters of Benjamin Tillman, who physically assaulted him.[38] Deas had been lobbying the Roosevelt administration for Koester's removal since his appointment in October 1901, and he had enlisted the aid of Booker T. Washington in the cause.[39] Koester claimed that Deas and other black politicians were in league with Koester's journalistic rivals at the *Columbia State* and falsely accused him of participating in a triple lynching at Gaston in 1893.[40] Koester denied the charge and insisted that he had only been present at the lynching as a reporter. Koester claimed that he had personally captured one of the victims, Tom Preston, and that he had forced the mob to shoot Preston rather than burn him by threatening "to blow out his [Preston's] brains the moment a match was applied to the rosin." Contemporary accounts make no mention of Koester's heroics, but he insisted that President Theodore Roosevelt believed his story. Deas and the *Columbia State,* however, organized a massive letter-writing campaign against Koester's appointment.[41] In the aftermath of the multiple lynching at Colleton, the Roosevelt administration apparently agreed with Booker T. Washington that "it would clear the atmosphere wonderfully and serve as the greatest encouragement to our race if it could be understood that this man lost his position because of having taken part in a lynching."[42] The Roosevelt administration probably saw little risk in sacrificing a "Gold Democrat" like Koester to satisfy the demands of Republican activists, who wanted the administration to issue a strong, albeit largely symbolic, condemnation of lynching.

About fourteen months after Koester's resignation, and partially in response to a lynching that occurred in the Inner Coastal Plain region, African Americans organized a statewide conference on lynching in Columbia. The African American Ministerial Union sponsored the event, which was held at Bethel Church in Columbia on 25 August 1903.[43] About 150 persons attended, including ministers, teachers, and political officials, and the major newspapers in the state sent reporters to cover the proceedings. White newspapers attempted to downplay the political implications of the speeches, but several speakers directly addressed the connection between human rights and lynching. A Charleston minister, G. C. Rowe, for instance, argued that lynching "cheapened human life" and that it represented the "rape of the public conscience." Lynching, said Rowe, was not punishment for an unspeakable crime but rather the "self-imposed degradation and condemnation of a so-called superior people!" Whites lynched, according to Rowe, mainly for "degrading the negro," and the only effective remedy was the elimination of "race distinctions" that fomented violence.

Former U.S. representative George Washington Murray connected lynching to the "narrow, bigoted spirit of slavery," which bred violence and hatred between whites and blacks. If the unjust economic and social disparities that existed between blacks and whites were removed, Murray claimed, then lynching would cease.[44] The summary statement from the conference condemned the racial bigotry of U.S. senator Benjamin Tillman, called for judicial equality between whites and blacks, and requested more educational assistance for African Americans, which the signatories believed was indispensable to the improvement of race relations.[45] In commenting on the conference, the *Charleston News and Courier* condemned Rowe for arguing that "the existence of the gorilla negro" was not "the chief cause of lynching." The "better class of whites," said the paper, wanted African Americans to be "useful and happy in due subordination to the superior race," but the radical opinions of black leaders like Rowe and Murray were a hindrance rather than a help to resolving the lynching problem.

During the fall that followed the conference, South Carolina suffered no further lynching, but during the winter of 1903–4, two black men were lynched in Dorchester County in separate incidents. Not surprisingly, both incidents allegedly involved attempted assaults on white women, and the second lynching prompted Governor Duncan Heyward to ask the state legislature for more money to combat lynching and to pass legislation that would make it easier to arrest suspected members of a mob.[46] About five weeks later, the Outer Coastal Plain region endured another lynching, which occurred in Berkeley County and involved a disorderly man named Robert Williams, who may have been shot with the active cooperation of a local law-enforcement official.[47]

Five months later, Berkeley County was the site of the depraved lynching of Kitt Bookard, which seemingly confirmed the opinions of African American leaders like Rowe and Murray concerning the causes of lynching.[48] Bookard was a twenty-one-year-old black tenant farmer, who in mid-July 1904 went fishing with five white men, including three brothers, Benny, Andrew, and Piney Martin, and two other white tenants, Henry Edwards and Adgar Butler, all of whom worked on the farm of Lewis Martin, who was the father of the Martin brothers. On the trip home, the men had an argument in which Bookard threatened to "spank" Henry Edwards, whom the African American tenants on the Martin farm apparently disliked. The same day, Edwards had Bookard arrested and fined five dollars. When Bookard could not pay the fine, however, he was sentenced to fifteen days in jail.

Four days later, six white men, including Edwards, town marshal John Palmer, constable S. A. Eadons (who was married to Lewis Martin's sister), Adgar Butler (who was a son-in-law of Lewis Martin), Penny Martin (a nephew of Lewis Martin), and Benjamin Martin took Bookard from the Eutawville calaboose supposedly intent on whipping him. When the men reached the Santee River, however, they told Bookard that he had reached the banks of the River Jordan and that they were going to kill him. After tying Bookard's limbs and stuffing cotton in his mouth to muffle his screams, the six men tortured Bookard. The lynchers scalped Bookard, cut off his genitals and ears, removed his eyes and tongue, and inflicted numerous knife wounds on his body. Following the torture, the men tied Bookard's body to an iron bar and threw it into the river. Bookard's body was found a week later. Outraged over Bookard's lynching, one thousand African Americans from the surrounding area attended the coroner's inquest.

Whites in the area feared that a race war might erupt unless authorities made some arrests. Governor Duncan Heyward told the press that he was "utterly disgusted" with the lynching, and he quietly used his own money to employ a Pinkerton detective to investigate the murder. For weeks, nothing appeared to happen in the case, but whites from Eutawville became so paranoid about undercover detectives that they banned traveling salesmen from the town.

In early August 1904, Aaron P. Prioleau, a prominent African American politician from Berkeley County and a perennial candidate for Congress, attempted to generate some progress in the case when he wrote a letter that suggested that African Americans had lost patience with waiting for the law to provide protection from such outrages. The *Columbia Record* opined that Prioleau's threatening words would "doubtless be remembered" by any future jury "even though they are sworn to find a verdict according to the law and evidence." The *Charleston News and Courier* condemned Prioleau and "his ignorant and viciously inclined friends," and worried that his letter might be "an excuse" for a jury to acquit anyone charged with Bookard's murder.[49]

In late October, the residents of Eutawville were shocked when authorities finally arrested six white men for Bookard's lynching. At a preliminary hearing in December, Bookard's wife, Mamie, revealed reluctantly that the animosity between her husband and Benjamin Martin resulted from Martin's coerced sexual relations with Bookard's sister, Eliza. The state's primary witness in the case was Henry Edwards, who admitted that the men had been drinking before the murder. Edwards claimed that Palmer and Eadons had killed Bookard. When asked about the condition of the body, however, Edwards denied that the men had tortured Bookard. Instead, Edwards conjectured that predatory fish had probably removed the various body parts. Ridiculous testimony of this sort did not help the state's prosecution of the case. State senator E. J. Dennis conducted the defense and portrayed the defendants as devoted family men whom the system had abused, in contrast to the cowardly and traitorous Edwards. A jury deliberated sixteen minutes before acquitting the defendants.

The state's inability to obtain a conviction in the Bookard lynching chagrined Governor Heyward, not only because he had spent his own money to bring the lynchers to justice but also because he was a rice planter from nearby Colleton County and violence of this sort offended his paternalistic sensibilities. Heyward probably believed that the state's reputation for grisly vengeance could suffer no further, but in August 1906, a Dorchester County mob proved him wrong. The lynching of Willie Spain, which involved the active collaboration of the county sheriff, Heyward lamented, was "about as much as folks ought to be asked to accept."[50]

Spain was in his early twenties and was described as a "sullen, worthless negro" who had recently migrated from North Carolina. He occasionally found work at the Dorchester Lumber Company, where he ostensibly tried to break into the house of the company manager, S. L. Connor. The screams of Connor's eleven-year-old daughter, however, supposedly frightened Spain, who had a brief altercation with Connor before he fled the scene. Within two hours, a posse had apprehended Spain and turned him over to the county sheriff, M. M. Limehouse. Spain was in jail for about thirty minutes before a mob arrived to lynch him. The pusillanimous Limehouse allowed the mob to take Spain from the jail without resistance before he wired Governor Heyward for assistance.[51] After a perfunctory identification by the Connor girl, the mob hanged Spain and riddled his body with bullets until it was beyond recognition. Limehouse later claimed that he thought the men had only wanted to interrogate Spain for attempting to break into Connor's house.

African Americans in the area were infuriated over the lynching and began expressing their dissatisfaction at the coroner's inquest. At the time of the inquest, African Americans organized a "caucus" to prevent other blacks from helping to bury Spain. They also began to construct a plan to punish the coroner, S. E. Kizer, whom they blamed for not doing enough to investigate the lynching. In order to ease racial tensions, Heyward called a special term of court to prosecute Limehouse and to indict some of the lynchers. In October 1906, Limehouse became the first sheriff in South Carolina indicted for malfeasance in office under a provision of the 1895 constitution. He was subsequently tried in Orangeburg County and acquitted in 1907.

Although Kizer became sheriff upon the removal of the cowardly Limehouse, his troubles were far from over. Kizer was one of the wealthiest and most influential cotton planters in the area, and he had apparently ordered some of his African American laborers to bury Spain's body. Local African American leaders deeply resented Kizer's actions, which ran contrary to the sentiments that blacks had expressed at the inquest. African Americans often refused to bury the remains of a lynching victim, not only because they were unwilling to bear the expense, but also because they wanted to emphasize that lynching was an affront to the human rights of all African Americans. By requiring that whites bury a victim of mob violence, African Americans subtly forced whites to acknowledge the humanity of a person whom a mob had claimed was inhuman and therefore beyond the protection of the law.

To Kizer's amazement, African American leaders organized a boycott of his plantation, and he later complained of constant threats and the loss of thousands of dollars of income because he could not hire enough workers to harvest his cotton. Other whites suspected of being involved in the lynching faced similar threats and boycotts. The economic pressure on Kizer forced him to use the courts to strike back against the suspected leaders of the protest. Kizer secured indictments against four African Americans who had allegedly organized the labor boycott, which presumably ended his labor problems, at least in the short term. Chastened by the experience, however, Kizer resigned as sheriff, and few whites seemed to want the position.[52] The protests that African Americans organized in response to the killing of Spain did not end lynching in the region, but afterward racial violence and terrorism began to wane. The Outer Coastal Plain and the Southern Pee Dee regions were the only two regions of South Carolina where lynching ceased before 1920.

In contrast to the Outer Coastal Plain, where five of the seven counties in the region had three or more lynching incidents, lynching in the Inner Coastal Plain was confined primarily to Barnwell and Orangeburg Counties. Orangeburg County had once been the most productive cotton-producing county in the nation, and it remained one of the nation's richest agricultural counties into the 1940s.[53] Outside of the Piedmont regions, the Inner Coastal Plain had the highest level of African American tenancy in the state. Not surprisingly, alleged murder and property crimes accounted for more than 61 percent of lynching incidents. Although the Inner Coastal Plain had 25 percent fewer lynching incidents than did the Outer Coastal Plain, lynching lasted longer in the Inner Coastal Plain. After 1910, the African American population in the Outer Coastal Plain began to decline significantly, perhaps due to the region's poor economic prospects. The percentage of black population in the Inner Coastal Plain, however, remained more stable, declining only about 5 percent from 1910 to 1940 (in the Outer Coastal Plain, the same figure was approximately 13 percent). Predictably, the Inner Coastal Plain had double the number of lynching incidents of the Outer Coastal Plain in the 1910s. After 1919, the Outer Coastal Plain was free from lynching, while the Inner Coastal Plain had two lynching incidents in the 1920s.

One of those lynched in the 1920s was a black tenant farmer from Appleton (Allendale County) named Ed Kirkland, who was accused of murdering his landlord, Eugene Walker, in a dispute over a rent settlement. Kirkland fled after the shooting incident but was quickly captured and turned over to Sheriff Bennett. Bennett wanted to take Kirkland to Columbia for safekeeping, and the two boarded a train at Gifford. But a mob intercepted the train at Fairfax and returned Kirkland to Appleton, where an estimated one thousand men burned Kirkland inside the Negro Lodge building. The lynching supposedly was devoid of excitement, which prompted the *Charleston News and Courier* to comment that it was "dangerously wrong when men who probably are simply average citizens appear actually to feel that it is incumbent upon them to take the law into their own hands and do so, as at Appleton, not under the stimulus of excitement, but 'in a quiet, matter-of-fact way.'" Three years later, the state supreme court ruled that Allendale County was liable to pay Lillian Kirkland two thousand dollars in reparation for her husband's lynching.[54] The Kirkland lynching was another example of how disputes between a landlord and a tenant often precipitated a spate of racial antagonism that culminated in lynching.

To the immediate north of the Inner Coastal Plain was the more urbanized and industrialized Midlands region, which contained the three counties of Aiken, Lexington, and Richland. Farmers from this sandhills region grew less cotton than farmers from surrounding regions, and many farmers engaged in dairy or truck farming. The Midlands was majority black until 1910, but always had a significantly smaller African American population than either its northern or southern neighbor. The Midlands had one of the lowest levels of white farm tenancy in the state, second only to the Outer Coastal Plain. Levels of African American tenancy hovered around the 80 percent range from 1900 to 1930, but this was substantially less than either the Western Piedmont or the Inner Coastal Plain.

The Midlands had eighteen lynching incidents, the same as the Inner Coastal Plain, all of which occurred in either Aiken or Lexington County. Richland County, which contained the state capital of Columbia, had no lynching within its borders. Seventeen of the thirty-seven executions (45.9 percent) that occurred in the region, however, took place within Richland County.[55] During Reconstruction, the Midlands was a center of Wade Hampton's Red Shirt movement, which violently reestablished white supremacy. Two of the state's bloodiest Reconstruction race conflicts, the Hamburg and the Ellenton riots, happened in Aiken County. The worst lynching years in the Midlands occurred during the administration of Governor Benjamin Tillman, who rode the sentiments of racial demagoguery and economic discontent to the governorship in 1890. Tillman's inflammatory rhetoric about lynching black rapists did much to encourage racial violence in the region.

The bloodiest lynching in the Midlands occurred at Gaston in July 1893.[56] Whites accused two black men, Will Thompson and Handy Kaigler, of raping and beating the wife of Archie Sightler, a respected white man. After leaving the woman's house, Thompson encountered his employer, Perry Goodwyn, in the woods. Goodwyn told Thompson that a mob was searching for him, and Thompson fled from the area. Hundreds of whites scoured the swamps south of Columbia for an entire night in search of Thompson, who finally was captured six days later. Thompson also implicated Tom Preston, who worked for Sightler, in the attack. The eighteen-year-old Thompson admitted that all three of the men had raped the woman, but Thompson alleged that Kaigler had forced him to participate at gunpoint.

After interrogating Thompson, a mob returned him to Gaston so that Archie Sightler could confront him. Sightler demanded that Thompson tell him about the attack, which he did in a "sing-song sort of way" that infuriated the mob. When some of the mob suggested that Thompson should be burned, he grabbed at Goodwyn and begged him to persuade the men otherwise. Goodwyn managed to convince the mob to hang and shoot Thompson rather than burn him, but he could do nothing to prevent Thompson's torture.

The mob took Thompson to a large clearing near a railroad track and tied him by the neck to a pine trunk that lay on the ground. While some of the mob held Thompson's legs, Sightler beat Thompson with several buggy traces. As Sightler and others pounded him, Thompson writhed in agony until the rope around his neck had nearly strangled him. Others kicked and struck the adolescent until his body became a bloody pulp, with one eye almost kicked out its socket. After the brutal beating, the mob made Thompson stand on a pile of rail ties with a rope around his neck that was attached to a branch of a large oak tree. A firing squad assembled along the railroad tracks, but was told not to shoot until Thompson had undergone the last agony. When the crossties were kicked from under him, Thompson managed to wrench his arms loose and grab the rope around his neck. This apparently amused the lynchers, who watched Thompson struggle wildly for a few moments, but the gurgling sounds that accompanied strangulation soon could be heard. After the body stopped swaying, the shooting commenced, which sent blood and flesh flying everywhere. The mob fired so many shots that "it was hard to tell anything about the body," which fell to the ground. After stringing what remained of Thompson's corpse up again, the mob cheered and left in search of Kaigler and Preston.

Around 11:00 a.m., Preston was captured seven miles from Gaston and returned to the clearing near the railroad. Preston was stripped, flogged, hanged, and shot, exactly the same as Thompson. Throughout the afternoon, men from the surrounding area fired at the bodies, which left "certain portions . . . shot entirely away." Meanwhile other mob members went to the Lexington courthouse to retrieve Kaigler from the local sheriff, who offered no resistance to the mob. The next morning, Kaigler was tortured and lynched at the clearing in the same manner as the other two victims, except that the mob left Kaigler's hands free so that he could struggle, as Thompson had done, after being hanged.

The depravity of the Gaston lynchings prompted the *Charleston News and Courier* to editorialize: "It appears to be useless to condemn and denounce lynching for this crime. The denunciations have been earnest and oft repeated, and new lynchings have followed always in a few weeks or days." The torture of the three victims demonstrated, in the words of the paper's editorialist, that the "evil is growing worse instead of better." Thompson's torture in particular, the paper sternly warned, "ought to set every sober-minded man who cares for the future welfare of the State, to thinking very seriously about this lynching business." Now that torture had become an accepted part of mob proceedings, the *News and Courier* observed with trepidation, "further steps will lead only to more and greater extremes of cruelty."[57]

Neither contemporaries nor subsequent observers doubted that Governor Tillman's approval of lynching for the crime of rape had precipitated this “most horrible state of affairs.”[58] Two months later, after an Aiken mob had lynched Calvin Stewart in retaliation for the murder of a white man, Tillman conceded that “there are some cases in which it is proper, but, the barrier once broken down, there will at last come some case where the evidence is so insufficient that public sentiment will punish someone so severely that lynchings will have to be stopped.” Despite these misgivings, Tillman saw no point in conducting a “farce of an investigation” into the lynching of Stewart.[59]

Beyond the mid-1890s, the worst lynching incident in the Midlands occurred during yet another race riot in Aiken County. In June 1902, a fight broke out between whites and blacks on a train going from Augusta, Georgia, to Langley, South Carolina, a mill-town hamlet. During the racial fracas, eleven white men were cut or shot and another was mortally wounded. Two black men, one named Wyatt Holmes and the other named Coleman, were arrested and jailed at Langley. A few hours after the fighting had ended, a mob arrived, overpowered the guards, and cut and shot the two black men to pieces. In the days following the lynching, whites feared retaliation from African Americans and organized patrols to interrogate any group of three or more blacks and prohibited groups of African Americans from boarding trains in the area.[60]

The two South Carolina regions with the fewest lynching incidents were the Northern and Southern Pee Dee regions, which lay in the northeastern quarter of the state. Both regions had eleven lynching incidents, although the last lynching to occur in the Southern Pee Dee happened in 1915, while the Northern Pee Dee had a lynching in 1921 and another in 1932. The Southern Pee Dee had a greater percentage black population, averaging nearly 70 percent black throughout the period, while the Northern Pee Dee became a white majority region in 1910 and averaged approximately 50 percent white over the entire period. The Northern Pee Dee was primarily a tobacco-producing region centered around the town of Florence. The Southern Pee Dee was more rural than its northern neighbor and more oriented toward cotton production, although some truck farming did occur. More than half of the lynching incidents that occurred in the Southern Pee Dee happened in Williamsburg County, where lynching exhibited a particularly vicious nature.[61]

The two regions had the same number of lynching incidents, but the more heavily white and urban Northern Pee Dee region had over 40 percent more executions than did the Southern Pee Dee. The emergence of bright-leaf tobacco production in the Northern Pee Dee during the early 1890s was largely the work of a dynamic class of entrepreneurial farmers, bankers, and merchants who eagerly embraced the New South ethic of market capitalism, agricultural innovation, and social progress.[62] The greater number of executions in the Northern Pee Dee as compared to its southern neighbor probably resulted from these market-oriented reformers, who strongly favored state-sanctioned executions over the more communal but "backward" values that lynchers embraced.[63] The Northern Pee Dee had approximately one lynching for every three executions, the lowest ratio in either South Carolina or Mississippi, while the Southern Pee Dee had the third-lowest ratio in the state (see table 2).

The spatial distribution of lynching in South Carolina was rather different from that of Mississippi. The majority-black, cotton-producing Western Piedmont was by far the worst lynching region in South Carolina, and it was also the region where African Americans faced the greatest statistical likelihood of lynching (see table 2). The heavily white, textile-oriented Upper Piedmont region was also a dangerous place for African Americans in terms of both lynching and legal executions.[64] The heavily black Southern Pee Dee region, however, was where African Americans had the least to fear from mobs; on the other hand, the same region experienced some of the state's most notorious lynchings.

Most of the lynching activity in South Carolina occurred in the Piedmont regions and emanated from political and economic conflicts that had first appeared during Reconstruction. Segregated working and living arrangements limited lynching incidents in some parts of the Piedmont as did the extensive use of legal executions in response to behavior among African Americans that whites found intolerable. Desperate poverty fueled lynching activity in the heavily black Outer Coastal Plain, especially after the turn of the century. Concerted efforts by elected officials and local black activists to curb lynching, however, eventually led to a decline in mob violence. High rates of black tenancy contributed to lynching in the neoplantation Inner Coastal Plain, while racial demagoguery incited lynching outbreaks in the Midlands. The Pee Dee regions, especially the Northern Pee Dee, had a market orientation that supported the emergence of middle-class entrepreneurs who preferred state-sanctioned executions as opposed to unpredictable mobs as a means of preserving racial order.

3

"No Rights for the Negro Which a White Man Is Bound to Respect"

LYNCHING AND POLITICAL POWER IN MISSISSIPPI AND SOUTH CAROLINA

The desire among some southern whites to invalidate the effects of emancipation and the enfranchisement of black males contributed to an onslaught of terroristic violence that manifested itself in lynching and other forms of repression and coercion. Whites attempted to dehumanize African Americans so that they could rationalize the apparent need to lynch allegedly depraved black criminals and exclude blacks from the body politic. The emergence of black fiends, who preyed purportedly on the innocent and defenseless, confirmed in the minds of many whites that blacks should never again be allowed unfettered access to political power.

Prior to disfranchisement, whites in Mississippi used terroristic violence most frequently in Republican regions of the state, in part because these same regions formed the core of the New South cotton kingdom. Republican regions in South Carolina, on the other hand, were in economic decline before disfranchisement. In the years before disfranchisement, economic marginalization and a gerrymandered lowcountry "black district" insulated African Americans in these South Carolina regions from racial violence. The desire of whites to demonize African Americans that culminated in legal disfranchisement and segregation, however, made lynching worse in both states. In Mississippi, disfranchisement unleashed class tensions among whites, especially in majority white regions, and the denial of the franchise did little to ease the interpersonal tensions that fueled lynching. In South Carolina, the decimation of the Republican Party made African Americans, especially in heavily black regions, more susceptible to violence from whites, and lynching for alleged crimes, such as murder or assault, became commonplace.

Just a few months before South Carolina enacted a new constitution that would impose a literacy test and a poll tax, ban interracial marriage, and segregate public schools, Frederick Douglass excoriated the white-supremacist South for using lynching as a means of disfranchising African Americans of their political rights. The claims of white southerners that black males had suddenly become menacing rapists, from Douglass's perspective, lacked credibility. Whites had made no such charge during the Civil War, Douglass noted, when white women had lived unprotected among black men while white men served in the Confederate army. Given the political climate of the United States in the 1890s, Douglass charged that the old shibboleths concerning black supremacy were no longer tenable; hence, whites created a myth of black criminality to inflict terror on African Americans and to deliberately deny them their constitutional rights.[1]

Other black leaders agreed that lynching was inseparably intertwined with whites' concerns about African American political power. David Augustus Straker, a former candidate for lieutenant governor of South Carolina, the first dean of law at Allen University in Columbia, South Carolina, and an accomplished criminal defense lawyer, claimed that southern disfranchisers fabricated the rape complex to "destroy Northern sentiment in the favor of the Negro by charging him with committing, as a class, the most heinous offense, next to murder." Straker argued that the "true purpose" of lynching was not punishment but to "cast odium upon . . . [blacks] . . . and thus show unfitness for political suffrage."[2] Robert C. O. Benjamin, an accomplished African American attorney and journalist, insisted that the charge of rape resulted from the "pretended and baseless fear of Negro supremacy" and was nothing less than "an effort to divest the Negro of his friends by giving him a revolting and hateful reputation."[3]

For many whites, lynching and violence became "a sort of final solution" to the problem of black political participation in the South.[4] Of course, whites lynched for a variety of transgressions, both real and imagined, but the unprecedented wave of lynching that beset the South in the last quarter of the nineteenth century was a direct result of emancipation. Emancipation enabled African Americans to strive for social and political equality in the South, and many white southerners regarded such prospects as inherently threatening.[5] Although whites frequently claimed that they tolerated lynching only for the unspeakable crime of rape, in calmer moments they often admitted that racial violence was an outgrowth of social and political competition between blacks and whites. The former Alabama Supreme Court justice Henderson Somerville, for instance, claimed that lynchings (and alleged rapes) were few in sections where "the negro vote has been eliminated as a controlling political factor," but numerous where blacks held "the balance of political power."[6] To many white southerners, the "negro problem" was essentially a political one for, as one white Mississippian put it: "If the Negro is permitted to engage in politics his usefulness as a laborer is at an end. He can no longer be controlled or utilized." Because the economic well-being of many whites was built upon the coercion of black laborers, the white South was "forced to assert its control over him [black laborers] in sheer self-defense."[7]

The psychological, social, economic, and political elements of white racism merged in lynching, which whites used to brutally subjugate African Americans to white caste conventions and to dehumanize black males so that whites could deny them any semblance of political power.[8] African American leaders bitterly resented the hypocrisy of whites who preached that if rape stopped so also would lynching, even while black men were lynched "for murder, arson, burglary, attempt at murder, impertinence, and also on suspicion of having committed a murder, on suspicion of knowing where a criminal is concealed, and for being a United [S]tates postmaster. Yet the cry goes forth: 'Stop the crime and lynching will stop.'" The political ramifications of lynching were all too apparent to black leaders, who claimed repeatedly that "the lynching habit was simply an expression of . . . race prejudice . . . that it was simply designed to be used against the negro."[9]

Although every lynching was a political statement about the social inferiority of blacks, researchers have not reached a consensus about the political dimensions of lynching partially because investigative efforts have been focused narrowly on the so-called power-threat hypothesis. According to this theory, the rate of lynching should have been higher in counties with a higher percentage of black population because the greater the percentage of blacks, the greater the potential for black political dominance. Following this logic, several scholars have tried to prove that disfranchisement had a negative impact on lynching but have found the evidence wanting.[10]

Lynching was political terrorism, but it was predicated primarily upon social rather than political competition. Three years after South Carolina had disfranchised blacks, for instance, the *Saluda (S.C.) Advocate* lamented that it was becoming increasingly difficult for blacks and whites to live with one another in the South. Since the Civil War, the newspaper noted, blacks had been busy educating themselves, expanding their minds, capabilities, and ambitions. Not only were blacks competing with whites for jobs and resources, the political equality that the Reconstruction amendments had granted blacks made it harder for whites to keep blacks in "their place." When blacks refused to accept the subservient status that whites accorded them, the *Advocate* concluded, whites readily took "to the shot gun, a primitive remedy but the final and supreme one, and so [did blacks]." The bloodshed and brutality that plagued the South after the Civil War would not dissipate, said the *Advocate,* "while we continue the experiment of trying to hold together in one body of citizenship a race which will always hold itself to be the superior and a race which is less and less inclined each year to accept a place as the inferior."[11]

Efforts to prove that disfranchisement had a uniformly negative impact on patterns of lynching are futile because whites never understood the threat that blacks posed exclusively in electoral terms. Furthermore, the notion that disfranchisement would necessarily cause a decrease in

TABLE 3. Lynching and African American political power in Mississippi and South Carolina counties

MISSISSIPPI

Had African American state legislator, 1881–1890	No.	Lynching incidents per county, 1881–1890	Lynching incidents per county, 1891–1900
Yes	15	2.1	2.3
No	60	1.3[a]	1.9
All counties	75	1.5	1.6

SOUTH CAROLINA

Had African American state legislator, 1881–1890	No.	Lynching incidents per county, 1881–1895	Lynching incidents per county, 1896–1910
Yes	6	0.5	1.7
No	38	1.6[b]	1.6
All counties	44	1.4	1.6

Notes: Excludes lynching incidents known to have been committed by an African American mob.
[a]One county was formed after 1890.
[b]Three counties were formed after 1895.

lynching ignores the considerable political power that blacks wielded in some areas of the South before disfranchisement and excludes the possibility that disfranchisement could make blacks more, rather than less, susceptible to lynching.[12] Indeed, in parts of both Mississippi and South Carolina, lynching became worse after disfranchisement because it constricted the autonomy and independence of blacks, aggravated tensions within the white community, and encouraged whites to believe they could use extralegal violence with impunity.[13]

Lynching was a consequence of racial and political conflict, but this conflict ebbed and flowed over time and place. Before disfranchisement in Mississippi, for instance, whites applied the lessons of lynching most severely in the Republican counties and regions of the state. Tables 3 and 4 show that Republican counties in Mississippi (as measured by the presence of African American state legislators) had a higher incidence of lynching than their non-Republican counterparts and that Republican regions had 55 percent more lynching than non-Republican regions be-

TABLE 4. Lynching incidents in Mississippi and South Carolina regions

MISSISSIPPI

Regions with black state legislators, 1881–1890			Regions without black state legislators, 1881–1890		
Region	Lynchings, 1881–1890	Lynchings, 1891–1900	Region	Lynchings, 1881–1890	Lynchings, 1891–1900
Bluff Hills	18	11	Black Prairie	10	13
Old Natchez	24	37	Pine Hills	7	22
Yazoo Delta	26	24	Pontotoc Hills	5	8
			Piney Woods	6	12
			Red Hills	14	20
Total	68	72	Total	42	75

SOUTH CAROLINA

Regions with black state legislators, 1881–1895			Regions without black state legislators, 1881–1895		
Region	Lynchings, 1881–1895	Lynchings, 1896–1910	Region	Lynching incidents, 1881–1895	Lynching incidents, 1896–1910
Inner Coastal Plain	6	5	Eastern Piedmont	13	5
Outer Coastal Plain	7	14	Midlands	7	7
Southern Pee Dee	3	5	Northern Pee Dee	1	5
			Upper Piedmont	11	7
			Western Piedmont	14	22
Total	16	24	Total	46	46

Note: Excludes lynching incidents known to have been committed by an African American mob.

fore disfranchisement.[14] Black political power in Mississippi was strongest in the Yazoo Delta, the state's richest agricultural region, which intensified white concerns about the possibility of a resurgence of the Republican Party. In South Carolina, conversely, Republican regions experienced less than 40 percent of the lynching committed in non-Republican regions before disfranchisement. Black political power in South Carolina was located in regions of declining economic significance, hence the need to use violence was less apparent than in Mississippi.[15]

The political position of African Americans in Mississippi was more tenuous than in South Carolina, partially because the black population in Mississippi was more concentrated than in South Carolina. Although Mississippi had a higher percentage of black population than South Carolina, it had only four predominantly black regions compared to seven in South Carolina. The most important of these regions was the Yazoo Delta, which was the center of the postbellum cotton kingdom and also the bastion of the Republican Party. Unlike the Western Piedmont in South Carolina or the Black Prairie in Mississippi, which were rich agricultural regions where minority white populations had quashed black political aspirations during an orgy of Reconstruction violence, the Yazoo Delta had been an undeveloped frontier during the 1870s. Hence, during Reconstruction, widespread violence had been unnecessary in the Delta.

Racial tension and violence in Republican regions of Mississippi stemmed in large part from demographic changes that occurred after the Civil War. After Reconstruction, a huge influx of black agricultural workers provided the small minority of white planters in the Yazoo Delta with a statewide political influence that greatly exceeded their numbers. Hill farmers from white regions resented this and other inequities and began to demand the exclusion of African Americans from the political process to diminish the power of Delta planters. In an attempt to remain in power, conservative Democrats emphasized that if whites divided, blacks would conquer, and thereby revived the specter of "negro domination."[16] Sectional conflict among whites caused racial politics to resurface much earlier in Mississippi than in South Carolina, where the creation of a lowcountry "black district" in 1882 in combination with the relatively benevolent practices of "tolerant white supremacists" defused racial politics until the early 1890s.[17]

The Yazoo Delta was the worst lynching region in Mississippi during the 1880s, but contrary to the protestations of southern apologists, alleged murder rather than the "usual crime" of rape was the driving force behind lynching in the Delta. The frontier-like conditions of the Delta produced a fluid social structure that enabled some blacks to buy their own land, and thousands of others came to the region with similar aspirations. The heavily black populations of the Delta translated into a modicum of black political power as well, and not surprisingly, the Delta produced more black legislators than any other Mississippi region. Delta whites were keenly cognizant of the overwhelming demographic presence of blacks and often conducted brutal reprisals in response to racial violence, especially after attacks on white landlords that threatened the prevailing order. Also important were black mobs that lynched with some regularity during the 1880s and made the precarious political and social predicament of Delta whites painfully apparent.[18]

In September 1889, the Yazoo Delta experienced an orgy of violence when whites massacred about twenty-five blacks in Leflore County.[19] The pogrom in Leflore County grew out of the attempt of black farmers to overcome their "peasant status."[20] Under the dynamic leadership of Oliver Cromwell, the Colored Farmers' Alliance in Leflore County became a force for independence among Delta blacks. Through personal contact and charismatic speeches, Cromwell convinced many African American farmers to join the Alliance and to trade with a cooperative store (for which Cromwell was also the commission agent) some thirty miles south of Leflore County instead of with local white merchants, upon whom blacks had traditionally relied for credit and supplies. Cromwell's activities coincided with a slumping economy, and white merchants became concerned that his success would come at their expense.[21]

Cromwell's activities threatened the economic hegemony of whites, and Leflore County whites worked quickly to undermine his leadership. In August 1889, rumors began circulating that Cromwell was an ex-convict and that he had used Alliance membership dues for personal enjoyment. Shortly thereafter Cromwell was threatened with physical harm if he did not immediately leave Leflore County. When black Alliance members resolved to defend Cromwell against aggression, whites feared a race war, and Governor Robert Lowry sent the militia to maintain order. Before sending off the troops, however, Lowry gave a rousing speech in which he declared that "he was from the crown of his head to the soles of his feet a white man's man, and should always uphold the superiority of the Anglo-Saxon race." Lowry nevertheless insisted that he wanted African Americans to have a "fair showing" and justice done.[22]

While apprehending some forty black Alliance leaders, the militia and white posses killed approximately twenty-five blacks, although white authorities never acknowledged the deaths. Whites specifically targeted four prominent leaders of the Alliance, whom they shot and killed.[23] Days after the initial massacre, whites continued to search for other African American leaders and lynched those who resisted. When some blacks, including one of Cromwell's close associates, burned a white merchant's store to the ground after the merchant refused to sell them ammunition, whites retaliated and hanged four blacks at Shell Mound, ending the efforts of African Americans at resistance.[24] The massacre and lynchings decimated the leadership of the Alliance, and soon thereafter the movement collapsed.[25] Leflore County whites brutally crushed the organizational efforts of black tenants in order to protect their economic and political power.

But the hopes and dreams of African Americans died hard, and not even the extraordinary bloodshed of the massacre could quell the conflict between whites and blacks for long. A little more than a year after the massacre, Leflore County whites found it necessary to lynch two more African Americans: one for killing a merchant in an argument and another for attempting to organize blacks to avenge the first lynching.[26] Despite the violence, blacks were not cowed into submission and refused to accept obsequiously the will of whites. The fear of black militancy prompted Delta whites to abandon their misgivings about a constitutional solution to the problem of black political power, and in 1890, Delta whites joined their white brethren in other parts of the state to revise the constitution to legally disfranchise most of the African American voters in Mississippi.[27]

Not all Republican regions in Mississippi and South Carolina were as prone to lynching as the Delta, however, because different historical experiences and precedents resulted in different patterns of lynching. Republican regions and counties in South Carolina, for instance, had less lynching before the passage of the 1895 disfranchising constitution because African Americans in these locales were relatively independent of whites (both economically and politically) and because these areas were of declining economic significance. Republican Party strength in South Carolina was confined primarily to the lowcountry regions, which had the highest percentage of black population in the state. Here, especially in the Outer Coastal Plain, African Americans had a strong and well-developed political organization that remained unchallenged until the mid-1880s. These regions had experienced little Reconstruction violence, partly because of their large black populations, but also because they were no longer prime agricultural areas. Many blacks in the lowcountry were able to purchase land, which made them less susceptible to the attacks of whites because independent black farmers did not have to deal regularly with white landowners.[28]

In addition, blacks in the South Carolina lowcountry were well organized and effectively resisted white aggression on a number of occasions.[29] In 1883, for example, a mob of one thousand Colleton County blacks threatened to lynch a white store clerk who had killed a twenty-eight-year-old black man of questionable reputation in an argument. The standoff was not resolved until a coroner's jury of eight blacks and four whites was impaneled and ruled that the deceased had been murdered by the white man, who came from a prominent family and was a graduate of the Citadel.[30] The prospect of blacks dictating to whites the outcome of a racial confrontation was unthinkable in the upcountry regions of the state, which helps explain why lowcountry regions experienced relatively few lynching incidents before the passage of the 1895 South Carolina constitution that disfranchised African American males.

Prior to disfranchisement in South Carolina, whites were most likely to lynch blacks in non-Republican, tenant-filled regions. Although South Carolina had only one majority white region, the Republican Party did not fare well outside of the lowcountry, particularly in the most productive agricultural regions, such as the Western Piedmont. In much of the upcountry, whites had vigorously contested black political power during Reconstruction and continued to subject blacks to periodic pogroms for the rest of the century. The high black tenancy rates in upcountry regions ensured that the brunt of lynching in South Carolina would always occur here, primarily because of the violent conflict that became a habitual part of white landlord-black tenant relations. In the fifteen years prior to disfranchisement, nearly three-quarters of all South Carolina lynchings occurred in upcountry regions; the corresponding figure for the fifteen years after disfranchisement was only about 66 percent.

A series of three lynching incidents in Barnwell County, South Carolina, demonstrated how lynching, even for alleged murder or rape, had political ramifications and eventually encouraged whites to use lynching in an attempt to inflict abject terror among the African American population. Barnwell County was within South Carolina's Inner Coastal Plain, a region of moderate Republican strength. On 28 December 1889, a mob of one hundred masked white men broke into the Barnwell County jail during the predawn hours, removed eight black prisoners, tied them to trees, and shot them to death. Two of the victims, Ripley Johnson and Mitchell Adams, were accused of murdering their landlord, James Heffernan, in late October 1889. The other six victims were charged with murdering the son of a plantation owner for whom they worked. In the weeks following the Heffernan killing, three other white men had been either shot or killed by black men, which had aroused "a state of indignant resentment among our [white] people that can be better imagined than described, but cannot be imagined by any one not present in our midst."[31] Rural whites were utterly fearful of black-on-white violence and felt that these racial affronts merited a swift and deadly response.

In the aftermath of the massacre, whites maintained that local blacks had been completely demoralized, but blacks appeared indignant at the funeral of Johnson and Adams a day or so later. Barnwell African Americans regarded the two lynched men as martyrs and had even raised funds to pay for their defense. At the funeral, some 550 blacks lined the streets of Barnwell in a demonstration of solidarity. Black women were conspicuous in their rage, shouting and gesticulating wildly, and asking "that God should burn Barnwell to the ground." Although Johnson and Adams were buried in the African American cemetery, African Americans refused to bury the other men, claiming that whites had killed them and therefore whites should bury them. Whites eventually buried the other victims in a potter's field.[32]

Both blacks and whites understood the massacre in political terms. Governor John P. Richardson asserted that the massacre proved that the two races must be separated. "Unquestionably the two races cannot live together in peace while both are aspiring to supremacy," he told a reporter. The appeals of African Americans "to Congress to give them [political] control of the South," Richardson insisted, had aggravated the racial antagonisms that were the underlying cause of lynching.[33]

In early January 1890, African American leaders from all over the state assembled at the Bethel Methodist Episcopal Church in Columbia to protest the Barnwell massacre. A committee consisting of representatives from three-quarters of South Carolina's counties drafted a statement that claimed that lynching stemmed not from black-on-white crime but from the pervasive notion "that there are no rights for the negro which a white man, whether worthy or unworthy, is bound to respect, when the observance of these rights is judged by a white man as in any way contrary to his personal views or prejudices."[34] A few weeks later, Barnwell blacks gathered at the county courthouse and passed resolutions that recommended that African Americans leave Barnwell for safer locales.

Some three years later, Barnwell County was the scene of another controversial lynching after the fourteen-year-old daughter of a prominent white farmer, J. D. Baxter, was allegedly assaulted on 14 April 1893 by a black man named Henry Williams. Captured in Orangeburg County, Williams was returned to Denmark, where Mamie Baxter identified him on two separate occasions. On 20 April 1893, a mob of several hundred men, including many prominent citizens, broke down the doors to the jail and removed Williams to lynch him. State senator S. G. Mayfield, however, somehow convinced the mob to allow Williams to spend the night in his office until definitive proof became available.

The next morning people from all directions began flooding into

Denmark, prompting the mayor to ban the sale of liquor. Some of the crowd took Williams from Mayfield's office and paraded him through the streets for all to see. The mob made it clear that it would hang Williams at noon, despite doubts about his guilt. One "hard-featured, horny-handed old farmer" expressed the sentiments of many when he declared, "Barnwell's reputation is at stake, and by [God] somebody has got to die."

About an hour before Williams was scheduled to be lynched, however, "four reputable and well-to-do farmers" arrived from Orangeburg County with an alibi for Williams. When the news spread about an alibi, the mob assembled in front of the jail and demanded that the farmers and Williams be interrogated in their presence. Williams appeared with a broad smile on his face, and he quickly called each of the white farmers by name. Each of the farmers claimed that they had seen Williams on their land on the day of the attack, and two of them said that Williams had helped them load phosphate on the morning of the attempted rape. After Mayfield and some of the others present conducted a spirited cross-examination, Mayfield asked the crowd for its verdict. Although some still wanted to hang Williams, the general opinion was that he was innocent but should be kept in jail.[35]

The desire among whites to punish African Americans for the alleged rape resulted in the arrest of more than twenty black men in the days that followed. Mobs assembled daily for over a week in the hope of lynching someone. Consequently, when John Peterson, a local black man who frequented gambling dens and prostitutes, learned that a warrant was out for his arrest, he fled to Columbia and arranged for a meeting with Governor Tillman. Peterson hoped that Tillman would protect him and hold him in Columbia until his trial occurred. After all, in Tillman's inaugural address of 1890, he had described lynching as "a blot on our civilization" and noted that since whites controlled every aspect of the criminal justice system, it was "simply infamous that resort should be had to lynch law." After his first term, however, Tillman's views on lynching changed. Using antiblack rhetoric for political gain, Tillman gave his unequivocal support to lynching during the 1892 election campaign, saying: "Governor as I am, I'd lead a mob to lynch a man who had ravished a white woman. . . . I justify lynching for rape, and, before Almighty God, I'm not ashamed of it."[36]

When Henry Williams had been threatened with lynching, Tillman sent a private letter to Senator Mayfield intimating that he would do nothing to prevent the crime. After a brief meeting with Peterson, Tillman turned him over to the Columbia police. During his interrogation, Peterson convinced the police of his innocence, but Tillman decided to return Peterson to Denmark anyway. Fully aware of the potential for violence, Tillman sacrificed Peterson for political expediency.

When Peterson arrived in Denmark, a crowd of hundreds met his train at the depot. An impromptu trial was held at the offices of Senator Mayfield, who apparently did what he could to save Peterson. When a committee of prominent citizens brought Peterson before Mamie Baxter, she admitted that he was not her attacker. After hearing the news of yet another suspect who could not be identified, the mob became greatly excited, more so when Baxter's father broke down and sobbed that his daughter would never be able to identify her assailant. Despite the tension, Mayfield again convinced the mob to disperse after he promised to have the evidence against Peterson transcribed and read to them at a later time.

Some in the mob, however, were unwilling to wait any longer. Shortly after dark, about twenty-five men battered down the jail door and removed Peterson to the scene of the attack on Baxter. Along the way, people jeered and taunted him. At the lynching scene, about two miles from Denmark, a large crowd of citizens, including farmers, laborers, and professionals, all gathered around a fire. Some talked of burning Peterson while others wanted to mutilate him. When Mayfield learned that the mob had Peterson, he rushed to the scene and pleaded that the black man not be lynched. Mayfield's insistence that Peterson was innocent perhaps persuaded the mob that Peterson should only hang. Six or eight men put a plow line around Peterson's neck and pulled him up over a tree limb. Someone then ordered all those present to retreat to the railroad tracks, from where hundreds of men took shots at Peterson's body.[37]

No evidence existed against Peterson, but this mattered little to those in the lynch mob. The mob acted not because it wanted to purge the community of a known rapist, but because it wanted to send a message to African Americans that their lives were outside the protection of the law. Few if any of those present believed that Peterson was guilty, but as one reporter observed, "Barnwell realized that it had to preach a sermon to its negroes and use unmistakable illustrations." Unwilling to accept the consequences of emancipation, which had accorded black men the same theoretical rights as whites, white men lynched to affirm the notion that no African American could challenge the authority, honor, or property of whites without endangering his or her personal safety.

The African American community responded vociferously to the Denmark lynching. On 26 April 1893, five hundred blacks gathered at the Columbia courthouse to denounce Governor Tillman for his complicity in the lynching and to exhort blacks to resist. Resolutions passed at the meeting called Tillman's actions "unwarranted, unprecedented, and inhuman" and charged that the lynching of blacks proved that the state could not protect African Americans, whether guilty of a crime or not. A predominant theme at the rally was that blacks could no longer wait for a "higher court" to intervene on their behalf. The last speaker to appear, a black mail agent named Shelton, seethed that blacks were "too submissive" and were too dependent on whites for protection. Asserting that the blood of Peterson was dripping "from the fingers of the Governor," Shelton exhorted those gathered to "rise up and defend ourselves against mob law and lynchers."[38] Some blacks did respond to lynching with political action. After a mob of York County whites lynched Jefferson Crawford in June 1894, for instance, African Americans proceeded to register to vote in the "greatest numbers of the past ten years."[39]

The race-based terror that bedeviled Barnwell County culminated in the June 1895 lynching of a sixty-year-old black fisherman named John Barnwell. Barnwell lived alone in a shanty about a mile from Branchville. One Saturday night, four white youths came to Barnwell's house, broke down his door, and shot him for no apparent reason. The next morning a constable took Barnwell's dying statement, in which he identified two of the youths involved. The lynching plague in Barnwell had reached its natural conclusion. Although whites justified lynching in terms of avenging crime, its larger meaning was always directed at the black community as a whole. That four white youths should murder a lonely and defenseless old black man in his home was entirely reasonable under the circumstances. The four boys involved, in the opinion of the *Charleston News and Courier,* had "learned only too well" the lessons that were taught at the "lynching school in which all boys of the State are being educated."[40]

Lynching, which was a violent rejection of the concept of black equality, ironically became worse after disfranchisement in both Mississippi and South Carolina. To be sure, lynching activity resulted from a boiling cauldron of social tensions, not just political conflict, but in Mississippi, lynching incidents increased by a third in the ten years following the passage of the 1890 constitution as compared to the decade immediately prior. In South Carolina, the situation was similar: lynching incidents increased by 25 percent in the fifteen years following the new constitution that had disfranchised blacks.

Lynching grew worse after disfranchisement because the court system became one of the last spheres of public life where blacks had at least theoretical equality with whites. Southern courts were far from benevolent toward black defendants, and no doubt became harsher after Jim Crow, but the southern judicial system did not always adhere to the rigid precepts of white supremacy.[41] Even when a case involved the inflammatory charge of rape, the courts (or the state) sometimes acted against the presumed will of the white community. In 1890, for instance, Willie Leaphart was sentenced to death for rape in Lexington, South Carolina, but after evidence surfaced about the veracity of the charge, Governor John Richardson granted Leaphart a reprieve. When the presiding judge ordered Leaphart to be jailed in Columbia for safekeeping, the local white community became so outraged that they sent a committee of fifteen prominent citizens to request that the governor return Leaphart to Lexington. After the men pledged their "law-abiding" reputations as a guarantee for Leaphart's safety, the governor agreed to return him, but ordered an undercover detective to remain in Leaphart's cell as a precaution. Shortly after Leaphart was returned to Lexington, a mob broke into the jail and shot Leaphart in his cell (the detective was wounded in the fracas). The mob adorned the jail with a sign that blamed Richardson and the judge for the lynching. The next day a drunken mob threatened Leaphart's white attorney and his family with violence, apparently in anger over the attorney's defense of an alleged rapist.[42]

After the removal of blacks from politics, whites began to doubt the wisdom of having courts enact "justice" for interracial crimes besides rape. Disfranchisement had repudiated the specter of political equality that existed in the federal constitution, but courts still operated under a theoretical premise of equality. Disfranchisement was a salve for the wounded patriarchal authority of white males, but it could do little to prevent intractable blacks from continuing to resist the demands of their alleged superiors. Lynching violently repudiated any notion of black-white equality and served notice that blacks who challenged white hegemony were beyond the protection of law. After disfranchisement, which was intended to shore up the power of white males, the primary cause of lynching changed from the purported defense of white female virtue to direct attacks against the person or interests of white males themselves. This was especially apparent in Republican regions, where disfranchisement had eliminated the need to cry rape. Prior to disfranchisement, whites frequently resorted to lynching for alleged sexual crimes to demonize black males and to show that they were unfit for the franchise. Before 1895, more than half of all lynching incidents in Republican regions of South Carolina, for example, resulted from alleged sexual assaults of one kind or another; but after disfranchisement, only about 30 percent of lynching incidents in these same regions stemmed from alleged sexual crimes (see fig. 5). Lynching in retaliation for murder or assault-related crimes, conversely, increased dramatically from approximately 13 percent of all lynching incidents in the decade and a half before 1896 to nearly 29 percent of all lynching incidents from 1896 to 1910. In Republican regions of Mississippi, the same pattern was evident: rape-related lynching declined substantially while lynching for murder or attempted murder increased from about 36 percent of all lynching incidents during the 1880s to approximately 43 percent of all lynching incidents in the decade that followed disfranchisement (see fig. 6).

The removal of black males from politics did not end the "negro question" as whites had hoped, but sometimes made it more likely that

FIGURE 5. Alleged causes of lynchings in South Carolina regions, 1881–1915 (percent)

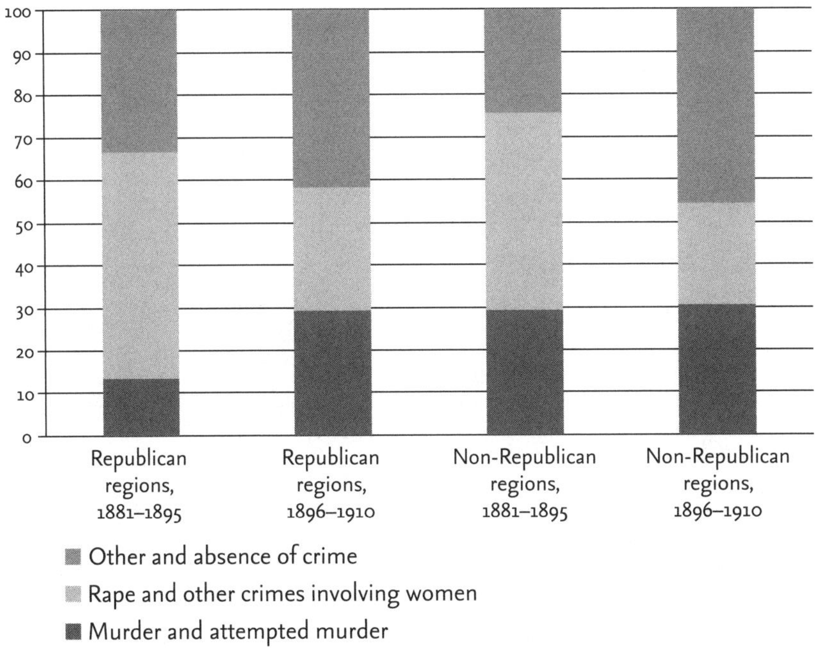

interpersonal confrontations between blacks and whites would result in lynching. The conflict between caste and justice, which had always plagued southern courts, became exacerbated after disfranchisement. In February 1904, for example, Cairo Williams shot and killed a white farmer, Thurston McGhee, during an argument over an animal trade.[43] McGhee apparently had his eye on Williams's mule and tried to browbeat him into trading the animal for a horse. Williams refused the "offer," but McGhee ordered a companion to take the mule from Williams anyway. When Williams attempted to take his mule back, McGhee hit Williams several times and repeatedly knocked him down. Terrified, Williams attempted to flee, but tripped over a buggy shaft, only to find McGhee charging at him, gun in hand. A crowd, which had gathered at the scene, started chanting "shoot him, shoot him!" Fearing for his life, Williams attempted to flee, but a group of whites cut him off. In desperation, Williams fired two shots in the direction of McGhee that mortally

FIGURE 6. Alleged causes of lynchings in Mississippi regions, 1881–1900 (percent)

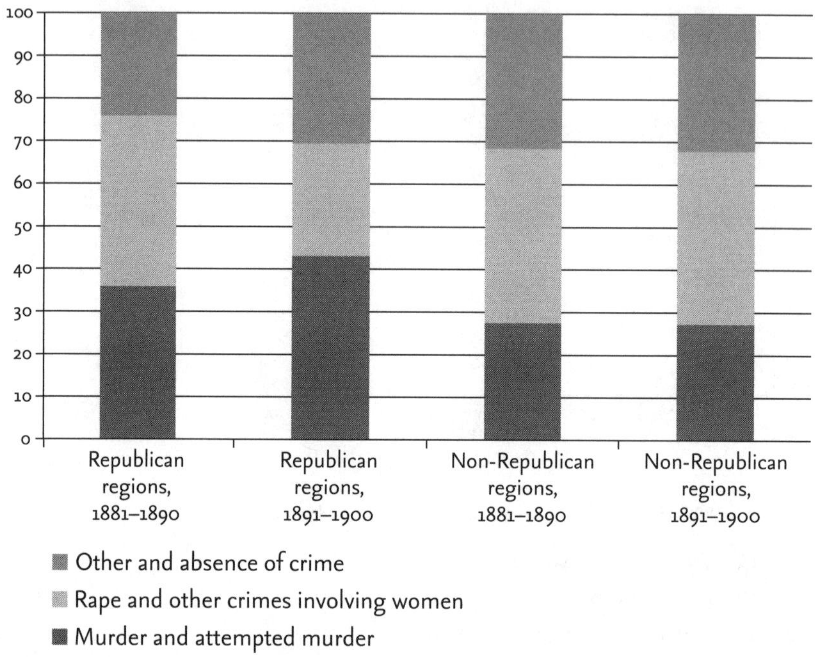

wounded the farmer. Williams probably would have been lynched on the spot had it not been for the local sheriff, who later that night surreptitiously removed Williams to Kingstree for safekeeping.

Williams was held in Columbia until April, when his trial was scheduled to open at Lake City. In a decision that shocked the sensibilities of local whites, the presiding judge decided to continue the case because the judge claimed that Williams could not obtain "anything even remotely resembling justice" in Lake City. In defending his decision, the judge argued that the courts guaranteed every person equal protection under the law and that he had a duty to "see that substantial justice is done, be the party on trial white or black." The judge admonished Lake City whites that they were "doing themselves and their community a great wrong when they allow their feelings to crop out in the presence of the Court and of jurors who must unconsciously be influenced by their neighbors." Under the circumstances, the judge blamed the community that a speedy trial could not be held. Adding insult to injury, the judge appointed two of Kingstree's best lawyers as defense attorneys for Williams and continued the case until the June term of court.

When Williams's four-day trial began in late June 1904, black and white spectators, who for different reasons were intensely interested in the outcome of the case, packed the courtroom. To the disbelief of the white population, the jury could not reach a verdict because they could not agree whether Williams was guilty of murder or of manslaughter. A mistrial was simply too much for local whites to endure, and that evening a mob took Williams from the custody of officers and shot him dozens of times. The court, which had accorded Cairo Williams the appearance of impartiality and fairness, had affirmed the equality of whites and blacks at least in respect to the law. This was antithetical to the outlook of whites who used violence to coerce and control the behavior of blacks. A black man who resisted the violent intimidation of a white man was a threat to white ascendancy, and whites not only lynched Cairo Williams but the law as well.

Sometimes disfranchisement intensified divisions within the white community itself, which in turn provided the impetus for a new wave of lynching. After disfranchisement, most of the growth in lynching activity in Mississippi, for example, occurred in white regions of the state. In regions with no black legislators, lynching increased 64 percent, from forty-five incidents during the period from 1881 to 1890 to seventy-four incidents between 1891 and 1900. Table 4 demonstrates that in the Piney Woods, the Pine Hills, and the Red Hills, all of which were predominantly white regions, lynching increased dramatically after the adoption of the constitution of 1890. In these regions, the disfranchising constitution helped trigger an unprecedented outbreak of lynching, no doubt made worse by the knowledge that whites could now lynch blacks with impunity. John Tommas, a black tenant farmer from Mississippi, for instance, wrote the Justice Department in 1899, lamenting that because whites had "all the advantage of us We are Shot down for nothing We are killed by the white people in the State of Miss. just like were . . . some . . . pherocious beast."[44]

Although the severe economic depression of the 1890s contributed to the increase in lynching, political considerations were also important. The suffrage restrictions contained in the new constitution disfranchised not only blacks but also poor whites, which meant certain defeat for the Populist Party in Mississippi.[45] Denied any legitimate role in the political process, disfranchised whites lashed back by destroying property and terrorizing black tenants, who often worked for wealthy, white, absentee landlords. The two white regions that had the most lynching activity in the decade after disfranchisement, the Pine Hills and the Red Hills, also experienced the largest decline in numbers of voters between the presidential elections of 1896 and 1900. Disfranchisement exacerbated class tensions that sparked an increase in lynching in white regions of the Mississippi.

Sensing the threat that terroristic violence posed to the prevailing order, establishment whites began to condemn lynching of all kinds. In the mid-1890s, the *Natchez Democrat* decried the number of lynchings that occurred in the state and "hoped that some means may soon be derived by which these extra judicial methods may have a stop put to them."[46] The *Jackson Evening News* condemned lynching as "wrong from beginning to end" and, reflecting its own racist attitudes, commented that a recent increase in brutality "would disgrace the center of Africa."[47] In early 1897, the *Vicksburg Commercial-Herald* counseled African Americans not to feel vengeful over lynching but to "watch and wait" because time would prove Shakespeare's dictum that "bloody instructions, being taught, return to plague the inventors." Until then, the black man should console himself, the paper counseled, "with the thought that for the crime of taking life without warrant or process of law, for the reproach and stain it brings upon the state, he and his race are blameless."[48]

During the 1890s, the white region of Mississippi that suffered the most from lynching was the Pine Hills. Here terroristic bands of "whitecappers" wreaked havoc on the lives of African Americans for more than a decade. Located immediately to the east of the more fertile Old Natchez lands, much of the Pine Hills was filled with longleaf yellow pine trees. Because of its sandy soil, most of the Pine Hills was of little use for farming, which enabled some African Americans to buy land in the region.[49] As late as the turn of the century, more than 18 percent of all farmers in the Pine Hills were black landowners, the highest percentage in the state.

When northern timber companies began harvesting pine trees in the region, land values increased tremendously, more than 40 percent in the 1880s.[50] Higher land values improved the financial position of African American landowners, which earned them the enmity of their whitecapper neighbors. In addition to the relative prosperity of some blacks, whites resented the labor practices of sawmill owners and merchants, both of whom preferred cheaper black labor to white.[51]

Merchants found African Americans more amenable to their needs than white "Cane Hill Billies." Merchants often employed blacks to work farms foreclosed on whites for supplies furnished. The region also had many Jewish merchants, who generally preferred black tenants because they were less likely to share the anti-Semitic sentiments of whites.[52] Some whites begrudged the good reputation that black tenants had among white merchants, which often made it easier for black farmers to obtain credit than their white counterparts.[53] The relative independence of black tenants who worked for absentee landlords prompted further resentment among some whites.[54]

Whitecappers threatened and destroyed the lives of blacks and the property of whites, which caused authorities to respond vigorously to whitecappers' terrorism. In early 1893, for instance, Hiller & Company, a Jewish firm in Pike County, Mississippi, claimed that during the previous two months, twenty-seven of its houses had been burned and fifty thousand dollars in property had been destroyed. The firm threatened to sue the county for its losses. Even after whites formed "Law and Order" clubs to combat the whitecappers, the depredations continued unabated.[55]

From 1891 to 1895, no fewer than sixteen lynchings occurred in the eight counties that composed the Pine Hills region. After a one-year hiatus in 1896, at least six more lynchings occurred in the region before 1901. Although whitecappers were not responsible for all of these lynchings, they committed at least eleven (50 percent of the total) and possibly more. A typical incident involved Jesse Pittman, an "inoffensive" black man from Marion County, whom ten whitecappers shot in the middle of the night as Pittman slept. Authorities charged the men involved with Pittman's murder, but a grand jury failed to return an indictment.[56] Although the historian William F. Holmes concludes that whitecappers embodied the "dark side" of populism, whitecappers should not be distinguished from other terroristic mobs that operated in the region, especially because whitecappers reappeared in the early twentieth century, years after the demise of populism.[57] Terroristic mobs continued to lynch well after the South had solidified politically, often out of a sense of frustration with economic and social conditions.

White mobs directed their dissatisfaction at African Americans who advocated black equality or at black institutions of advancement. In July 1894, for instance, a group of seventy-three whites from Amite County, among them "some of the coolest of the law-abiding element," lynched a black schoolteacher named Hood, whom whites claimed had insulted the local school superintendent by accusing him of "showing particularity in his appointments[,] discriminating between whites and blacks." Similar to the practice of whitecappers, the mob appointed a smaller committee to confront the man at a local schoolhouse.[58] The mob claimed that they only wanted to warn Hood to leave the county, but Hood apparently thought otherwise and killed the committee spokesman, Nolan Hanks, who was a young husband with three children. After a mob riddled Hood with bullets, whites held a mass meeting to exonerate themselves from responsibility for their actions and to establish a relief fund for Hanks's family.

A few weeks later, the terror began anew when whites burned two black schoolhouses.[59] The local paper blamed the atrocities on "a low down set of whites who are taking advantage of the present state of affairs." The paper expressed regret over the violence but said that such incidents could not be helped because God had decreed that "the sons of Ham should be the servants unto their brethren, and it is flying in the face of Providence to disobey a Biblical injunction." The paper warned "the negro to respect the white man always and to so live that the white man will respect him." In an ominous reminder to African Americans, local whites decreed the day that they lynched Hood as Nolan Hanks Memorial Day.[60]

In South Carolina, disfranchisement also helped to create a "racialized" social milieu in which whites increasingly vented their anger and frustrations on blacks. Table 4 shows that total lynching incidents in South Carolina increased by a fourth in the decade and a half after disfranchisement as compared to the fifteen years before. More than 70 percent of this increase occurred in what had been Republican regions, especially the Outer Coastal Plain. After disfranchisement in South Carolina, lynching became more wanton and terroristic. Lynching for no apparent crime or for minor offenses, for example, increased dramatically from about a third of all lynching incidents in the years before 1896 to more than two-thirds from 1896 to 1910.[61]

The lynching of Frazier Baker and his family at Lake City, South Carolina, starkly revealed the racial realities that disfranchisement helped spawn. Lake City was a small town situated in the northwest corner of Williamsburg County, which was nearly 63 percent black in 1900. Lake City, however, was a "white man's town" that had fewer than a dozen black residents, none of whom owned "a foot of land" within the corporate limits of the town. Hence, the white citizens of Lake City were shocked in September 1897 when Frazier Baker, a forty-year-old "coal black" schoolteacher and Colored Farmers' Alliance man from Florence County, was appointed postmaster of Lake City. E. H. Deas, the black deputy collector of internal revenue for South Carolina, had recommended Baker for the job, and racial tensions flared almost immediately after Baker assumed office. Whites considered Baker "uncivil, ignorant, and lazy." The previous white postmaster had delivered mail three times per day, whites complained, but Baker managed only one daily delivery.[62]

Although Baker did reduce service, he did so only after whites repeatedly tried to kill him. In December 1897, Washington sent a postal inspector to investigate the complaints. When the inspector recommended that the office be closed, whites burned the post office to the ground in the hope that Baker would be forced to resign since no white person would rent the government space in town. Seeking to ensure Baker's safety, the U.S. postmaster general ordered Baker to restrict mail delivery to daylight hours. After the government acquired an old schoolhouse in the "suburbs," however, the tension dissipated, and Baker felt safe enough to send for his wife and six children in early February 1898. Some local whites were determined to remove Baker from office at any cost, however, and shortly after the Baker family arrived, a mob conspired to kill the postmaster. A few days before the lynching, Baker received new threats on his life, which he reported to Washington.[63]

On the night of 21 February 1898, the Baker family went to bed as usual, but around 1:00 a.m. Baker awoke to find the post office (which doubled as the family's residence) in flames. Baker leapt from his bed and tried to douse the fire lapping at his door with some jugs of water but to no avail. As he gathered his family, Baker told his son Lincoln to run for help, but as soon as the boy opened the door shots rang out. Realizing the danger, Baker dragged his son back from the door, screamed at his attackers, and paced frantically in the small room, praying for God's deliverance. As the heat became unbearable, Baker told his wife, Lavinia, that the family "might as well die running as to die standing still." With his family behind him, Baker started for the door, but before he could open it, a bullet killed two-year-old Julia Baker, who was in her mother's arms. After he realized that his youngest child was dead, Baker desperately opened the door to a deadly barrage of bullets that blasted him onto his wife's lap. Although wounded in the arm, Lavinia Baker somehow managed to calm her panicked family, and they crawled out of the house and hid in some nearby bushes. Two of the children, Sarah and Millie, who were seven and five respectively, managed to escape unharmed; but eighteen-year-old Rosa had her left arm broken from a gunshot; fourteen-year-old Cora had a bullet lodged in her right hand; and eleven-year-old Lincoln suffered a severe abdominal wound and a broken right forearm. Although the surviving family members remained in Lake City for three days after the lynching, whites provided the Bakers with no medical treatment for their injuries.[64]

The ghastly lynching of the Bakers elicited condemnation from nearly all quarters. Although South Carolina senator Benjamin Tillman defended the white residents of Lake City as "proud people" who "would not receive their mail from a nigger," South Carolina governor William Ellerbe described the lynching as "the worst incident that had happened in the state in years." Upon hearing of the lynching, South Carolina congressional representative William Elliot exclaimed, "My God, it can't be true," and argued that such "hot-headed action" was not reflective of the attitude of most whites.[65]

While most white newspapers condemned the lynching, many also regarded it as a predictable consequence of Baker's appointment. The *Charleston News and Courier,* for instance, described the lynching as "one of the most dastardly crimes ever committed in this blood-stained State," but said that Baker's appointment was an "outrage" and that such an incompetent person "would not have been appointed postmaster for any town North, East or West." The *Augusta (Ga.) Chronicle* accused the McKinley administration of the worst "folly" for "trying to force upon a community a public official who was repugnant to the people," but conceded that "an unacceptable postmaster does not furnish justification for the murder and massacre of women and children." The *Louisville Courier Journal* called the lynching "the most revolting crime ever perpetrated by white men in South Carolina," but noted that the McKinley administration had refused to remove Baker from office despite the objections of both South Carolina senators and the local congressional representative.[66]

The *Columbia State* bluntly described the lynching as a "bitter shame" for South Carolina that demonstrated that "mob savagery" had reached "its apex." The *State* conceded that Baker's appointment had been offensive to whites, but pointed out that Baker was not the first African American postmaster in the South. With racist irony, the *State* wondered if "Apache savages [could] be more cruel, more ruthless, more lustful of blood than these civilized white men of Williamsburg County?" The white people of Lake City, the *State* claimed, had descended to "the moral and religious level of the aboriginal African." "Where," the *State* decried, "are the white man's characteristics in this deed? Where is his superiority shown? Where do we find the fruits of his thousands of years of civilization and self-control and cultivated conscience?" Clearly concerned about the political backlash that the lynching might engender, the *State* predicted that the cowardly crime against Baker and his family would haunt South Carolina for decades to come. The Baker lynching, the paper warned, "will be a taunt in the mouths of our enemies and, we must bow our heads under the lash of their scorn."[67]

Some northern newspapers viewed the lynching as not only a stain against South Carolina but also as an affront to the moral standing of the United States in the international community, especially at a time when the United States was admonishing Spain about alleged atrocities in Cuba. The *New York Tribune,* for instance, acknowledged that Baker's appointment was probably unwise, but noted it was deeply disturbed by the "savage" connotations that the lynching evoked. "The crime was not done by wild Kurd tribesmen on the women and children of an Armenian village, nor by some Afghan on the family of the British invader, nor by a Russian martinet on some Siberian exiles, nor by Turkish masters of wretched Cretans, nor by Spanish soldiery on Cuban rebels, nor even by red Indians dancing naked about a prairie-schooner camp," intoned the *Tribune.* "It was done by white men, descendants of the founders of one of the thirteen original states of the American Union, the boasted leader of the world's latest and best civilization." This fiendish murder resulted not from a "noble if ungovernable rage," according to the *Tribune,* but instead was disturbing evidence of the "measure of South Carolina's barbarian debauch."

The next day, the *Tribune* compared the lynching to the attack on Fort Sumter because both incidents were direct assaults against the authority of the federal government. The *Tribune* urged that "every one concerned in the attack ought to hang" because the "infant-murdering, women-slaughtering savagery" of South Carolina needed a severe reminder "that the United States Government is not to be trifled with, and that assassination is not to be naturalized in this country as a political force." If the federal government did not take decisive action against the lynchers, the *Tribune* said, then the United States "had better not preach humanity to the rest of the world."[68]

Other northern white papers agreed that the lynching was not only a challenge to the authority of the federal government but also to the racial policies of the Republican Party. The *New York Post,* for example, argued that the "central fact" to emerge from the lynching was the "simple truth" that "Southern whites resent, not simply the appointment of a bad negro as postmaster, but of any negro, and the same is equally true of other offices." Southern whites, according to the *Post,* could not countenance any pretense of black equality, which was why whites in both South Carolina and Mississippi had disfranchised the black populations living in those states. The North, the *Post* admitted, was little better, and the paper asserted that a Republican administration would never have dared to appoint a black postmaster in the North. According to the *Post,* the Baker lynching cruelly confirmed that "the experiment of having two races live side by side on equal terms . . . is not working well." Therefore, the *Post* argued, the country should approach the prospect of annexing Hawaii, "with its native Kanakas and imported Orientals," and Cuba, "with its heterogeneous population of Negroes and Spaniards" with caution.[69]

Given the international tensions that had arisen from the *Maine* disaster, some northern newspapers recognized that the federal government could hardly ignore the political challenge that the Baker lynching presented. The *Chicago Tribune,* for instance, advised the administration to use troops, if necessary, to bring the perpetrators to justice and said that not taking vigorous action in the case "would be tantamount to condoning a crime against the United States." The *New York Times* agreed that "some exemplary hanging" was in order, but said that after the law had been vindicated, the Republican Party should abandon "its ill-judged laws of thirty years ago." The attempt to "make black white" had been a "terrible mistake," according to the *Times,* that was "an unendurable exasperation to white and a cruel illusion for black."[70]

Some African American newspapers agreed with white papers that it was wrong for the McKinley administration to appoint black officials in the South. The *Indianapolis (Ind.) Freeman,* for example, said that Baker's appointment was "reprehensible" in a community that suffered from such obvious racial antipathy. The *Freeman* argued that it was pointless to sacrifice individual lives in a futile effort to eradicate racism. The fact that blacks had supported McKinley for president was, according to the *Freeman,* irrelevant to whether or not blacks should be appointed to patronage positions. Lynchings, the *Freeman* asserted, were directed not against individuals but against the entire black race. "A blow at a white man is a blow at the man only," said the paper, but "a blow at a Negro under certain conditions is a blow at the race." If the federal government was not strong enough to protect black officeholders from malevolent whites, the *Freeman* asserted, then the government should not appoint African Americans to these positions.[71]

Other African American papers, however, contended more caustically that the only way to prevent such atrocities in the future was for blacks to resist vigorously the mob tactics of whites. The *Omaha (Neb.) Afro-American Sentinel,* for example, condemned southern whites as "the most brutal, cruel and cowardly element of humanity known to modern times," but chastised southern blacks as "arrant cowards" who seemed "incapable of offering any effective resistance to their fiendish persecutors." Lynching, the paper stated, was a degrading legacy of slavery that stemmed not only from a lack of respect among whites for the rights of blacks, but also from a shameful dearth of "manly resistance" in the African American community. "Could any man of reflection believe," wondered the *Sentinel,* "that had the 100 white savages who assassinated Baker and his family known that even as many as 25 courageous Negroes were awaiting their coming, that they would ever have persisted in the execution of their fiendish plan?" Despite the obvious signs that Lake City whites would physically harm Baker and his family in order to force him from office, the *Sentinel* despaired "that there was not even ONE Negro in the whole community that possessed courage enough to move a finger in self-defense." Blacks were the majority population in South Carolina, and "as a general thing, one Negro in the South—and especially in South Carolina—is equal in physical ability to two whites," which made the failure of the black community to resist white aggression all the more exasperating for the *Sentinel.* Southern African Americans would wait in vain for the federal government to protect them from the depredations of whites. When it came to lynching, warned the *Sentinel,* the federal government "is as powerless under the Constitution to protect them [African Americans] as is the government of Great Britain."[72]

Other African American newspapers worried about the divisive consequences of the Baker lynching at a time when the country needed to present a united front against Spain. The *Washington Bee,* for instance, claimed that the Baker atrocity eclipsed all other lynchings in terms of "malignity and deep-dyed prejudice and hatred" and "open defiance of national authority." The *Bee* cautioned that the "uncertainty of life and property" that African Americans endured in the South would sap the patriotism necessary to fight a war against Spain. Furthermore, the "spirit of desperation" that had descended upon southern blacks might lead to vindictive reprisals against whites. Under the circumstances, the *Bee* urged the McKinley administration "to stay the hand of crime and insult and murder which is systematically and eternally raised against the striving colored people."[73]

The *Springfield (Ill.) Record* sounded a similar theme and noted that Baker had been lynched on the same day that President McKinley had extolled the virtues of American freedom and had told a Philadelphia audience that the United States had never failed to honor a "just obligation." But the stain of lynching, which the government was apparently powerless to remove, made African Americans wonder if "the God of justice is blind and that they have no country, no home, and no nation." Future generations, the *Record* predicted, would "marvel at the criminal negligence of the statesmen who have in their hands the power to right this wrong, in-so-far, as it is possible, and to punish the guilty ones who have no regard for the rights of American citizens, whose skin happens to be black."[74]

Most African American newspapers only indirectly rebuked McKinley for the government's responsibility in the affair, but some editors were less circumspect when it came to southern politicians. The *Salt Lake City (Utah) Broad-Ax,* for example, denounced South Carolina senators Benjamin Tillman and John McLauren as "unmitigated and barefaced prevaricators" for suggesting that the lynching had resulted from a visceral desire among whites to avoid contact with blacks. Had the senators forgotten, the *Broad-Ax* asked, that during slavery, "all of the handsome female negroes were compelled to occupy a bed in the room which was used for sleeping purposes by the sons of the aristocratic slave holders . . . for no other purpose but to satisfy their carnal desires and passions?" Male slaves had also been house servants who had been "compelled to wash the white ladies' feet." If, during slavery, southern white men had no objection to sleeping with female slaves and males slaves were allowed "to bathe the feet of the fair blue-eyed Saxon ladies," then the *Broad-Ax* mockingly wondered why a gentleman like Baker could not "be permitted to serve in the capacity of postmaster?"

It was ludicrous for the country to debate the propriety of converting foreign "heathens" to Christianity, according to the *Broad-Ax,* when the South was full of sadistic hypocrites who harbored an intense hatred for African Americans. Until white Christians radically changed their behavior toward blacks, the *Broad-Ax* declared, "we shall continue to hold the religion of the cross in derision and regard it being nothing more than an empty sound which signifies nothing and which is as false as h—ll itself." A few weeks later, the *Broad-Ax* commented that the only hope for southern blacks was for McKinley to declare martial law in Lake City and "have every devil implicated in the awful crime shot to death." The cowardly whites who committed lynchings would understand only one thing: "a prompt dreadful warning . . . such as will make their souls tremble."[75]

The *Kansas City (Kans.) American Citizen* also denounced the hypocrisy of southern politicians. "The southern statesmen who plead for cuba [*sic*]," the paper declared, "could learn a valuable lesson by looking around their own blood curdling confines of butchery." Southerners claimed to respect the Constitution, but the *Citizen* asserted that "there is about as much respect for the constitution of the United States, in the southern states, as there is for the bible in hades [*sic*]." The "highly civilized" mob that killed Baker and his child defied "all law, state, human or divine." Southern states, said the *Citizen,* were "black with treason and anarchy," and if the federal government could not protect the lives of its "humblest citizens," it "should be wiped from the face of the earth." The mob reigned supreme in the South, the *Citizen* bemoaned, and "to its sulpharious dictum, all law and reason bend the quivering knee."[76]

Partially in response to such criticism, the McKinley administration offered a $1,500 reward for the apprehension and conviction of the lynchers. At a cabinet meeting in early March 1898, Attorney General Griggs advised the president that the federal government would have jurisdiction in the case unless South Carolina authorities first arrested those involved.[77] A few days later, however, a Williamsburg County grand jury proved that white men in the area were not willing to take up the gauntlet for the law, and the grand jury did not even mention the lynching in its presentment. Bitterly disappointed, the *Charleston News and Courier* commented that the grand jury's silence had "condoned the most horrible crime ever committed in South Carolina."[78] The grand jury's inaction assured that any attempt to prosecute the lynchers in state court would be nothing more than a farce.

Federal officials, however, conducted a vigorous investigation of the case, providing Abial Lathrop, the U.S. attorney in Charleston, with "unlimited means" to pursue the perpetrators.[79] Despite assigning two postal investigators and a private detective to the case, however, the government found it difficult to secure evidence against the lynchers. In mid-April 1898, Lathrop wrote the attorney general in Washington that while some progress had been made in the case, the government lacked sufficient evidence to obtain warrants. Lathrop complained that citizens in Lake City were "terrorized to such an extent that it is difficult to get anyone to speak to a person supposed to be interested in the investigation, it being generally understood that to do so will place their lives in jeopardy." In order to entice witnesses to come forth, Lathrop asked that the attorney general grant him the authority to remove witnesses from Lake City under government protection and to compensate them for lost income.[80]

Approximately two months later, Lathrop reported that two men who were present at the lynching and who could identify nearly all those involved had expressed a willingness to testify on behalf of the government.[81] Eleven men were eventually tried in the case for murder, assault, conspiracy to commit murder, and destruction of mail.[82] None of the accused were persons of importance in the community, nor did they possess much wealth. Hence, Lathrop found it curious that so many of Lake City's prominent citizens came to the preliminary examination in Charleston in July 1898. Lathrop informed the attorney general that although the accused were poor, they were "well supplied with means . . . and in case bail should be granted will be able to obtain any amount that may be required."[83] Obviously, the alleged lynchers had the support of at least some of Lake City's more prosperous citizens.

The trial of the accused lynchers began in April 1899 and lasted almost two weeks. The jury, which Lathrop described as "one of the best juries ever impaneled for the trial of any case in this State," was composed of businessmen from all over South Carolina.[84] The government's star witness was Joseph Newham, an illiterate forty-seven-year-old North Carolina native who had lived in Williamsburg County for nearly thirty years. Newham had done a little bit of everything to support himself, including "teamstering, shoemaking, harness making, etc." He testified frankly about those involved in the lynching, claiming that eight of the eleven men on trial had participated in the crime. Newham admitted to lighting the post office fire and said that he felt little remorse over the death of Baker and his daughter. Under cross-examination, the defense attorney and South Carolina congressional representative George S. Legare impugned Newham's credibility and intimated that Newham had concocted his story to obtain money from the government. Newham admitted that he now worked in a Washington, D.C., mail-bag repair shop for fifty dollars per month and that he had earned only about eighteen dollars per month from his wagon business in Lake City.[85]

Another important government witness was M. B. Springs, a twenty-eight-year-old bicycle repairman who had a shop in Lake City. Both Newham and Springs testified that the instigator of the lynching was Henry Stokes, a newcomer to Lake City who owned a small grocery in the eastern part of town. Springs said that Stokes had first approached him about intimidating Baker in mid-February. Springs agreed to join the mob, with the understanding that "we were to shoot and scare Baker away without killing him." After the mob decided to murder Baker, however, Springs claimed that he backed out of the group.[86]

Springs paid dearly for his testimony. Before the lynching, Springs had been well regarded in Lake City. Three months after the trial, however, Springs feared for his life and wrote the Department of Justice that he had "lost all hopes as I cant get any thing to do any wheare around L.C." Springs complained that he could get no work around Charleston either because "those People have [m]any Friends and I have asked for help untill it is of no use to ask any more . . . I am afraid I will have to leave for good and change my name if I Stay South and I have bin Broken up By telling the Trouth and I thought the Goverment would help me but they have not done so and I think it a Poore Dept of Justic that would take up a Poore man like me and ruin him."[87] Unable to find a job for Springs, Lathrop eventually had Springs arrested and placed under court protection.[88]

At least two African Americans testified at the trial, and one claimed that he had been at the post office the night of the lynching. Henderson Williams testified that he had clearly seen seven or eight armed white men leaving the burning post office, but that he only recognized one of them. Although Williams attended the coroner's inquest held at the scene, he was afraid to say anything and claimed that if he had spoken up, he would have been killed.

Two weeks after the lynching, Williams personally experienced the lingering aftereffects of the Baker tragedy, when he had a dispute with a white store owner named Jones. Williams had gone to Jones's store to collect a debt that Jones owed him, but Jones wanted Williams to "trade it out." When Williams refused, Jones warned him that if he did not leave town immediately, "we'll do you like they did Baker." In 1887, Williams claimed that he had almost been lynched on a "wrong report for nothing," and Jones's threat prompted Williams to flee immediately for Florence.[89]

After nearly two weeks of testimony, the jury deliberated almost twenty-four hours before adjourning in a mistrial. Eleven of the jurors reportedly wanted to convict Henry Stokes, but one "lone juror did not intend to see Stokes convicted and his friends set free, and on this account the body failed to agree."[90] Although Lathrop told the attorney general that he would press the case again in November, he admitted that he "would gladly be relieved of the terrible strain and responsibility of another trial of this case."[91]

After the first trial, the notoriety of the case prompted the government to leave it on the docket for nearly a decade, but no second prosecution ensued.[92] In the aftermath of the trial, the *Charleston News and Courier* commented that no one doubted that at least some of the accused were guilty. Political and race prejudice was the only thing, according to the *News and Courier,* "that stood between them [the accused] and the punishment provided by the law."[93] Still the *News and Courier* hoped vainly that the trial would be a "triumph for order and a promise of better things in the future."

African American newspapers initially stated that the trial would have a salutary impact on southern race relations, but this optimism dissipated quickly. The *Indianapolis (Ind.) Freeman,* which followed the conciliatory path of Booker T. Washington, described the news of the indictments as "welcome intelligence" that demonstrated that the Republican Party was still a strong ally of blacks. The *Freeman* hoped that the trial would shed a "great light" upon the "very ugly race problem."[94]

The *St. Paul (Minn.) Appeal* wrote that the nation's 10 million black citizens would carefully watch the judge and jury in the trial to see if the white South would live up to its own exalted conception of itself. "Let us see," asked the *Appeal,* if white southerners, who claimed "to be the embodiment of all the best of mankind, physically, mentally, morally, the best in honor, in the administration of exact and blind justice; the best in all the Christian virtues which make men better," would "make the punishment fit the crime?" If those responsible for committing "one of the blackest crimes in the nation's history" were not convicted, the *Appeal* despaired, then "in the name of God and humanity, what are we to hope for?" Just a week later, however, the *Appeal* lamented that "the whole thing is a stupendous farce and before they get through we expect them to prove that Baker and his children 'came to their deaths by natural causes or were frozen to death.'"[95]

The *Washington, D.C., Colored American* considered the Lake City case as nothing less than "Republican government on trial." A "lack of centralized governmental authority," in the opinion of the *Colored American,* was "breeding the train of evils which threatens the life of our republic." The *Colored American* took solace from the fact that "thinking white men" shared this sentiment. In support of this claim, the *Colored American* reprinted an editorial from the *Philadelphia Evening Bulletin* that argued that if the "unspeakable atrocity" that befell Baker and his family had been committed by a "band of Tagals" against an American family in the Philippines, "the whole country would have thrilled with indignation and the demand for instant vengeance would have been unanimous." A white mob had attacked a black family in South Carolina, however, and the supposedly superior Christian civilization of the United States had waited more than a year to bring the accused to trial. "If this country cannot legally punish the assassins bred in its own bosom," the *Evening Bulletin* claimed, then "in some part of the United States . . . republican government is a failure."[96]

The *Cleveland (Ohio) Gazette,* an African American weekly, also asserted that the trial would "test the good faith and integrity of the nation." The government would either vindicate the rights of its citizens, no matter what the color, or "ignominiously surrender its power to rebels and traitors." "The right to participate in the blessings and affairs of the national government is a privilege conferred under the fundamental law," wrote the *Gazette,* "and it is not the province of an individual nor [*sic*] of a state to interfere." A mob had interfered infamously with Baker's rights, and the government had a duty "to ferret out the assailants and bring them to justice." Although past decisions of the Supreme Court made it unlikely that justice would be served, the *Gazette* expressed hope that the country was "gradually coming to the realization of the solemn truth, that enjoyment of the rights of the people individually and collectively depends upon their security."[97]

After a mistrial was declared, the *Washington, D.C., Colored American* lashed out bitterly against the McKinley administration. In a front-page story, the reporter John E. Bruce argued that the administration should have known that a conviction was impossible in South Carolina and demanded a change of venue. If Ulysses Grant had still been president, Bruce argued, the trial would have been moved, but the timid McKinley had "unlimited faith . . . in the honor of the southern white man." Bruce was indignant that African Americans had played no role in the trial, and he charged that the whole trial was nothing more than a case of "political bunco."[98]

When Lake City whites asked the government to reopen the post office, most African American newspapers bitterly denounced their hypocrisy. "The contention of this uncivilized burg," wrote the *Colored American,* "is the height of impudence." Lake City whites had "committed an outrage against humanity," and "trampled upon the authority of the government," but now they wanted their mail privileges restored. The *Colored American* advised that the government should reopen the Lake City post office when Baker's murderers were convicted and not before. The *St. Paul (Minn.) Appeal* rebuked the *Atlanta Constitution* for supporting the reopening of the post office. The *Appeal* claimed that the mob had brought the situation on themselves through "their treasonable actions in refusing to accept the postmaster . . . simply because he was an Afro-American." Whites, the *Appeal* claimed, were "getting off entirely too easy by simply having their mail stopped."[99]

The *Cleveland (Ohio) Gazette* warned that if McKinley acquiesced in this matter, the president's actions "would be generally regarded as a sanction of mob violence in those sections where it is so common." If McKinley wanted to reopen the post office, the *Gazette* claimed, then he had to appoint another African American postmaster to teach the people of Lake City that "the mandates of the federal government must be everywhere obeyed." The *Freeman,* however, argued that the walls of prejudice were so impenetrable that nothing could be gained by insisting that the post office remain closed. The *Freeman* stated that white papers could demand this punishment if they wanted, but urged the black press to forgive the perpetrators because the many should not have to suffer for the crimes of the few. "Let the government see to it," the *Freeman* counseled, "that in the event of the repetition of the deed, that 'no guilty man escapes'"; in the long run, such action would be "a far more efficacious antidote than years of dislocated post offices." The *Freeman* admitted, however, that the law in the South had become nothing more than "senseless mummery," which was why it advised African Americans that the only reasonable course was "always espousing the country's interests" so that "a glow of patriotism . . . should overshadow all other considerations."[100]

In one sense, the *Freeman*'s emphasis on patriotic patience proved prescient: the loyal service of millions of African Americans during two world wars laid part of the necessary foundation for the modern civil rights movement. However, the virulent racism that inspired lynching made it impossible for many African Americans to wait patiently for a better future. Baker's lynching made it painfully evident that violence was the crucible in which whites crushed the social and political aspirations of African Americans.

White newspapers implicitly recognized the racial terrorism that explained lynching when they admitted that the only explanation for Baker's lynching was the fact that he was black. "We do not plead the color of the victims of the mob as an excuse for mob violence," said the *Charleston News and Courier,* "but we simply state the fact as an explanation of such outbreaks of lawlessness." Racism rather than an alleged desire for retributive justice was now at the heart of lynching, according to the *News and Courier,* for it was not "the enormity of the crime, but the color of the victims that controls in such matters." Another white newspaper, the *Dallas Baptist Standard,* expressed the same sentiment more clearly. According to the *Standard,* the reason that Baker had been lynched was "that the white people of the South, and of the North, too, for that matter, do not believe that to kill a Negro is murder." The *Standard* claimed that racism had clouded public sentiment to such an extent that "Negroes are classed with dogs and mules, and to kill a Negro is a pastime rather than a crime."[101] The *Standard* expressed hope that over time, newspaper editors, ministers, and other southern leaders would succeed in changing the perception that African Americans were not entitled to the same rights as whites, but most African American newspapers understood that without constant pressure from the African American community itself, such a change would be a long time coming.

Other white papers, however, were more recalcitrant than the *Standard.* The *Saluda (S.C.) Advocate* blamed the lynching on the McKinley administration for appointing Baker in the first place and said that "we need not expect anything else when black negroes are put in office over white men. . . . We in the South have never stood it, and never will."[102] Although progressive voices like the *News and Courier* could not understand why white mobs would lynch and treat the law with contempt, many whites regarded lynching as the "law of the survival of the fittest," which was superior to any constitutional law.[103] If blacks refused to acknowledge their inferiority to whites, whites would respond with lynching, hence the upsurge in murder and assault-related lynching and lynching for no apparent crime that occurred after disfranchisement.

Frenzied political racism was also responsible for South Carolina's worst postdisfranchisement lynching incident, the Phoenix election riot that occurred in the Western Piedmont in November 1898. Phoenix was a small hamlet in newly formed Greenwood County, which bordered Edgefield and Abbeville Counties. Living in the area since the 1820s was a wealthy family of white Republicans, headed by the sixty-three-year-old patriarch Colonel John R. Tolbert, who farmed more than 2,800 acres of land with the assistance of numerous black tenants. Before the war, Tolbert had not supported secession, but he fought for the Confederacy and rose to the rank of colonel. After the war, the Tolberts supported Ulysses S. Grant for president, much to the dismay of their neighbors, who reacted so violently that the legislature closed the Phoenix polls in 1868 and did not reopen them until 1897.

Republican administrations in Washington liberally rewarded the Tolberts for their loyalty with patronage plums. In 1898, the elder Tolbert was collector of customs at Charleston; one of Tolbert's sons, Robert "Red" Tolbert, was state Republican chairman; one of his nephews was Republican township leader in Phoenix; and the wife of another of Tolbert's nephews was in charge of the post office at McCormick. The Tolberts' preference for black tenants combined with their "egalitarian beliefs," Republican politics, and privileged status elicited enmity from many whites in the area, especially landless whites struggling against poverty.[104]

The "Ben Tillman Constitution," as African Americans derisively referred to it, had severely weakened the political clout of the Tolberts, but not their spirit of independence. In 1898, Red Tolbert united the Republicans behind his candidacy for the Third District congressional seat, which he hoped to contest before the Republican Congress. For weeks before the election, Tolbert encouraged all eligible Republicans to go to the polls and tender a ballot. Tolbert prepared blank affidavits for Republicans who were denied the right to vote at the polling place, which he intended to use in his case before the House of Representatives. When Democrats learned of Tolbert's plan, they made it known that they would rather kill two or three white men "than let the niggers vote and have to kill a whole lot of people later."[105]

On election day, Tom Tolbert and an African American body guard named Joe Circuit were at the Phoenix polling place collecting the affidavits of black Republicans who had not been allowed to vote. Early that morning, two Democratic enforcers, J. Giles "Bose" Etheridge and Robert "Bob" Cheatham, came to the polling place, which was a dry-goods store, to prevent Tolbert from collecting the affidavits. After Etheridge struck Tolbert on the head with a piece of wood, Circuit hit Etheridge with an iron rod. Shooting then ensued, and Etheridge was killed with a bullet through the head. When a crowd of heavily armed whites who were at the polling place opened fire, the African Americans fled for their lives in all directions. Tolbert was severely wounded during the shootout, but relatives rescued him. Although it was unclear who had killed Etheridge (some thought it was Cheatham), whites predictably blamed Circuit for the killing, which precipitated a pogrom against the African American community.

The next day, white men from Newberry, Edgefield, Abbeville, and Saluda Counties responded to the call of "Color and Country" that emanated from Greenwood. Mobs rounded up eleven blacks accused of wounding three whites in an ambush that occurred the night of the riot at Rehoboth Methodist Church, the church that the Tolbert family had helped establish after being expelled from a Baptist congregation for opposing secession before the war. In the churchyard, the mob of three hundred extracted confessions from some of the accused through "such persuasions as a pistol at the ear or a rope around the neck." The mob then ordered the men to sit on a log and opened fire on them. Four of the men were perforated from head to foot with bullets, two were mortally wounded, but five others somehow escaped with their lives. One of the men killed was named, ironically, Wade Hampton McKinney, after Wade Hampton, the hero of the "Redemption" movement and the patriarch of the South Carolina Democratic Party. The next day, whites brought McKinney's father, "Old Uncle" Loudon McKinney, to the church to identify the bodies. Although whites considered

Loudon McKinney an "old school darkey" and a good Democrat, some of the mob wanted to lynch him simply because "his skin was black." The reporter August Kohn noted that this "anti-negro expression was characteristic of the mob" and pointed out that it was "just such expressions and the final whoops and breaking away of the hot-heads that are accountable for the dead and dying in the county."[106]

Earlier that day, Kohn had witnessed another lynching at Rehoboth Church. Around the time that Kohn had arrived at the scene to view the bodies of the first victims, a mob of fifteen or twenty white men came marching down the road with a black man named Essex Harrison in front of them. The mob ordered the trembling Harrison to stand in front of the stiffened corpses and face them; when Harrison began to move, the mob killed him in an instant, and his body collapsed on top of the others. When Kohn asked the mob why they had killed Harrison, one man responded that Harrison had gone to Phoenix and voted.

Terror reigned over the area for four days. Bands of whites scoured the countryside in search of African Americans allegedly involved in the riot. Ben Collins and Jeff Darling were lynched in separate incidents on the evening of 10 November 1898 for allegedly firing shots at the Phoenix polling place (Collins was the tenant of a white man who had been elected captain of the Democratic forces at Phoenix). Red Tolbert claimed that two black tenants who had worked for his brother Tom were found dead in a pasture, killed by unknown persons. On 13 November 1898, a black woman named Eliza Goode was killed from a shot to the abdomen after a mob fired indiscriminately into her cabin. African American community groups were also singled out for attacks, including one church that was badly damaged and desecrated.

Although the mobs were motivated primarily by the belief that "an occasional clearing up of the race atmosphere by a killing does good and makes the negro remember his place," class tensions were also evident. A white mob nearly lynched a wealthy white planter named Andrew Stockman, for instance, after Stockman refused to participate in the atrocities. The mob accused Stockman of renting lands to blacks, which he acknowledged, claiming that black tenants "gave less trouble and were more easily satisfied with their homes." Stockman apparently was saved by the intervention of his wife, who shamed the mob when she insisted that they would have to kill her before they killed her husband. Stockman's tenants, however, were not as fortunate. The mob drove them from their homes and in all likelihood lynched some of them.

The threat of class warfare and the fear of losing black labor finally convinced elite whites to end the violence. "Conservative" citizens formed a "Committee of Safety" that insisted that the indiscriminate killings must stop. At mass meetings held in Greenwood and Ninety-Six, resolutions passed that called for "a turning in the tide, not only because [of] the brutality and shamefulness of further killings, but because . . . further killings will only result in driving away colored labor."

Not even Senator Tillman could deny that the Phoenix lynchings were the result of "race antagonism." Tillman claimed that under "ordinary circumstances," Tolbert's farcical election campaign would have merited only derision but that the Wilmington, North Carolina, race riot had heightened racial tensions. Tillman insisted that the race question was dormant in other parts of the state and added that the disfranchisement of blacks in South Carolina had ensured "as far as possible, a cessation of angry race feeling."

The aftermath of the Phoenix massacre, however, proved otherwise. For a year after the riot, whitecappers routinely whipped black men and sexually assaulted black women in the hope of driving black families from their lands and securing lower rents. Whites accused blacks who struggled to make a living and to educate their children of promoting the "diabolical doctrine" of social equality. Although Tillman blamed the Phoenix melee on selfish white men like the Tolberts who dared to interject the issue of race prejudice into politics, he eventually had to visit Greenwood and threaten federal intervention to put an end to the class-based violence that was directed against "poor Negroes who have nothing to do with the Tolberts."[107]

The connection between disfranchisement and lynching escaped Tillman's myopic vision, but it was more than apparent to the *Charleston News and Courier*. The newspaper observed that the white man's constitution gave whites license to kill blacks against whom "no offence was proved or even charged." The paper noted that a new mob, which no longer rode in the night and wore masks while carrying out its bloody work, had arrived on the scene. Mobs now organized as troops "in full light of day," and not only killed innocent men in churchyards, but, even worse, also killed women and children. The state apparently was impotent against mobs, which, the paper admitted, had become "stronger than constitutional authorities." In Reconstruction days, the *News and Courier* reminded its readers, whites had justified lynching "because we were living under what we called 'an alien form of government,'" but what need was there to kill blacks "under our own constitution without let or hindrance?"[108]

After 1890, African Americans in the South entered the second stage of their "dark journey," which was concerned less with political equality than economic or social advancement.[109] But white supremacy demanded the subservience of African Americans in all phases of life. With blacks and many poor whites excluded from political participation, lynching assumed a new character of indiscriminate violence, and increased dramatically in parts of Mississippi and South Carolina that had been relatively free of lynching before disfranchisement. Disfranchisement was not the only cause of this orgy of violence, but it was the most public manifestation of the social and economic tensions that engendered lynching. Whites disfranchised blacks to confirm in law the alleged "uneradicable differences" between the races and the second-class status of African Americans.[110] When blacks refused to acquiesce to the dictates of white hegemony, whites sometimes lynched in order to sear the sentiments of racial superiority into the consciousness of southern society.

The African American civil rights activist Ida B. Wells-Barnett dissected the insidious connection between disfranchisement and lynching when she explained:

> With no sacredness of the ballot there can be no sacredness of human life itself. For if the strong can take the weak man's ballot, when it suits his purposes to do so, he will take his life also. Having successfully swept aside the constitutional safeguards to the ballot, it is the smallest of small matters for the South to sweep aside its own safeguards

> to human life. Thus "trial by jury" for the black man in that section has become a mockery, a plaything of the ruling classes and the rabble alike. The mob says: "This people has no vote with which to punish us or the consenting officers of the law, therefore we indulge our brutal instincts, give free reign to race prejudice and lynch, hang, burn them when we please." Therefore, the more complete the disfranchisement, the more frequent and horrible has been the hangings, shootings, and burnings.[111]

Disfranchising constitutions were but a part of the hardening of racism that occurred during the Jim Crow years. Disfranchisement, however, enshrined the color line in the highest law of the state, and thereby strengthened the notion that whites could treat African Americans as they pleased. The removal of many poor whites from the political process, moreover, unleashed a reaction of terroristic violence that was aimed not only at African Americans but also at the privileged whites for whom they worked. Whites disfranchised African Americans because of African Americans' supposed inferiority, and they lynched when African Americans refused to accept the social, economic, and political constraints that white racism demanded.

4

"The Equal of Some White Men and the Superior of Others"

AFRICAN AMERICAN VICTIMS OF LYNCHING

African American resistance to racial oppression resulted in lynching becoming an integral feature of the southern caste system. In the predominantly rural states of Mississippi and South Carolina, landlord-tenant relations were rife with racial conflict; hence, the majority of African American lynching victims were agricultural workers who refused to acquiesce to white domination. African American farmworkers regularly challenged the actions of whites who oppressed them. When a black person got the better of a dispute with a white superior, whites sometimes responded with lynching in the hope of discouraging future affronts to white supremacy. The itinerant, isolated, and unsavory working conditions of some African American laborers also invoked suspicion and fear among the white population. The unusual living conditions and habits of some African Americans workers provoked anxiety among many whites, and nonfarm black laborers were lynched more often for alleged sexual crimes than were agricultural workers. African Americans who achieved success in southern society also could be targeted by a lynch mob. Whites lynched successful African Americans for maintaining their dignity in the face of white harassment or because their achievements were an affront to some whites. Occasionally, whites also lynched African American women, often with extreme brutality, to reinforce the notion that every member of the black community could be held accountable for the "undisciplined freedom" that inspired African Americans to resist the daily constraints of racial oppression. Only about one in twenty lynching incidents, on the other hand, involved a white male victim, who often held a prominent place in a community. White-on-white lynching, however, usually involved the desire to render impotent a vexatious exception to the moral or social order. White-on-white lynching was aimed at individual reprobates and contained few of the terroristic attributes that characterized white-on-black lynching.

Lynching, whether directed against a black or a white victim, was an expression of a mob's desire to maintain appropriate boundaries of behavior, which in the case of blacks were usually predicated upon racial subordination. The desire of black men for social, economic, and political autonomy could threaten the communal and personal power of white men from any status or background. A popular social Darwinistic conception of white supremacy demanded that the "LOWEST white man in the social scale is above the negro who stands HIGHEST" and undermined appeals from some white elites for "law and order." If southern whites wanted to "keep nigger in his place," then they sometimes had no choice but to use violence against "obnoxious" blacks who were determined to thwart white oppression. "The black must submit to the white," bellowed William P. Beard, the racist, iconoclastic, Bleasite editor of the *Abbeville (S.C.) Scimitar,* "or the white will destroy."[1]

Beard's jarring assessment of the status of race relations in the South had been prompted by the October 1916 lynching of Anthony Crawford, a wealthy African American landowner from the Western Piedmont town of Abbeville.[2] Abbeville had been the home of John C. Calhoun and proudly claimed to be both "the cradle and the grave" of the Confederacy. Abbeville's storied past was reflected in the majestic oak trees that lined its streets and the stately mansions and manicured lawns of its genteel elite. Beyond the town's elegant façade, however, was a mill district where working-class whites made no secret of their desire to use violence to intimidate blacks. Violence against "uppity" African Americans was commonplace in Abbeville. "When a nigger gets impudent," commented a local gin manager, "we stretch him out and paddle him a bit."[3] The

Abbeville elite did nothing to counteract such attitudes, which they regarded as a necessary evil. Confident and aggressive blacks disturbed the entire white community and had to be controlled at all costs.

Anthony Crawford was a fifty-six-year-old freedman who lived about seven miles from Abbeville on the Little River, where he owned more than 400 acres of prime cotton land.[4] As a boy, Anthony Crawford had helped his father farm a small cotton patch, which became the basis of his future fortune. The young Crawford was ambitious and routinely walked several miles to and from Abbeville to attend school. Over the years, the dapper and determined Crawford transformed his ambition and perseverance into a considerable fortune. In his early twenties, Crawford purchased nearly 200 acres of land for $830. Just five years later in 1888, Crawford bought about 100 acres of land for $670 that bordered the farms of his father and his brother. By the mid-1890s, Crawford had achieved enough prominence to help found the Industrial Union of Abbeville County, which was dedicated to promoting the "material moral and intellectual advancement of the colored people." Around the turn of the twentieth century, Crawford completed his land holdings when he acquired about 170 acres of land for $700 in 1899 and then another 113 acres of land for $800 in 1903.[5] At the time of his death in 1916, Crawford's estate was worth an estimated $25,000.[6]

Crawford's prosperity did not go unnoticed in the white community. In November 1904, for instance, the *Abbeville Medium* reported that Crawford had raised a "splendid" 1,000-bushel crop of corn along with forty-eight bales of cotton. The paper also reported, somewhat enviously, that Crawford owned six horses, twelve head of cattle, eighteen hogs, two wagons, a McCormick rake, a new top buggy, and a substantial bank account.[7]

Material success bolstered Crawford's innate self-confidence, which made him an outstanding figure in the African American community. For nearly two decades, Crawford was the chief benefactor and secretary of the Chapel AME Church, which he dominated as completely as any bishop. When a preacher who had a personal conflict with Crawford dared to suggest in his sermon that the congregation was a "boss-ridden" institution, for example, Crawford sprang to his feet, slapped the preacher, and fired him on the spot. The self-assured Crawford deferred to no man, black or white. Crawford's success and personal charisma convinced him that he was "the equal of some white men and the superior of others."[8]

Crawford had a large family of sixteen children, and he was determined to provide his children with all the advantages of his material success. Some of Crawford's sons attended college, and all of the children had farms in close proximity to their father.[9] The material success of the Crawfords inevitably brought them into conflict with whites, and four of Crawford's sons were convicted of aggravated assault as a result of an altercation in which a white man named James Rodgers was shot. Crawford's material resources enabled his sons to avoid jail in lieu of a five-hundred-dollar fine, but the incident left lingering animosity among whites toward Crawford and his family. A few years after the incident, Crawford wrote an open letter to the white community in which he apologized and promised that his family would "strive to make as good citizens in the future as we have in the past."[10] Crawford's contrition did little to mollify some whites, who "had been figuring on giving him a licking for a long time."[11] Years later, when Crawford was lynched, the mayor of Abbeville happened to be a relative of James Rodgers. Although Mayor C. C. Gamble witnessed much of the lynching, he did nothing to stop it.

Race relations in Abbeville County were far from amiable in the years that preceded Crawford's lynching. In March 1910, for instance, whites burned a local black college to the ground, and three black male students died as a result.[12] In 1913, some Abbeville whites castrated a black youth because a young white woman thought the boy was going to insult her. One of the perpetrators of this atrocity took an active part in the Crawford lynching, bragging about his prior exploits and encouraging those present to lynch that "dam nigger Crawford."[13] Fifteen months before Crawford's death, whites lynched a black man named Will Lozier after Lozier mortally wounded the son of a well-known white farmer during an argument.[14] Just a few weeks before Crawford was killed, a young black man was severely whipped for supposedly insulting a white store clerk. A more circumspect person might have modified his behavior in light of such atrocities, but Crawford feared no one and once bragged that "the day a white man hits me is the day I die."[15]

On a Saturday in late October 1916, Crawford arrived in Abbeville with two loads of cotton and a load of seed. While he waited in line for the gin, Crawford went to sell his seed at the store of W. D. Barksdale. Crawford knew that cotton seed was selling for ninety cents a pound, so when Barksdale offered eighty-five cents, Crawford told him that he already had a better deal. When Barksdale called Crawford a liar, the proud farmer cursed Barksdale for trying to cheat him. Barksdale then retreated inside his store, but Crawford continued his tirade saying that he would not sell "to any dam white man only at his price." Two of Barksdale's clerks, one of whom was the son of the president of the People's Bank of Abbeville, then armed themselves with ax handles and attempted to whip Crawford, but Crawford fended them off. As Crawford fled across the town square, Sheriff Burts arrested him. Before Burts could escort Crawford to the municipal building, however, a crowd gathered to whip Crawford for his animadversions, but the sheriff easily dispersed them.[16]

While Crawford arranged his bail, Barksdale asked McKinney Cann, a local ruffian whom Barksdale knew from church, to organize a mob that would whip Crawford and "cure him if possible," but the merchant wanted no part in the beating.[17] When Crawford began to make his way back to the cotton gin, someone alerted the mob, and a man blocked the jail door from the outside to prevent Sheriff Burts from leaving. Sensing danger, Crawford fled for the cotton gin. Inside he found a four-pound hammer and waited in a partially covered pit in the boiler room. When McKinney Cann entered the pit, Crawford smashed his skull with the hammer and probably would have killed Cann if another man had not restrained Crawford's arm as he delivered the blow. Someone then crushed Crawford's head with a rock, and Crawford collapsed unconscious. The mob, which included three brothers of McKinney Cann, took Crawford outside to the street, where he regained consciousness and tried to escape. Fighting his way some fifty feet, Crawford beat six of the men rather badly before someone stabbed Crawford in the back with a knife. The gin superintendent and two furniture dealers tried to prevent further mayhem, but as Crawford lay in the street a crowd of a couple hundred men kicked and beat him unconscious.

Crawford probably would have been lynched then and there had it not been for Sheriff Burts, who pleaded with the mob to release Crawford to his custody. For forty-five minutes, Burts implored the men not to tarnish his reputation and violate his oath of office by lynching Crawford. Finally, after Burts promised Lester and Jack Cann that Crawford would not be moved until the condition of their brother had stabilized, the mob relented and allowed Burts to take the bloodied Crawford to the county jail. At the jail, Mayor Gamble, who was also a doctor, treated Crawford, who was beaten so badly that Gamble thought Crawford would probably die.

When the mob learned of Crawford's condition, they decided to lynch him before he could die. Later in the afternoon, a rumor started that Burts was planning to remove Crawford on the 4:00 p.m. train. The drunken mob then stormed the jail, and neither Sheriff Burts nor the jailer resisted. Crawford was dragged down three flights of stairs and thrown into the street amidst a chorus of cheers. Men pummeled Crawford with rocks while others beat him with wagon boards. The mob repeatedly lifted Crawford by the arms and feet, tossed him on the ground, and jumped, spit, and beat on him. A white woman named Dewey desperately phoned Mayor Gamble to stop the lynching, but he refused to intervene. The mob then dragged Crawford through the African American district as a warning to "good niggers." Upon reaching the wealthier part of town, however, the mob threw Crawford's lifeless body on a passing load of slabs so as to not offend the "better class of people," who were "strongly opposed to work of this character, but . . . were all helpless before the frenzied mob."[18]

When the mob reached the fairgrounds, Crawford was surely dead, but they hanged him anyway and then emptied several hundred rounds into his body. At sunset, Coroner F. W. R. Nance led a jury up the lynching hill. Aware that his grandson had taken an active part in the lynching, Nance appointed two members of the lynch mob to the jury, which decided without taking any evidence that Crawford had been killed by parties unknown.[19] That night, liquor flowed freely, and the drunken mob decided to drive the Crawford family from the area. Fearing that if the mob "ever started they'd shoot every nigger along that seven miles of road," several leading businessmen convinced the mob to disband in lieu of a community meeting that would decide the fate of the Crawford family.[20]

The meeting, which was held a couple of days after the lynching, attracted several hundred persons, some from as far away as Anderson County, twenty miles to the north. A faction allied with the Cann family wanted to take immediate action against the Crawfords, but Abbeville's "better" element, led by clerk of the court Jack Perrin, bank president J. Allen Smith, and merchant J. S. Stark, asked for a chance to convince the Crawfords to leave voluntarily. When Perrin, Smith, and Stark returned, they assured the men in attendance that the Crawfords were "good niggers" and that they would leave if necessary, but they wanted to stay on their father's farm. Someone then fired a revolver that elicited shouts of "Run 'em out today!" and "Lynch the black bastards!" The meeting then decided unanimously that the Crawfords should leave the state by 15 November.

The community leaders hoped that the trouble would then end, but the terror began anew, when a mob forced all the black businesses in Abbeville to close. The only black business that remained open was the blacksmith, which one of the town leaders refused to let the mob close. After shooting broke out, a group of terrified blacks fled to the house of the aforementioned Mrs. Dewey, who appeared with a rifle and drove the mob from her lawn. Mrs. Dewey assured her husband that she would have opened fire to ward off the attackers, but she was reluctant to shoot "dogs in the back as these people were dogs of the lowest type."[21]

In response to the atrocities, African Americans refused to shop at the stores of white merchants. Mayor Gamble, who had done nothing to quell the violence, admitted that business had fallen off significantly and that blacks were fast leaving the area. The loss of business combined with the exodus of African American labor finally prompted white businessmen to publicly condemn the actions of the mob. In mid-November, a twelve-person "reconciliation committee" was formed, and the Crawford family was allowed to remain on their land.[22]

The Crawford lynching had far-reaching consequences for Abbeville County. Whites were unable to stem the outflow of black labor, which increased greatly after the lynching. The *Columbia State* hoped that the out-migration and economic boycott might finally convince whites to refrain from lynching. Whites had "lynched their own pocketbooks," observed the *State,* and the coming of the boll weevil would only make the situation worse. Unless mobs ceased, the *State* feared that lynching and boll weevils would "drive away the labor from farms and bankrupt this Southern country." White farmers needed more black labor not less, and the paper reminded its readers that the "flight of the Israelites from Egypt still has its lessons." At least from the perspective of white landowners, the *State* claimed, the deleterious effects of mobs were "hard facts [that] are unlynchable." The 1920 census confirmed the negative impact: Abbeville County lost 8 percent of its black population in the 1910s compared to an average of less than 1 percent in other South Carolina counties.

"Property ownership," said one prominent white South Carolina newspaper editor, "always makes the Negro more assertive, more independent, and the poor whites can't stand it."[23] The success of a man like Anthony Crawford, however, was intolerable to poor and rich alike. The president of the Farmers Bank in Abbeville, for instance, commented that Crawford had been insolent toward whites and got what he deserved. Although the banker wanted the law upheld, he did not want "a white man's right to whip a negro once in a while interfered with."[24] A lawyer and journalist from Abbeville described Crawford as a "vicious Negro" who was "too eager to curse and abuse a white man and assert his manhood." After the investigative reporter Roy Nash interviewed many of Abbeville's leading citizens, he concluded that Crawford had been lynched simply because "he lacked the humility becoming a 'nigger.'"[25]

The desire among many whites to strip African Americans of every vestige of economic and political power allowed the more vicious members of the white community to use violence with impunity. Despite the well-intentioned efforts of Governor Manning to bring Crawford's murderers to justice, the bloodletting in Abbeville County continued. Amazingly, just three years after Crawford's death, the Cann family figured prominently in another lynching. Lester Cann, who was now an Abbeville sheriff deputy, provoked the wrath of a black man named Mark Smith. In retaliation, Smith shot Cann but was acquitted. Shortly thereafter a mob riddled Smith with bullets in the presence of his wife and mother.[26]

The lynching of Anthony Crawford stemmed in large part from the desire among whites to eliminate an unsettling exception to the tenets of white supremacy. Although it started with an argument, Crawford's lynching was not a spontaneous event. Whites lynched Anthony Crawford because he refused to accept the notion that African Americans had to remain socially inferior to whites. Whites regularly lynched African Americans who openly (and often violently) defied the demands of white employers or who allegedly committed some egregious affront against white racial mores.[27] African Americans like Crawford who refused to accept their subordinate status often paid for their courage with their lives.

The vicious murder of Anthony Crawford demonstrated that lynching was often an outgrowth of whites' anxiety about the changing status of blacks. Lynching did not usually stem from a "crime" committed by a black desperado but instead from the violent conflict that emanated from the inequities of the southern racial system.[28] Although fears of black transients and sexual offenders did much to fan the flames of lynching, the root cause was the daily discord that existed between black and white southerners who knew and worked with one another. Lynching was not primarily an extralegal effort to quash black criminality, but rather a visceral and violent reaction to the intransigence and resistance of southern blacks to the daily manifestations of white supremacy.

The typical black person who became the target of a lynch mob was not an outcast in southern society. Most black lynching victims were agricultural workers, primarily tenants, who frequently had lived and worked in the same area for years. Tenants were often accused of some crime against their landlord or supervisor. Table 5 shows that more than 60 percent of all black lynching incidents in Mississippi and South Carolina involved African American agricultural workers.[29] In the overwhelming majority of agricultural lynchings, whites accused tenants of committing

TABLE 5. Status of lynching victims by race, Mississippi and South Carolina, 1881–1940

Status	Black	White
Agricultural workers (%)	62.4	12.5
Nonfarm workers (%)	19.4	31.3
Outlaws and felons (%)	11	6.3
Landowners, professionals, civil servants, etc. (%)	7.2	50
Total number lynched	264	16

a crime against their employer or a member of their employer's immediate family. Murder or assault accounted for more than 50 percent of all the crimes that agricultural victims allegedly committed. Contrary to the claims of contemporary white apologists, rape or attempted rape was cited in only about 15 percent of the lynching incidents that involved agricultural workers. Racial tensions plagued landlord-tenant relations, which was why tenants were lynched more often for alleged racial transgressions or property crimes than were other lynching victims.

The next-largest group of black lynching victims was nonfarm workers, which included rail workers, artisans, lumber and turpentine laborers, fisherman, and service workers like porters and mail carriers. Nonfarm black victims were involved in about 20 percent of lynching incidents in both Mississippi and in South Carolina. As was the case with agricultural workers, whites typically lynched nonfarm workers for allegedly committing a crime against their employer. Murder and assault-related crimes accounted for approximately 42 percent of the alleged causes of lynching incidents that involved nonfarm victims.

Unlike agricultural lynching incidents, however, alleged rape and other crimes involving women were the justification in almost 37 percent of nonfarm lynching incidents. Whites feared some working-class blacks, especially itinerant workers, who seemed to have little regard for the niceties of white racial etiquette. Semi-nomadic black laborers, such as those who toiled in isolated lumber and turpentine camps, lived in an almost separate society and usually had little contact with white people who lived on farms or in towns. Consequently, itinerant laborers were more than twice as likely to be lynched for an alleged crime against a white woman than were black agricultural workers.[30]

Despite the belief among whites that lynching was aimed primarily at "undesirable" elements in the African American population, criminals or outlaws were the victims in only about 11 percent of African American lynching incidents. Victims in this category included persons who supposedly belonged to an organized band of criminals, convicts, ex-convicts, and persons wanted for crimes other than the one for which they were ostensibly lynched. In Mississippi, more than 13 percent of black lynching incidents involved criminals, but in South Carolina the figure was only about 3 percent. The difference probably resulted from the frontier-like conditions that existed in some Mississippi regions (such as the Piney Woods, where more than one-third of black lynching victims were purported outlaws or criminals) and a greater sense of judicial efficacy that existed in South Carolina. Murder-related crimes topped the alleged reasons for lynching black criminals, being cited as the cause in about 45 percent of lynching incidents. The next most frequent charge against black "outlaw" victims was rape, which was indicative of white stereotypes about the criminal element in the black community. Anecdotal evidence suggests that outlaw victims typically had no apparent connection with the person whom they were accused of harming, which supports the notion that outlaw victims were less connected to white society than were other black lynching victims.

Black professionals and landowners occasionally fell victim to the sanguinary lessons of a white mob. If a professional or landowner, such as Anthony Crawford, acted in a manner that defied white racial etiquette, a lynching could result. Not surprisingly, most victims in this category were lynched in retaliation for murder and assault-related crimes or for no apparent crime. South Carolina had more professional or landowners who were lynched than did Mississippi (13.3 percent and 5.5 percent respectively) because landownership was more common among African Americans in South Carolina than in Mississippi.[31] As a group, however, African American landowners were underrepresented as lynching victims because landowners had more personal autonomy and less contact with whites than did African American tenants.

Although some scholars have suggested that blacks rarely challenged the dictums of their white employers, the lynching evidence from Mississippi and South Carolina indicates otherwise.[32] The accounts of lynching incidents that involved agricultural workers are replete with disputes and disagreements between African Americans and their employers that frequently resulted in the death or injury of a white person. Whites lynched agricultural workers not simply because they were black, but also because they dared to challenge (often physically) the supposedly superior social stature of a white landlord or supervisor.

In July 1903, for example, Cato Garrett, a young black tenant from the Natchez District in Mississippi, killed a popular and "well connected" planter named Harry Stout. Garrett had argued with Stout about placing a mule in a meadow, and when words came to blows, Garrett stabbed Stout in the heart with a small penknife. Although authorities convened a special grand jury to ensure that Garrett would receive a speedy trial, three days later, fifteen of Stout's friends took Garrett from a law officer and hanged him along a small road near the scene of the incident. Predictably, no arrests were made in connection with Garrett's death.[33]

A similar lynching occurred in the Inner Coastal Plain region of South Carolina, when Frank De Loache and his son John were lynched in December 1905 after the two tenants were accused of killing an "influential and prosperous" farmer named Hayne Craddock. Craddock had come to De Loache's cabin with two other black tenants to collect a ginning debt. When the elder De Loache refused to pay, Craddock assaulted him. The one-armed De Loache shouted for his son to help him, and after John De Loache appeared with a gun, a struggle ensued in which Craddock was killed from a gunshot wound to the back. The news of the killing spread quickly, but the local magistrate managed to arrest the two De Loache men before a mob could apprehend them.

Unfortunately for the De Loaches, the magistrate chose to lock them in an outhouse on the Craddock place and left them overnight in the care of a constable. The next morning, a large crowd of Craddock's relatives and friends gathered at Craddock's farm to lynch the De Loaches. The constable proved utterly incapable of preventing the lynching, even though some whites believed that Craddock might have been killed by the two black tenants who had accompanied him to De Loache's cabin. After the constable allowed some of the mob to beat the De Loaches for a half hour or so, some of the white men present argued against a lynching. But others insisted, "This is a white man's country and we ain't going to let it go just so." Around 11:30 a.m., the constable finally wired for help, but by noon the De Loaches were dead, shot to death near a little stream about 200 yards from a road.

The inability of authorities to protect the De Loaches from the mob prompted South Carolina governor Duncan Heyward to launch an official investigation. Heyward hired a private investigator to take charge of the case. Eventually seven "prominent" farmers were arrested in connection with the lynching. The *Charleston News and Courier* admitted that a conviction was unlikely but insisted that "the fact is being established in the public mind that the lyncher has to fight for his life and liberty." But the white public had little sympathy for African American tenants accused of killing a white employer. No doubt the *News and Courier* was correct when it claimed that "every man, woman, and child within a ten mile radius" of the lynching knew who the lynchers were, but on the day of the hearing all but one of the state's witnesses were black. All seven men arrested were eventually released because of insufficient evidence.[34] African American tenants who violently attacked their white employers provoked fear and outrage among the white community, which viewed such violence as a serious affront to racial hegemony.

Even when white employers were held in disdain by the white community and were guilty of egregious abuse of an African American worker, whites could still feel compelled to respond violently to tenant aggression. E. L. Johnston, for instance, was a thirty-five-year-old alcoholic dentist from Mobile, Alabama, who failed as a dentist in Mobile and then decided to become an itinerant dentist in the Red Hills region of Mississippi, where his father owned a profitable farm near the town of Shubuta.[35] Johnston was no more successful as a country dentist than he had been in Mobile, but during one of his trips through the country, Johnston met and seduced a twenty-year-old black woman named Maggie Howze. Later the philandering dentist invited Maggie and her younger sister Alma to live and work on his father's farm so that "he could have [Maggie] at his disposal whenever he wished." Although Johnston was married and had a child, he apparently felt no remorse over his many extramarital affairs.

After the Howze sisters moved to the Johnston place, they became acquainted with two brothers named Major and Andrew Clark. The Clark brothers were working for Johnston to pay the debt on a mule that their father had purchased from the dentist. Major Clark became romantically involved with Maggie Howze, and eventually the two decided to marry. Johnston became enraged over the relationship, however, and told Clark that he would kill him if he did not stop seeing Maggie. The animosity between Clark and his employer intensified when Clark learned that Johnston had impregnated both Maggie and Alma Howze.

One morning in mid-December 1918, Johnston was shot in his barn while milking a cow. Suspicion immediately centered on Major Clark, who carried the mortally wounded Johnston from the barn to his house. But Johnston's father, a former member of the Mississippi state legislature, did not believe that Clark had killed his son and later would plead with a mob to spare Clark's life. Many whites in Shubuta believed that a white man had killed Johnston because of another affair in which the dentist had been involved.

A week and a half elapsed between the killing of Johnston and the preliminary hearing to arraign the Howze sisters and the Clark brothers for murder. During that time, all four of the accused were held outside of Shubuta to prevent a lynching. Major Clark was kept in Meridian, some forty miles from Shubuta, where authorities extracted a confession from him by smashing his testicles in a vice. When the defendants were returned to Shubuta for a hearing, it was a foregone conclusion that they would be lynched. On the day of the hearing, scores of cars and people began pouring into Shubuta after dark, prompting the chief of police to simply leave town for Meridian. The deputy sheriff in charge of the jail allowed himself to be handcuffed at the mob's request. After removing the prisoners from the jail with no resistance, the well-orchestrated mob cut all power to the town.

The mob drove the four victims to a covered bridge over the Chickasawha River, a short distance from Shubuta. Four ropes were tied to a girder under the bridge and placed around the victims' necks. To their dying breaths, each of the accused claimed that they were innocent and begged for mercy. When Maggie Howze screamed for her life, a mob member silenced her with a monkey wrench to the mouth, which knocked out some of her teeth. Maggie then endured another blow to the head, which cracked open a half-inch-wide gash in her skull. The mob threw each victim over the bridge with a rope tied around his or her neck. The Clark brothers and Alma Howze each died instantly when their necks were broken. Maggie Howze, however, twice caught herself on the side of the bridge before finally succumbing a third time. The next day mob members laughed about how that "big black Jersey woman" had clung desperately to life.

When the bodies were "discovered," local African Americans refused to retrieve the corpses, saying that "the white folks lynched them and they can cut them down." After the bodies were brought to a white funeral home, some witnesses claimed that Alma Howze's child could still be seen moving. The victims eventually were buried without religious services, just outside of the white cemetery (African Americans refused to accept the bodies into the black cemetery). The lynching prompted many black tenants to flee from the area, leaving crops to decay in the fields. The brutal lynching was done in defense of a white man's "right" to treat African Americans as he pleased. The Clark brothers and the Howze sisters were lynched to demonstrate that African Americans had no inherent rights outside of what members of the local white community deemed tolerable. Mississippi governor Theodore Bilbo bluntly rejected the notion that the lynching was unjust and told the NAACP "to go to Hell" when it requested that Bilbo investigate the brutal murders.

African American tenants routinely resisted the attempts of white employers to impose their will on work arrangements, crop settlements, monetary matters, freedom of movement, or interpersonal relations, and scores of lynchings resulted from disputes between tenants and employers.[36] Whites felt compelled to act in the Johnston case, for instance, not because they doubted the ability of the legal system to impose an acceptable punishment nor to salvage the honor of a moral degenerate but because they worried that if they did nothing, "no white man who had

FIGURE 7. Demand for farm labor and white-on-black lynching incidents in major cotton-producing regions, 1881–1940

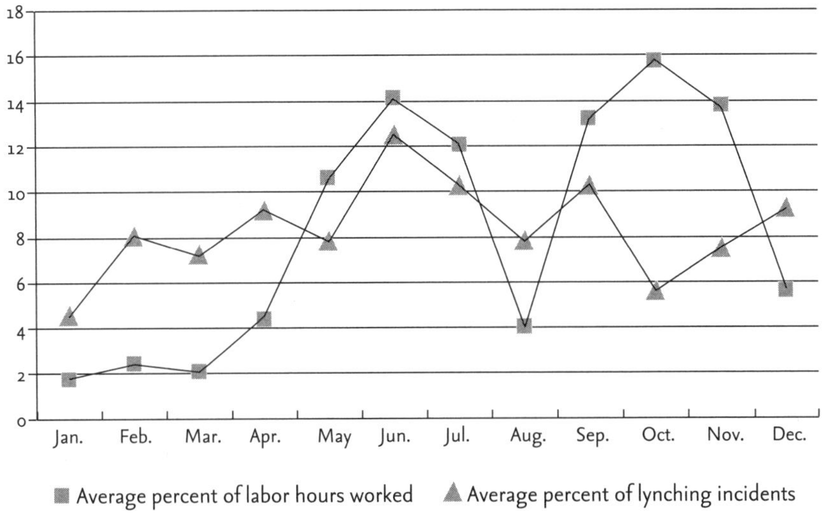

wronged a Negro would be safe." The coercive nature of landlord-tenant relations made such fears palpable. Contemporary observers, including NAACP activists James Weldon Johnson, William Pickens, and Walter White, all believed that the exploitation of African American tenants by white landlords was the fundamental cause of lynching.[37] In essence, many lynchings resulted from the refusal of African Americans to submit to the indignities and oppression that many landlords attempted to impose.

Additional evidence that lynching resulted from landlord-tenant conflicts can be seen in figure 7, which compares the monthly demand for farm labor in major cotton-producing regions with the proportion of white-on-black lynching incidents that occurred in each month over six decades.[38] The correlation between the demand for labor and lynching incidents was moderately strong, meaning that as laborers spent more time working in the fields, they were more likely to be lynched.[39] In fact, lynching often stemmed from work-related disagreements that tenants had with landlords.[40]

When tenants worked less, as in midwinter and especially in the month of August, fewer lynchings occurred. The decline in lynching incidents, especially during October and November, probably resulted from the improved position of tenants vis-à-vis landlords that occurred around harvest time. Landlords had to be more accommodating at this time of year because tenants might leave or refuse to work and allow the cotton to rot in the fields.[41]

The increase in lynching incidents in December probably resulted from the "settling-up" that occurred at the end of the season. Robert Motely, for instance, was an African American tenant who worked on a cotton plantation in the Mississippi Yazoo Delta.[42] When Motely objected to the settlement offered by the prosperous planter R. W. Silvey, however, Silvey attempted to horsewhip Motely. After Silvey kicked Motely in the face several times, Motely's brother William shot Silvey, mortally wounding the planter. William Motley escaped, but Robert Motely was not as fortunate and was jailed at Lambert. The night after the incident, an armed mob broke into the Lambert jail and hanged Motely. The problem for whites in the postbellum South was that black tenants were not the submissive slaves who supposedly had contentedly worked the land before the war. The concept of honor permeated black culture as well as white, and African American tenants resorted to violence when whites abused them or denigrated their sense of self-respect. Whites would often respond to such assertions with lynching in the desperate hope of convincing other African Americans that the price for challenging the caste system was too high.[43]

Although African American tenants understood that a violent confrontation with whites could result in lynching, some deliberately chose martyrdom rather than accepting the alternative. In 1923, for instance, a black tenant named Joe Pullen sent shockwaves through the Yazoo Delta when he killed a white planter and then engaged in a ferocious gun battle with a mob that came to lynch him. Pullen worked for W. T. Sanders on a cotton plantation near Drew, and at the end of the harvest season, Sanders apparently became angry with Pullen for spending money on repairs to Pullen's house and to purchase basic necessities. Pullen believed that the money belonged to him, however, because Sanders had never paid him for work that Pullen had done on the plantation. When Sanders demanded that Pullen repay the money, Pullen refused and Sanders shot him in the arm. Pullen then drew his .38 caliber pistol and shot Sanders dead. Knowing that a mob would soon be searching for him, Pullen grabbed a shotgun, hid in the bayou, and waited. When a sheriff's posse arrived, Pullen surprised the mob and shot one man in the face, another in the head, and a third in the torso. The mob then launched a fusillade of gunfire at Pullen, but the defiant tenant remained unharmed. Seeking to drive Pullen from his protective cover, the mob used gasoline to set ablaze the ditch in which Pullen hid. Pullen survived the flames, however, and managed to wound another member of the posse. The casualties prompted the posse to retrieve some automatic rifles and a machine gun from Clarksdale. After mounting the machine gun on the bank of a ditch, the mob once again started a fire in the ditch where Pullen was hiding and then engaged in a furious gunfight with Pullen that lasted more than an hour. When Pullen finally fled from the burning ditch, he was mortally wounded from a barrage of machine-gun bullets. The mob then tied Pullen's legs to a car and dragged his corpse to Drew, where onlookers could view the macabre remains. Someone cut off Pullen's ear, which later was displayed in jar of alcohol in a Drew storefront. Newspapers claimed that Pullen had killed five whites and wounded nine, but African Americans claimed that Pullen had killed thirteen and wounded twenty-six during the furious standoff. Whatever the actual casualties may have been, Fannie Lou Hamer recalled that "it was a while in Mississippi before the whites tried something like that again."[44]

The unwillingness of whites to accept the culture of freedom that blacks desired precipitated the "crisis of the New South," which involved a widening chasm of suspicion between whites and blacks who were born after slavery. In stark contrast to the loyal and peaceful slaves of antebellum lore, many whites now detected a "new sort of black character: the 'desperado' or 'bad nigger'" in the late nineteenth-century South. Unlike the beloved, docile, infantile "darkey" whom whites thought they knew and understood, "bad niggers" scoffed at the pretensions of white caste, authority, and honor.[45] Unable to accept the reality that black tenants who lived and worked in close proximity with whites frequently opposed white supremacy, some whites projected their racial anxiety on black workers who were supposedly far removed from southern society.

No African American worker generated more fear and suspicion among whites than an itinerant laborer, who could be an "outsider" to both the black and white communities. The "slave-like" status of many black manual laborers, moreover, made them a target of derision even among African Americans. The criminal background of some laborers and the rather unsavory moral conditions that prevailed in many of the camps exacerbated the stereotypical fears of whites, who seemed to believe that such men always were lurking in the shadows, waiting to prey upon the virtue of white women.[46] Indeed, the unexpected appearance of a strange African American worker could sometimes send ripples of fear through a white community. If such a worker attacked, threatened, or scared a white woman, moreover, his violent demise was often foreordained.

Abe Barrett, for example, was a powerfully built, dark-skinned turpentine worker from the Piney Woods of Mississippi whom whites lynched in June 1901.[47] Barrett lived around Rotten Bayou, the center of the turpentine industry in Hancock County, but had only recently arrived in the area from Georgia. Before the lynching, white people around Rotten Bayou had become increasingly fearful of "the dangerously impudent negroes working in the orchards and round the turpentine stills." Whites, who lived near the orchards, feared this "most dangerous class of humanity," and many whites worried that white women should not be home alone.

Whites accused Barrett of attempting to rape Anna Ladnier, the fifteen-year-old daughter of a prominent planter from Hancock County on the afternoon of 12 June 1901. The Ladnier home was situated near a creek that had a turpentine camp on one side of it. Anna Ladnier was apparently washing vegetables at a spring when Barrett encountered her. Barrett first exchanged some small talk with the girl about buying some of the vegetables before he allegedly grabbed her from behind. The girl's screams prompted Barrett to hit her on the head with a tree-trimming tool. Badly injured, the girl continued to resist while Barrett choked her.

Barrett tried to flee with the girl, but her screams attracted a local schoolmaster, who arrived as Barrett carried the girl away. Upon seeing the schoolmaster, however, Barrett dropped the girl and fled. Unfortunately, Anna Ladnier eventually died from her injuries.

After news of the attack spread, a one-hundred-man posse quickly assembled to search for Barrett. Six days later, two white men captured Barrett in a turpentine camp near Gulfport. After the early-morning capture, the small posse sent a message to Hancock County so that other posses would not endure another day in the hot sun for naught.

By late morning, the news of Barrett's apprehension had spread along the entire Gulf Coast. When the train carrying Barrett arrived in Gulfport, a crowd of white machine hands and railroad employees was waiting to lynch Barrett. The Hancock County men secretly took Barrett out of town, however, to allow the Ladnier girl the opportunity to identify her attacker. But three miles from the depot, a Gulfport mob hanged Barrett with a plow line from an oak tree. The lynching happened near a railroad, and several trains passed with passengers gaping at the bullet-ridden body. Mobs often displayed the corpse of a victim in a prominent place not only to terrorize other African Americans but also to implicate gawkers in their work and to lend communal sanction to their crime.

African Americans, whom whites perceived as a threat to women, were not the only blacks who engendered fear in the minds of whites. Some blacks openly flouted legal authority and seemed incorrigible to whites. Jordan Parker, for instance, was a sixty-five-year-old "hard case" who lived near Purvis in Mississippi's Piney Woods region.[48] Parker came from a family of habitual criminals, and each of Parker's three older brothers had suffered violent deaths at the hands of whites. Two of Parker's brothers had reportedly been killed by returning Confederate soldiers, who claimed that the brothers had robbed their homes while they had been at war. Another brother, Turner, allegedly had been a bandit who operated around the Pearl River swamp. After a series of robberies, whites organized a manhunt and shot Turner Parker to death at his hut.

Whites who lived around Purvis feared Parker and considered him extremely dangerous. Local lore had it that Parker had participated in a mass murder during Reconstruction and had sent eleven corpses adrift down the Pearl River, each bearing a sign marked "Free Ticket to Hell." A few years later, a brother of one of the murdered men supposedly shot Parker and left him for dead, but Parker somehow survived the attack and became a recluse who supported his family through hunting and fishing.

In mid-December 1884, a New Orleans and Northeastern train killed one of Parker's pigs, and Parker filed a claim against the railroad for $2.25. When the railroad refused to compensate Parker, whites claimed that he threatened to "ditch" a train. Three days before Christmas, a train carrying about one hundred passengers derailed on a curve about a mile north of Purvis. The wreck killed a white engineer and a black fireman, both of whom were scalded to death.

The railroad hired three detectives to investigate the accident, and on Christmas Day Parker and his ten-year-old son were arrested and jailed at Poplarville, where Parker received a preliminary hearing the following day. News of Parker's incarceration spread quickly up and down the railroad, and a large crowd attended the hearing. Although some of the "most respectable" citizens in Purvis testified against Parker, the state did not have a compelling case. The judge, nevertheless, remanded the case to county court in Columbia, about forty miles from Poplarville.

That same night, however, a mob of thirty-five unmasked men rammed a rail through the jail door at Poplarville, ostensibly while the guards inside slept. Around 3:00 a.m., the mob boarded a southbound train with Parker and his son in tow. As the train proceeded south toward Picayune, the mob tortured Parker with a red-hot poker, applying it to his sides and hands. After threatening to kill the younger Parker, who allegedly implicated his father as the perpetrator of the train derailment, the mob stopped the train at an abandoned sand pit about ten miles south of Poplarville. The mob then tied Parker to a pine tree that could be seen from the tracks and shot him to death. The mob left an ominous justification on the corpse that read in part: "Tried by Judge Lynch and sentenced to death. This should be a caution to all other train wreckers." The "respectable" citizens of Purvis and Poplarville remained silent about the lynching and felt relieved that a menacing black man had been given his due. No effort was made to prosecute the friends of the deceased engineer, who were believed to have been responsible for the lynching.

Although Parker was the first "hard case" that whites removed from the Poplarville jail and lynched, he was far from the last. In January 1909, a mob broke down the jail door and brutally lynched Pink Willis for the attempted rape of a former sheriff's daughter. About a decade later, a mob took Claude Singleton, who had been sentenced to life imprisonment for the murder of a white railroad worker, from the jail and hanged him. After grotesquely mutilating Singleton's corpse, the mob paraded his decapitated head around town on a pike. In 1959, Mack Charles Parker, who had been accused of the rape and kidnapping of a pregnant white woman, was brutally beaten by a mob of enraged whites as they took him from the county jail in Poplarville. After driving Parker to nearby Louisiana, the mob shot him at point-blank range and threw his battered body into the Pearl River. Despite an intensive FBI investigation that revealed the identities of most of those who participated in the murder, local and federal grand juries refused to indict any of the alleged lynchers.[49]

The lynching of black workers often stemmed from employer-employee disputes that resembled the conflicts that led to the lynching of many African American tenants. Ed Dunlap and Henry Campbell, both of whom were lynched in early November 1932, are but two examples. Ed Dunlap was a construction worker from Mississippi's Yazoo Delta. Dunlap argued with his foreman, R. A. Leist, over a work assignment on a government rock-paving crew.[50] When the disagreement became heated, Dunlap shot and wounded Leist in the right arm and then fled for his sister's house, who lived in the area. Realizing that his life was in danger, Dunlap tried to convince an African American taxi driver to take him to St. Louis but decided otherwise after learning that authorities knew of his whereabouts. A "posse" of about one hundred law officers and citizens eventually tracked Dunlap to a plantation cabin about six miles north of Greenville, Mississippi. When Dunlap refused to surrender, the mob set the cabin afire. As Dunlap fled from the flames, he was riddled with bullets.

Henry Campbell was also a road construction worker, from the Northern Pee Dee region in South Carolina, who allegedly shot and killed his foreman, H. L. Tolbert, after arguing with Tolbert about his dismissal.[51] Campbell, who was also Tolbert's chauffeur, fled in Tolbert's automobile, but a mob of three hundred followed in quick pursuit. Near the North Carolina state line, Campbell abandoned the car in attempt to evade his pursuers. The mob chased Campbell through the cornfields, where a South Carolina state highway department mechanic eventually shot and killed him. Campbell's body was brought back to Duford, South Carolina, where a mob intended to burn it. When some local white women objected to the burning, however, the mob allowed a prominent planter to put the body in a decrepit tobacco drag and bury it in a shallow grave on his plantation. Whites in the area reportedly felt that the lynching was a justifiable reminder to "the Negro of his subordinant position in Southern society."

When not in direct conflict with employers, some black workers found themselves in harm's way because of labor tensions within the white community or because whites wanted their jobs. Most conspicuous in this regard were rail workers. When workers struck the Illinois Central Railroad in the fall of 1911, for instance, the company hired black strikebreakers, who immediately became targets for violence.[52] The railroad had to close its shop at McComb, Mississippi, for example, until Governor Earl Brewer ordered more than four hundred national guardsmen to provide security for black workers. In order to protect African American workers, the railroad built a stockade around its facility and opened a commissary inside so that strikebreakers would not need to venture out.

Some of the black workers, however, returned home at the end of their shift. One evening in early January 1912, a group of African American workers was walking to nearby Summit when white strikers attacked them. The strikers killed two of the black workers and mortally wounded another. Six white workers were eventually charged with the crime, but a grand jury only indicted two of them. At the trial of one of the defendants, in March 1912, the state presented eyewitness testimony from two of the African American workers, who identified the striker as a member of the mob. Nevertheless, a jury deliberated for less than a half hour before returning a verdict for acquittal. The strike divided the white community, and African American workers were squeezed between the financial interests of the commercial class and those of white workers. Exasperated by the acquittal, the trial judge, who sympathized with the railroad, despaired that the "material progress" of Mississippi would continue to be slow as long as such crimes were "hidden out or winked at by many of our [white] citizens."

African American workers did not have to be scabs, however, to provoke the enmity of whites. During the first months of 1921, for instance, black rail workers were lynched and beaten along the Yazoo and Mississippi Valley Railroad in western Mississippi.[53] White rail workers resented African American brakeman who rode in the front of trains. In separate incidents, disgruntled whites shot and killed Horace Hurd, who had worked for the railroad for six years, and Arthur Tyler, who had twelve years of service. Other workers claimed that African American brakemen were being beaten and forced to leave their jobs on a daily basis. Workers typically were assaulted at night while they inspected a train. The violence against African American brakemen became so frequent that the NAACP appealed to the Justice Department to investigate the incidents. The status of some African American workers threatened some working-class white men, who lynched to enhance both caste and class solidarity.

If whites feared or loathed black workers, they often were positively terrified of African American felons and "outlaws." The crime wave that plagued the rural South in the last quarter of the nineteenth century helped change "the dominant image of blacks in the white mind . . . from inferior child to aggressive and dangerous animal."[54] In fact, the fear of black outlaws led some whites to regard lynching as a positive good. A young white female teacher from the Eastern Piedmont of South Carolina, for example, wrote her fiancé about the laudatory activities of a lynch mob that had hanged five notorious black "bandits." The woman was "overjoyed" at the lynching, saying that "the negroes deserved worse punishment." Far from acting rashly, the lynchers had, according to the white teacher, viewed the matter from "all sides" before deciding on a "wise" and "proper punishment" for the "desperate" band of outlaws.[55]

Unfortunately, "wise and proper punishment" of this kind was routine in some parts of Mississippi and South Carolina. In Mississippi's Old Natchez region, for instance, at least seven outlaws or convicts were lynched in less than thirty months in the early 1890s.[56] Two of these lynching incidents involved gangs of thieves who allegedly had committed a series of crimes over an extended period of time. Smith Tooley and John Adams, for example, were lynched in July 1892 at the Vicksburg courthouse after whites accused them of a series of robberies and a murder.[57] The sentiment against Tooley and Adams was so strong that the governor ordered the Warren County Light Artillery to guard the jail at night. On the night of 5 July 1892, however, a mob of more than six hundred men stormed the jail, which was surrounded by a brick wall twenty feet high. Although the troops had a Gatling gun and could have easily dispersed the mob, "it was useless to expect them to fire upon their relatives and friends," and only the first lieutenant reported for duty. The mob used a huge pole to ram the jail gate and was inside in about fifteen minutes. The mob then interrogated each of the victims for about an hour and even had a secretary record their statements. When it became apparent that the two victims continued to talk only to forestall their deaths, however, some in the mob clamored for the lynching to commence. Before an excited crowd, both men were hanged in the courthouse yard, although the leaders of the lynching supposedly remained calm. Ida B. Wells-Barnett later claimed that the lynching had been the idea of white men who profited from the goods that Tooley and Adams had stolen, and feared that their nefarious activities would become known.[58]

Just three months later, whites from the Old Natchez region dispensed with two African Americans named Gabe Meeks and Charles Goff, who were accused of belonging to a band of burglars who operated in the western portion of Mississippi.[59] The week before the lynching, the two men had allegedly robbed a store in Rankin County and pistol-whipped two white clerks who worked there. After Meeks and Goff were captured, Governor Stone wired local authorities and ordered that the prisoners be protected. The victims were given a preliminary hearing after which a judge remanded them to jail. On the ten-mile trip to jail, however, a mob of about one hundred men took Meeks and Goff from authorities and hanged them to a tree in the Pelahatchie swamp. Before killing the men, the mob extracted the names of other black men who supposedly belonged to the burglary ring. If the mob had captured these men, none doubted that a general lynching would have resulted.

Even more terrifying to some whites than a marauding band of thieves was an African American convict who allegedly had committed a heinous crime while escaped from prison. Many of these lynching victims were prison "trusties" who, because of their willingness to help discipline other prisoners, enjoyed special privileges that sometimes included leaving a camp or jail. Lawson Patton, for example, was a trusty lynched at Oxford, Lafayette County, in Mississippi's Pontotoc Hills region in September 1908.[60] Home to the University of Mississippi, Oxford had an enlightened reputation.[61] Patton was a habitual criminal who for years had run an illegal, "blind tiger" drinking establishment. Although Patton was in and out of the Oxford jail, he was not known for being impudent or disrespectful toward whites. One of the white prisoners in the Oxford jail was a tenant named McMillen who had been convicted the previous June of resisting arrest. McMillen's wife and three children lived on a nearby farm, and Patton sometimes brought Mrs. McMillen messages from her husband.

Early in the afternoon of 8 September 1908, Patton went to the McMillen farm to deliver Mrs. McMillen a message from her husband. Patton, who apparently was drunk at the time, for some reason argued with Mrs. McMillen, who ordered him to leave her farm. When McMillen's daughter went to check on her mother, however, she found the unfortunate woman murdered, with her throat slashed from ear to ear.

The local sheriff quickly organized a posse that included practically the entire white male population of Oxford. A running chase ensued in which Patton was shot at around one hundred times. Although wounded several times, Patton might have escaped had not two boys with shotguns filled his back with buckshot and held him at bay. Patton was brought to town under heavy guard and placed in jail. The bloodied and weakened Patton presented a "bestial appearance" as the mob paraded him through the streets. Almost immediately, Oxford was full of armed men and boys who openly talked of lynching Patton.

When Judge W. A. Roane realized that a lynching was imminent, he tried to persuade the mob to disperse. Roane was a circuit court judge and promised the crowd that Patton would be given a speedy trial when court convened in a week. The Reverend W. S. Spruggins from the local Methodist church also urged the mob to go home.[62] Following Roane's plea for restraint, however, former U.S. senator William Sullivan delivered a sensational harangue in which he demanded an immediate end for Patton. Later, when questioned about his actions, Sullivan fumed against the audacity of such a crime. "I led the mob," Sullivan declared, "and I'm proud of it. I directed every movement of the mob, and I did every thing I could to see that he was lynched. Cut a white woman's throat! And a negro! Of course I wanted him lynched. I saw his body dangling from a tree this morning, and I'm glad of it."[63]

The Lafayette County jail was regarded as the strongest in Mississippi, but after Sullivan's speech the mob set about its grim task with fierce determination. After rushing the jail and breaking through the front doors, the mob used chisels and sledgehammers to break open the steel doors. At this point, the sheriff decided that resistance was pointless, and he abandoned the jail so that he would not be forced to give up his prisoner. After two hours of work, the mob broke through a massive steel door as hundreds outside the jail cheered. The elation was short-lived, however, when the mob discovered that another steel door stood between them and Patton. The mob then decided that it would be faster to break through the brick walls of the prison, but this arduous work had to be done on ladders. It took the mob another three hours to penetrate the prison walls. Hundreds of men helped in the task, and reinforcements were brought in on the Illinois Central Railroad. "It is doubtful if ever before in the history of mobs," said one reporter on the scene, "there has been a more systematic and long-continued assault made on a jail or door than has been witnessed by hundreds of Lafayette, Marshall and Yallobusha citizens here tonight." All ages of men, including boys, participated. All the while, none of the participants attempted to conceal their identity. Working-class men and farmers made up much of the mob, but people from all backgrounds, including businessmen and professionals, watched eagerly as the mob went about its task.

When the mob finally breached his cell, Patton resisted with an iron bedpost and a spade. Patton managed to seriously injure three of the mob before he was killed in a fusillade of bullets. Those inside then tossed the body through the hole in the prison wall to the crowd that waited below. A rope was placed around Patton's neck, and about fifty men dragged the remains through the public square, where others scalped the corpse and hanged it to a telephone pole in the courthouse yard. The next day, Judge Roane, a group of ministers, and eighteen other citizens condemned the lynching. As usual, a coroner's jury declared that Patton had been killed by parties unknown. Most in Oxford seemed "satisfied with the actions of the mob," which once again had demonstrated the harsh, brutal reality that buttressed white supremacy.

The volatile mixture of fear and indignation that a heinous crime elicited from the white community, combined with the excitement that emanated from a convict manhunt, produced the largest crowd that ever witnessed a lynching in Mississippi or South Carolina, when trusty Charley Sheppard was burned alive near the infamous Parchman Prison Farm on New Year's Eve 1928.[64] The forty-one-year-old Sheppard was serving a twenty-year sentence for manslaughter before he supposedly beat and stabbed to death J. D. Duvall, a carpenter sergeant at the prison farm. The powerfully built Sheppard said he cut the fifty-five-year-old Duvall's throat because Duvall had beaten him for returning late from a leave of absence. After killing Duvall, Sheppard then abducted and allegedly raped one of Duvall's eight children, an eighteen-year-old daughter named Ruth.

For three days, more than one thousand armed men scoured several counties in search of Sheppard (who had released Ruth Duvall after twenty-four hours). Sheppard was eventually found on the plantation of Miss Laura Mae Keeler, where Sheppard's brother Tom was also a tenant. Because Keeler feared mob violence, she had Tom Sheppard brought to her house the night before his brother arrived. When a cook on the plantation found Charley Sheppard in one of the tenant cabins, Keeler notified authorities of his whereabouts and asked that armed guards and bloodhounds be sent to aid in Sheppard's capture.

Not wanting to see Sheppard lynched, however, Keeler thought better of the matter and decided to talk to Sheppard herself before a mob arrived. Unarmed, Keeler went to the cabin where Sheppard was hiding, and he agreed to surrender peaceably if Keeler turned him over to the sheriff. Sheppard warned Keeler that he would "shoot it out," however, if Keeler could not guarantee his safety. Miss Keeler then went back to the house and told the armed men who had arrived that she was going to escort Sheppard to the sheriff. Amazingly, the men reluctantly agreed and sent another convict trusty and a white man from Jackson to accompany Keeler and Sheppard.

The unlikely pair started for the sheriff early in the morning and took back roads to avoid the many posses in the area. But word spread quickly of Sheppard's capture, and shortly after noon, a caravan of at least fifty cars led by one of Duvall's brothers stopped Keeler's vehicle near Cleveland and demanded that Sheppard be given to them. Realizing that resistance was futile, Keeler pleaded with the mob to relinquish Sheppard to authorities.

The macabre entourage toured the countryside to allow every possible person to see Sheppard and "visited several negro camps in which Sheppard's impending fate was described with warnings to the blacks." At Lombardy, a makeshift platform was constructed in front of the May Brothers' store, from which Sheppard confessed to his alleged crimes. All the lights of the store were turned on Sheppard so that the crowd could see him. Word of Sheppard's impending burning at one of the prison farm gates was broadcast "by all possible means throughout the countryside." Thousands of cars joined a silent parade to Camp 11, where Sheppard had released Ruth Duvall some days earlier and now was to be burned. The onslaught of vehicles was so large that every gas station in the area was drained of fuel.

By early evening, six thousand people had gathered at the site of the burning. When Sheppard finally arrived, mob members methodically built a huge wood pyre. As the bound and strapped Sheppard lay on the wood, mob members doused the pile with gasoline that participants had carried to the scene. Fearing that Sheppard might die from the gas fumes, someone in the mob stuffed his nose and mouth with mud. The burning was delayed several more minutes when it was learned that Duvall's son and brother-in-law were on their way to the scene. When they arrived, the two men were taken to the front of the crowd and given the honor of shooting Sheppard if he tried to escape.

Shortly before the pyre was lit, a "wild-eyed" onlooker "leaped atop the pile of wood, straddled the negro's body and cut his ears off with a pocket knife." This was the only bodily mutilation reported against Sheppard. The burning began about quarter past seven. The crowd gasped in amazement as the flames shot high in the air. Women shrieked in terror as Sheppard "twisted and fought his ropes, cursing his captors and white people generally." As Sheppard roiled back and forth in the flames, he finally rolled completely off the pile of wood. When Sheppard attempted to get to his feet, some mob members raised their guns but were stopped by others who argued that Sheppard should suffer as much as his life would allow. The mob quickly tossed Sheppard back on the pyre and poured fresh cans of gasoline on the burning bier. Witnesses claimed that Sheppard continued to fight the ropes that bound him for an unbelievable forty-five minutes before he finally succumbed to the flames.

When the fire died out, souvenir hunters carried off body parts. The next morning, however, Sheppard's skull and other body parts could be seen strewn along the roadside; the sickening odor apparently had prompted some participants to discard their ghoulish mementos. The man who had cut off Sheppard's ears, however, proudly displayed them at a gas station in Drew the following day. As for the authorities, Governor Theodore Bilbo declared that they had "neither the time nor the money to investigate 2000 people."

The manner in which the mob had paraded Sheppard before other black convicts and the large crowd that gathered to see the burning was indicative of the morbid fear that African American criminals induced in whites. White justice demanded that Sheppard be burned, and white racism required that African Americans understand that whites held them responsible for Sheppard's crimes.

The horrific burning of Sheppard was reminiscent of a scene from *The Marrow of Tradition,* a novel by the distinguished African American writer Charles Waddell Chestnutt, who was one of the first authors to write serious fiction about blacks. In the novel, a Captain McBane, who was an ardent white supremacist, attempted to convince a mob to burn a black man. "We seem to have the right nigger," McBane exhorted the crowd, "but whether we have or not, burn a nigger. It is an assault upon the white race. . . . It would justify the white people in burning any nigger." Lynching was necessary, McBane explained, to "serve notice on the niggers that we shall hold the whole race responsible for the misdeeds of each individual."[65] When alleged crimes involved a convict or outlaw, whites often regarded lynching as the appropriate response. A recidivist had proven himself impenetrable to white criminal justice, hence lynching was necessary to preserve civil and social order.

Although whites lynched some African Americans supposedly for being unamenable to white law, they lynched other African Americans, such as landowners, businessmen, professionals, and civil servants, for not "knowing their place" in society. Ebeneezer Fowler, for instance, was the wealthiest black man in the Yazoo Delta's Issaquena County in the early 1880s.[66] A mob of whites shot and killed Fowler in the streets of Mayersville after it became known that Fowler was having an intimate relationship with a white woman. Black residents were so upset over the lynching that local whites feared a race riot and were unable to restore calm until a contingent of militia arrived from Vicksburg. Whites were sensitive to the actions and behavior of successful blacks and would often seize on any excuse to eliminate the good fortune of privileged blacks. Prominent African Americans, like Frazier Baker or Anthony Crawford, could be lynched simply because their status contradicted white notions of black inferiority.

The occasional lynching of African American women often resulted from a desire among whites to punish African Americans who challenged racial oppression. African American women were victims in at least twenty-six lynching incidents in Mississippi and South Carolina. More than half of the African American women lynched died with their husbands, lovers, or sons, who usually had been accused of murdering a white man. Of those black women lynched alone, however, only one-quarter were accused of a murder-related crime. Although some scholars have suggested that white men found black women less threatening than black men, African American women were also lynched for challenging the white caste system.[67] In the spring of 1881, for example, whites in the Western Piedmont of South Carolina lynched an old black woman named Eliza Cowan for allegedly burning the barn of a prominent planter.[68] In July 1894, whites lynched a black woman in Simpson County, Mississippi, allegedly for inciting a race war.[69] A white posse from the Yazoo Delta brutally beat and shot a black female tenant named Jennie Collins after she refused to allow them to search her cabin. The white men were looking for Jack Farmer, who had shot and wounded a white planter during an argument. Although Collins may have sheltered Farmer, she allowed a white posse to search her cabin and supposedly even treated them to ice cream. When a second group of white men demanded to search her cabin, however, Collins refused. The posse then knocked Collins down and shot her in the head. Collins was a longtime resident of the area, and her three sons, two daughters, and mother all lived in the community.[70] The white mob killed Collins to impress upon African Americans that blacks resisted the will of whites at their own peril.

Some African American women became the targets of vicious atrocities because whites wanted to spread an unmistakable message of terror in the African American community. Cordella Stevenson, for instance, was lynched in the Black Prairie region of Mississippi in December 1915 after her son was accused of arson. Stevenson and her husband, Arch, were hardworking people who had been tenants on the same farm for eleven years. Police had questioned the Stevensons about their son's involvement in a barn burning that had happened several months earlier, but the couple claimed that their son had left the farm before the barn had been burned and that they did not know their son's whereabouts so the police released them.

A mob, nevertheless, came to the Stevensons' cabin late one night and seized Cordella while they held Arch Stevenson at gunpoint. The mob then dragged Cordella Stevenson through the streets of Columbus, raped her at an isolated spot, and hanged her from a tree. The revolting sight of Stevenson's nude body, which was found hanging near the Mobile & Ohio Railroad tracks, served notice to African Americans that in the minds of the mob, blacks had no legal or human rights. The "thousands and thousands of passengers" who viewed this atrocious sight, moreover, lent implicit sanction to the mob's evil work.[71]

Although mobs who lynched African American women were condemned by many whites, the brutal nature of their actions often evoked a defensive response from whites who lived in the area where such terror occurred. In December 1895, for example, whites lynched a black man and his mother in South Carolina's Outer Coastal Plain. Broxton Bridge was a heavily black township of Colleton County that whites claimed had been beset by a recent crime wave. After a local white church was robbed of a Bible and some furniture, some white men apparently decided to make an example of a young African American named Isham Kearse, who was a suspect in several robberies and a store fire. Four prominent white men, including a doctor, organized a mob and went to confront Kearse, who stayed with his mother, Hannah Walker, near Broxton Ford.

When the mob encountered Kearse on the road to his mother's house, they immediately "arrested" him. They put a rope around Kearse's neck and tied him to a buggy. They then dragged Kearse two miles to a ferry, where they waited for two other mob members to retrieve Hannah Walker and Kearse's seventeen-year-old wife, Rosa. When the women arrived, the mob stripped the three naked and whipped them with an old buggy trace. Kearse and his mother were beaten so badly that a physician later described their bodies as "pulpified." Rosa Kearse, who had recently given birth, was also beaten from head to toe, but she survived the attack. The next morning Kearse's body was found lifeless at the spot of the whipping. About a hundred yards away from Kearse, Hannah Walker lay dead atop a log in a pool of knee-deep water. Although Rosa Kearse managed to crawl home, she was severely injured.

The depravity of the lynching elicited widespread condemnation from many of South Carolina's white papers. The *Baptist Courier* said that the six lynchers were guilty of an "inexcusable, unpardonable, brutal, heathenish" crime. The paper was outraged that the mob ostensibly had lynched the victims for stealing a Bible and wondered whether "those cruel hands that wielded the bloody buggy trace ever opened that blessed Book?" The *Anderson People's Advocate* compared the lynching to the atrocious brutalities that the Turks had inflicted on the Armenians. The *People's Advocate* found the mob wanting in comparison with the Turks, who at least had not been reared in a "civilized," Christian country. The *Charleston News and Courier* echoed these sentiments and declared that "If justice is rendered to them they will be tried and convicted and hanged as speedily as they would be if they were negroes and their victims had been white people. If they escape the gallows, no man should be put to death in this State for any crime hereafter."[72] Other papers that condemned the lynching included the *Palmetto Post,* the *Hampton Guardian,* the *Marion Star,* the *Yorkville Enquirer,* the *Rock Hill Herald,* and the *Sumter Freeman.*

Some local whites, however, reacted bitterly to such criticisms and claimed that in the months before the lynching a wave of arson had engulfed the area. Homes, tenant houses, barns, stables, ginmills, sawmills, stores, and crops all had been mysteriously burned. In addition, blacks allegedly had stabbed or shot at least six white men. "Notwithstanding all these crimes," wrote one irate resident, "only one negro has suffered. Numerous warrants have been sworn out, but never served from the simple fact that the fellows wanted could not be found." Local white residents had even petitioned the governor to help end the crime wave but had received no reply.[73]

In light of these circumstances, some local whites deeply resented the condemnations that emanated from more urban parts of the state. "City folk" who lived amidst a large white population and had the benefit of a local police force, according to one rural farmer, knew little about the "cares and trials" of white farmers who were "surrounded by barbarians, after thirty years of undisciplined freedom in our vast forest and fields." City residents, moreover, did not understand the obstacles to justice, racial and otherwise, that rural whites encountered.[74] In addition to the magistrate and constables' fees that often made justice a luxury, rural whites complained that they still had to contend with "negro juryman, whose sense of justice is measured by the color of the skin of the accused." Another rural resident was even more uncompromising: "Let the press howl; let the paid spy write of its infamy; let the governor boast of withholding his mercy; let the public become indignant; but so long as our people suffer as they have suffered; just so long will the press chronicle events equally as tragic."[75]

Governor John Gary Evans, who was the nephew of one of South Carolina's most notoriously racist politicians, assigned a state detective named Newbold to investigate the murders. Newbold claimed that the lynchers had a grudge against Isham Kearse and attributed the lynching to "pure cussedness." Four white men from "four of the largest and most respectable families in the State" eventually were tried for the murder of Hannah Walker. Although Rosa Kearse identified all of the men as her attackers, the defense claimed that it was ridiculous to accept the word of a black woman against four prominent white men. One defense attorney described Kearse as "sassy" and complained: "That woman wasn't whipped. Didn't get enough if she was." The attorney further characterized Kearse's testimony against the defendants as offensive and unconvincing because she admitted that she had never met the men before the night of the lynching, but she talked "as though she had been their companion all her life." In addition, the defense claimed that if Kearse had been taken away in the dark and dragged behind a buggy, she would have been in a state of such utter confusion that she would have been unable to recognize anyone. A jury deliberated for just four and a half hours before deciding on acquittal.[76] Whites were unable to accept, much less comprehend, the "undisciplined freedom" of blacks, which seemed inherently threatening to the property and security of whites. The "discipline of slavery" no longer existed, and if whites wanted blacks to respect the concept of "meum et teum," then whites would have to preserve their privileged position with violence.[77]

African American women were victims only in about 3.5 percent of all lynching incidents, but more than 11 percent of all lynching incidents that involved torture had black female victims. All lynchings were barbarous, but few surpassed the fiendish cruelty displayed in the lynchings of Hannah Walker, Cordella Stevenson, or Maggie Howze. Although whites lynched black females infrequently, the lynching of a black woman was a vicious reminder of the unrestrained mandates of white supremacy. The desire to send a brutal message to the African American community probably explains why more than 80 percent of lynching incidents that involved black females in Mississippi and South Carolina occurred in majority black regions. The extraordinary depravity exhibited in lynchings that involved African American women demonstrated, according to Walter White, how "the race problem in this country has resolved into the saving of the bodies of blacks and the souls of whites."[78]

Another group of lynching victims that merits analysis was white males, who were the target in about 5 percent of all lynching incidents (no white females were lynched in either Mississippi or South Carolina). Nearly 90 percent of white victims were lynched before 1905. The lynching of white males occurred mainly in the white regions of Mississippi, which experienced 54 percent of all the white lynching incidents that occurred in either Mississippi or South Carolina. The worst white region in this regard was the Red Hills of Mississippi, which had a tradition of lawlessness dating back at least to Reconstruction.[79]

Although half of white male lynching victims were landowners, professionals, or other prominent persons, less than 10 percent of black male victims were in this category (see table 5). While just over 35 percent of black victims were accused of murder-related crimes, nearly half of white victims were.[80] White men, on the other hand, rarely were lynched for sexual assault; and when this did occur, the accusation almost invariably involved a minor rather than an adult white woman. Manhunts and torture were common occurrences in many black lynchings but almost never happened in white lynchings. Although the lynching of a prominent black man typically attracted a large crowd, prominent white men were usually lynched in a more private setting, perhaps because of the fear of arrest. Arrests followed in half of white lynchings, but only 28 percent of black lynching incidents resulted in arrests of alleged perpetrators.

The 1885 lynching of Oliver Towles Culbreath, which occurred in South Carolina's Western Piedmont region in 1885, exemplifies the "culture of honor" that inspired many white lynchings and also revealed why black lynching occurred so much more frequently than did white lynching.[81] Culbreath came from a modest family that lived in the Pleasant Lane section of northern Edgefield County. During the war, Culbreath had served with distinction as a sergeant under the command of Captain William Francis Prescott, who apparently took a liking to the young man.

Prescott was one of the richest farmers in the area, and after the war, Culbreath married Prescott's daughter, Fannie. Culbreath quickly acquired a reputation for being an exceptionally able and industrious farmer. Culbreath owned a cotton gin and a grain mill and hired a few men to help him on the farm. As his wealth increased, he also became known as an unusually generous man. Fannie and her husband appeared happy and eventually had six children, including four sons and two daughters.

For many years, Culbreath was considered "an honorable gentleman and worthy citizen," but after his father-in-law died, Culbreath began to drink heavily and mistreat his wife. Culbreath became intensely jealous of his wife, and he began to suspect that she might be having an affair with one of his employees, twenty-four-year-old William H. Hammond. On one occasion Culbreath was in a drunken rage and allegedly scourged his wife and his mother with a buggy whip. A reporter claimed that Culbreath's "conduct was so offensive to the people of the county that it is surprising he was not lynched at an earlier day." Fannie Culbreath eventually balked at her husband's ill-treatment and to the great scandal of Edgefield demanded a separation in 1883 or 1884. After the separation, Culbreath became even more jealous of his wife and routinely spied on her.

William Hammond, however, continued to visit the family and to work on the Culbreath farm. During the summer of 1885, Culbreath threatened to kill Hammond unless he stopped seeing his wife and family. On the night of 12 September 1885, Hammond was shot and killed on the back porch of the Culbreath home, while he gave a drink of water to five-year-old Harry Culbreath. Hammond apparently was spending the night at the Culbreath house at the request of Culbreath's oldest son, Memphis, who was away on a visit.

Most people assumed that Oliver Culbreath either had killed Hammond himself or had paid someone else to do it. Memphis Culbreath also may have been involved, however, because he fled Edgefield for Virginia on the night of his father's arrest and never returned. Although the local papers reported that the motive for the murder was William Hammond's amorous interest in Culbreath's daughter Jenny, Fannie Culbreath may have had a relationship with Hammond since she eventually married his older brother Charlie in November 1888.[82] Oliver Culbreath's brother, Dr. William Aiken Culbreath, intimated in a private letter that the reason Oliver was lynched was to prevent such unseemly disclosures from being revealed at trial.

On the afternoon of 21 September 1885, authorities arrested Oliver Culbreath for Hammond's murder and brought him to the law office of his attorney, John Gary Evans, just off the Edgefield Courthouse square. A few hour hours later, a mob of some three dozen men stormed the law office and shot and wounded Culbreath. The mob then took Culbreath a few miles away, shot him several more times, and left him for dead. Later that night, a sheriff's posse found Culbreath struggling to get back to Edgefield. As his wounds were being treated, Culbreath claimed that his attackers had included his wife's brother, Dr. William E. Prescott, and her uncle, Wyatt Holmes. Rumors spread that Memphis Culbreath was also a member of the masked mob.

The lynching naturally generated strong sentiments in Edgefield. William Aiken Culbreath claimed that four-fifths of the local population was against the lynching, and local papers reported that citizens organized public meetings to denounce the atrocity. In a scathing sermon, the Reverend H. A. Whitman of the First Baptist Church blamed the lynching on public apathy concerning education and morality. William Aiken Culbreath bragged to a friend that he could have every one of the mob members lynched, but he chose a more restrained course of action because he was a law-abiding man.

Most of the thirty-three men eventually arrested for the crime were well-to-do farmers, each owning an average of 370 acres of land. When the trial judge granted the accused men bail in lieu of $2,500, a spontaneous night-long party broke out, "celebrated in the genuine Edgefield style," that included ample quantities of whiskey.

In August 1887, Wyatt Holmes and his neighbor, a struggling farmer named William Parkman, were tried for Culbreath's murder. The accused retained Senator Matthew Calbraith Butler as their defense counsel. The state called numerous witnesses during the course of the three-day trial, but Butler felt no need to introduce testimony on behalf of his clients. The jury deliberated forty-five minutes before returning a verdict of not guilty. In the aftermath of this crushing defeat, the state dropped the charges against the other mob members.

The editor of the *Edgefield Chronicle,* James T. Bacon, admitted that justice had not been done in the case, but he felt that the community could take pride in the fact that it had done all that it could to bring the lynchers to justice. According to Bacon, the Culbreath affair was "too emphatically out of the common to be reached by ordinary methods or usual processes of law." From the perspective of the white community, the lynching was a natural consequence of the tarnished honor that Culbreath had inflicted on the influential family of his wife.[83]

The response of the African American community to the lynching and trial, however, was perplexing to local white residents. Despite the sweltering summer heat, African American men attended the trial in large numbers. A dumbfounded James Bacon could not imagine why African Americans were interested in a trial that "was utterly and exclusively a white man's case." Bacon noted with consternation the disruption that the presence of so many African Americans brought to the courtroom. Bacon sensed that the men were making some sort of political statement, and he lamented that access to the "temple of justice" enabled African American men to publicly and proudly "realize old Abe Lincoln's emancipation proclamation." Whites occasionally lynched white men in order to redress the aggrieved honor of one party or another, but they routinely lynched blacks in order to affirm that the freedom that resulted from the aftermath of the Civil War would never afford blacks social and political equality with whites.

Although a typical elite white lynching was a rather staid and private affair, a working-class white lynching was often much more dramatic. John Knox, for example, was a Canadian stevedore who had come to Mississippi's Piney Woods to work in the lumber camps.[84] In January 1901, the hard-drinking Knox married a widow named Davis, who ran a boardinghouse in Scranton for lumbermen. The woman's twelve-year-old son, Don Davis, was a favorite of many of the lumbermen, who considered the boy their "mascot."

On the morning of 26 February 1901, John Knox had a heated argument with his wife. Two reputable witnesses testified that during the argument they saw John Knox approach the Davis boy with a Springfield rifle and shoot him at point-blank range. The boy died immediately from a gunshot wound to the abdomen.

When lumbermen learned that Knox had killed his own stepson, they "became mad as hornets and it was . . . almost certain from that moment that he [Knox] would be lynched." By midafternoon, some two hundred to three hundred men were milling around the courthouse. Around 3:00 p.m., a coroner's jury convened before a packed courtroom and after hearing testimony charged Knox with murder. The animosity toward Knox was palpable, and some white citizens wired Governor Andrew Longino to tell him that a lynching was imminent. Around 9:00 p.m., Longino wired Sheriff R. J. Loughridge to summon a posse to protect Knox. Loughridge claimed that he did so, but a mob nevertheless overpowered him and several deputies around 11:00 p.m. After breaking into the jail, a mob of about two hundred armed men took Knox to a lynching tree at the Louisville & Nashville depot. After hanging Knox, the mob waited a few minutes while Knox slowly strangled to death, before they riddled his body with bullets. The body remained hanging in the center of town until the afternoon of the next day.

Governor Longino tried to take a stand against the lynchers, going so far as to assign the state attorney general to the case, but few people in Scranton thought that the mob should be prosecuted. Eleven men were eventually arrested for the crime, but the state was unable to secure any hard evidence "for the reason that, although most of the people in the town know all about the lynching, nobody can remember anything." When Judge T. A. Woods released without bail nine of the men, but held two deputy sheriffs who allegedly had assisted in the lynching, whites from Scranton denounced Woods for not letting all the men go. Most people in Scranton reportedly felt that the arrests only were for political effect and complained that if the governor had not become involved, the whole matter would have been dropped. Many citizens resented wasting tax dollars on the incident, for as one man put it, "if they knew that every man in the city was guilty, no grand jury could be obtained that would indict a single one." Scranton had a tradition of lynching that made it seem commonplace. Knox was at least the eighth victim to be hanged from the same oak tree in the center of town. In April 1901, a grand jury investigated the case but returned no indictments.

Another popular and expeditious lynching of a laboring white man occurred in South Carolina's Eastern Piedmont on 1 October 1904. John Morrison was a "desperate sort of man" who lived with his wife on the edge of Kershaw, South Carolina, where he took care of a water-pumping station for the Southern Railway.[85] Morrison was known to have killed three black men, the most recent in the summer of 1904, when he shot a black man for cursing at him. Morrison had been tried for the most recent homicide but was easily acquitted since, according to the trial judge, "it was an ordinary case of a white man killing a negro." Sometime after his acquittal, however, the railroad fired Morrison for threatening to shoot a rail crew if they used coal that Morrison claimed belonged to him. Morrison remained in his company-supplied house, however, because no one in Kershaw had the courage to make him leave.

Morrison once bragged that he could commit any crime and be acquitted for it, which may explain his actions on 1 October, when he murdered a white man for refusing to lend him some small change. Around 6:00 p.m., Morrison met Willie Floyd, a popular young farmer from a well-known family, in the streets of Kershaw and asked Floyd to loan him ten cents for some liquor. Floyd refused, saying he did not have any change, and went about his business. A short time later, Morrison told Floyd that he had always treated Floyd like a gentleman but that he was going to kill Floyd for refusing him the money. When the terrified Floyd threw up his arms and begged Morrison not to kill him, Morrison shot twice and killed Floyd in front of many horrified witnesses.

Almost immediately after the murder, there "was an under-current of determination to make Morrison pay the penalty of his crime before the night had passed." In less than two hours, more than five hundred men had surrounded the poorly secured Kershaw guardhouse. Some citizens wired Governor Duncan Heyward about the mob's anger, and Heyward ordered the sheriff at Camden to call out the militia and protect Morrison. When the mob learned that the militia was on its way, they quickly stormed the jail, removed Morrison, and hanged him to a hickory tree just outside of the town limits. After the lynching, no local residents would bury Morrison's body, so he was eventually interred in a potter's field.

Governor Heyward said he was "utterly disgusted" with the lynching, and he ordered the local solicitor to employ a private detective to investigate the case. Thirteen men were eventually charged with the crime, but the state was unable to uncover any conclusive evidence. The local solicitor told Heyward that "this was the most orderly, quiet and sober lynching that ever occurred—a real pious lynching, with the preachers in the background, almost audibly saying amen."[86] The solicitor explained to the governor that he had appealed personally to the town leaders for their help but found most in sympathy with the lynchers. The conscience of Kershaw was, in the solicitor's opinion, debauched in Morrison's blood, which made prosecution of the case impossible. In April 1905, the case against all thirteen men charged in the lynching was dropped.

As with black men, white men were lynched for murder, rape, theft, and political terrorism. Lynching was private law, to be used in defense of honor, communal values, white male hegemony, and property. The willingness of whites to lynch a white man indicated that lynching did not contravene white law but supplemented it.[87] The purpose of a white lynching, however, usually was to purge a community of a deviant individual. Although black lynching was also directed against individuals, it was intended to reinforce the subjugation of African Americans to whites. Consequently, white lynchings were an extraordinary occurrence, while black lynchings were an essential element of the racial oppression and violence that bedeviled the South.[88]

5

"An Example Must Be Made"

LYNCH MOBS AND THE RESPONSE OF AFRICAN AMERICANS

The size, purpose, and nature of lynch mobs varied across time and space. During the first phase of the lynching epidemic, white-only mobs avoided directing their fury against the African American community as a whole, and some African Americans participated in lynch mobs that were punitive in purpose. Black mobs generated anxiety among whites, however, who found the prospect of African Americans inflicting extralegal vengeance disquieting. As lynching became racialized, larger mobs became more frequent and African Americans abandoned the practice. Large mobs often formed where the perceived depredations of rootless black laborers generated anxiety among whites, who worried about the negative effect that aimless blacks might have on the local economy. In regions where African Americans formed a large majority of the population and had more independence from whites, however, lynch mobs tended to be smaller and often killed for offenses such as assault or property crimes. In the lynch-prone Yazoo Delta, mobs tended to be smaller not only because of the high concentration of African Americans but also because Delta whites preferred to repress tenant transgressions with privately sanctioned vengeance. Smaller mobs also formed in regions where class divisions divided the white population. On a state level, Mississippi mobs were larger, more resolute, and more cruel than mobs in South Carolina because the racial climate in Mississippi was more acrimonious than in South Carolina. African American resistance to lynching eventually reduced the size of mobs, but lynching continued in regions where conflict between white landlords and black tenants remained part of the daily fabric of life. As the lynching era waned, however, the ability of a mob to elicit communal support in defense of its murderous work became less evident.

The collective behavior of mobs has usually been explained in terms of the need to regularly reaffirm white male supremacy.[1] The ritualistic aspects of mob behavior have received particular attention because racial ritual was the mortar of white solidarity and helped define caste roles that prevailed in the South.[2] Many mobs first wanted to redress individual grievances, however, and only secondarily acted in support of communal white supremacy. Given the social, economic, political, and legal predominance of whites in the post-Reconstruction South, white southerners frequently wondered why mobs lynched. "There is not a negro Judge on the Bench in any Southern State, nor a negro prosecuting attorney, and the jury box is almost exclusively filled with white men," observed the *Charleston News and Courier,* which asked, "Why should there be a resort to mob violence when the law and the Courts are competent?"[3] Mississippi governor Edmond Noel also struggled to understand mobs. With white people in complete control of "every power of our state government" and the punishment of black criminals a virtual certainty in the South, Noel could not comprehend why "the superior and ruling race" should "contest for the evil distinction of preeminence in lawless savagery."[4]

Mobs often acted in support of white supremacy within an emotionally charged context of violent confrontation between individual whites and blacks. The inequities of the southern caste system created an underlying tension that was the catalyst for much lynching. Mobs did not necessarily reinforce white solidarity, however, when they lynched to make an example of a black man who had violently resisted the constrictions of caste. After a senseless lynching from a communal point of view, for instance, the *Charleston News and Courier* observed that a "man described as a 'lyncher' is one accused of having joined in a community act," but many lynch mobs were not a "community in the colloquial sense." Instead, the paper charged that mobs were often nothing more than "bloody assassins" who had revenge as their primary motive.[5]

The desire of a mob for retribution could often overwhelm the preference of authorities for a legal affirmation of white supremacy. When a mob lynched Bob "Snowball" Davis, for example, it ignored the impassioned plea of South Carolina governor Duncan Heyward, who viewed mob violence as a stain on the character of whites. Davis, who was a day laborer with extremely dark skin, had a bad reputation in Greenwood County, which was in the Western Piedmont of South Carolina.[6] Local whites considered Davis mentally deficient, and thirteen years previously a mob of whites and blacks had lynched Davis's half-brother Jake, ostensibly for raping the wife of a local Mexican War hero.[7] Davis was in his early twenties and had already served a sentence on the county chain gang.

In August 1906, whites accused Davis of the attempted rape of Jennie Brooks, the twenty-year-old daughter of a prosperous Greenwood County farmer and merchant. The brutal nature of the attack on the young woman, who was severely cut on the hand and throat, enraged local whites. As news of the assault spread, white men gathered at the woman's home, where her bloodstained dress hung in the backyard.

For two days, squads of men searched the surrounding countryside in vain for Davis. Despite Davis's bad reputation among whites, local African Americans tried to help Davis escape by providing search parties with false and contradictory information about the wanted man's whereabouts. An old black woman, for instance, told a group of whites that Davis had been to her house three times during the night and that he had fled in the opposite direction from which the white men searched. The manhunt was hindered further because Davis had been on a chain gang, and he had trained the bloodhounds used to track him. On several occasions, searchers claimed that the dogs had caught up with Davis but had not bothered him at all.

When Governor Heyward learned that as many as one thousand men were in pursuit of Davis, he tried to contact the sheriff and other prominent citizens in the area but was told repeatedly that no communication lines were working in Greenwood County. Heyward knew that a mob would want to burn Davis and considered sending the militia to protect him, but the governor later claimed that he did not know where to dispatch the troops. Finally, after talking with the local sheriff, Heyward decided that the only way to prevent a lynching was to make a personal appeal before the mob.

Heyward and two newspaper reporters took a train to the Piedmont and then drove a buggy through the rain to the Brooks home in the Mount Moriah section of Greenwood County. About fifty men were at the house when Heyward arrived, and the woman's family frankly told the governor that "there was no earthly chance" that he could save Davis from death. When Heyward expressed his hope that the law would be respected, the woman's female relatives rebuffed the governor, saying that "they would act as men if need be." The woman's father, J. Pett Brooks, bluntly told Heyward that he wanted Davis burned.

After a mob brought Davis to the house for the woman to identify him, the crowd quickly swelled in number. From a makeshift podium that was constructed at a corner of the front yard rail-fence, Heyward made his appeal for the law. Many in the mob might have expected that Heyward would deliver a Tillman-like speech and condone the use of violence, and as the governor mounted the platform, the crowd cheered. But Heyward was a Bourbon Hamptonite, one of the last large rice planters in South Carolina, and he despised lynching as an act of wanton lawlessness. Heyward informed the crowd that he could have ordered troops to protect Davis but that he did not want more trouble. Instead, he came as governor to plead on behalf of the law.

Heyward told the mob that he knew how they felt, that he had a wife and family and that he had experienced the dangers of living in one of the remotest parts of Colleton County. But Heyward emphasized that South Carolina was on trial "before the civilized world." He appealed to the "manhood" of those present, to their citizenship and their pride in their state, and pleaded that the law be allowed to punish the "brute" in their midst. Heyward promised that Davis would be tried within two weeks. The governor reminded the crowd that some of them would be jurors and that they would surely convict Davis of his crime (Heyward neglected to mention that neither attempted rape nor attempted murder were capital crimes in South Carolina). In a rhetorical flourish, Heyward even offered to cut the rope at the legal execution of Davis. But lynching, Heyward warned, was a dark cloud on the state's horizon. Heyward reminded his listeners about the negative effects that lingered after the Phoenix lynching in 1898. Heyward pleaded with the mob to suppress its passions and to show the world that "the vindication of the law was higher and nobler than simple vengeance." Heyward admitted that the mob might "enjoy" lynching Davis, but he claimed that in the long run it would be better if Davis was legally executed. Finally, "fagged out and hopeless," Heyward descended from the platform. "The circumstances of the assault, the young woman in the room fifty feet away, the long and wearying search, the record of the negro, the bloody garments all conspired," wrote a reporter at the scene, "to make the eloquence, the force and earnestness of Governor Heyward's appeal for law fall on deaf ears."

After Heyward's speech, the mob took Davis to a small clump of woods near the Brooks' home, but Heyward continued to press for Davis's legal execution. Many in the mob resented the governor's efforts, and Heyward was told that if he continued to interfere, a bag would be placed over his head to keep him quiet. Some in the mob had participated in the Phoenix massacre and insisted that Davis should be lynched. The "men with gray hairs and determination" who urged the mob to complete its sanguinary task were "fairly representative of the citizenship that makes the State." To allow the maximum number of men to participate in the lynching, the mob ignored J. Pett Brooks's stated wish that Davis be burned and instead decided to shoot him. After Davis was tied to a pine tree about ten feet above the ground, mob members shot him to a pulp during a ten-minute fusillade that could be heard all the way to Greenwood.

Bob Davis was lynched because the demands of white caste conflicted with the constraints of the law.[8] The mob ignored Governor Heyward's appeal on behalf of the law because the desire to kill Davis had become "the whole story." Mob members besmirched the "fair name" of South Carolina because local circumstances demanded that "an example must be made." Around the time of the Davis lynching, whites in the Western

Piedmont and the Inner Coastal Plain regions of South Carolina frequently resorted to lethal racial violence. After 1900, these two plantation regions accounted for almost half of the large mobs that occurred in the state. These regions experienced endemic landlord-tenant conflicts, which made mobs more determined and vicious because of fears that emanated from disputes with African Americans.

A similar pattern can be seen when comparing Mississippi to South Carolina. Mississippi mobs generally were larger, more resolute, and more cruel than those in South Carolina. Nearly 60 percent of Mississippi mobs contained fifty persons or more, while the majority of mobs in South Carolina (52.4 percent) had fewer than fifty people (see fig. 8). If mob size was an indication of community sanction, then alleged rape and other crimes that involved women and murder or attempted murder were seen as the greatest threats to white solidarity (see fig. 9). In South Carolina, where whites were keenly focused on undermining the political autonomy of African Americans, alleged sexual crimes against white women were more evident than in Mississippi, especially in the years before disfranchisement. Incessant conflict between landlords and tenants was more prevalent in Mississippi, however, which is why alleged murder or attempted murder spawned a greater percentage of lynchings than in South Carolina. Lynching for minor crimes or no apparent crime did not garner as much community support and hence involved smaller mobs. The most secretive mobs often lynched to frighten African American tenants from their farms and almost always operated under the cover of darkness because they feared that elite whites would press for the prosecution of such crimes.

Ironically, lynching had not always been an exclusively white affair. During the early years of the lynching plague, African Americans often participated in lynch mobs, and on one occasion whites even asked African Americans for permission to lynch an alleged rapist.[9] When lynching was more punitive in nature, it was also more frequent and less racialized. Two-thirds of lynching incidents that involved African American participation in mobs occurred before 1900, but only 42 percent of white-mob lynching incidents happened before the turn of the century.

The personal characteristics of alleged crime victims had an im-

FIGURE 8. Mob size in Mississippi and South Carolina (percent)

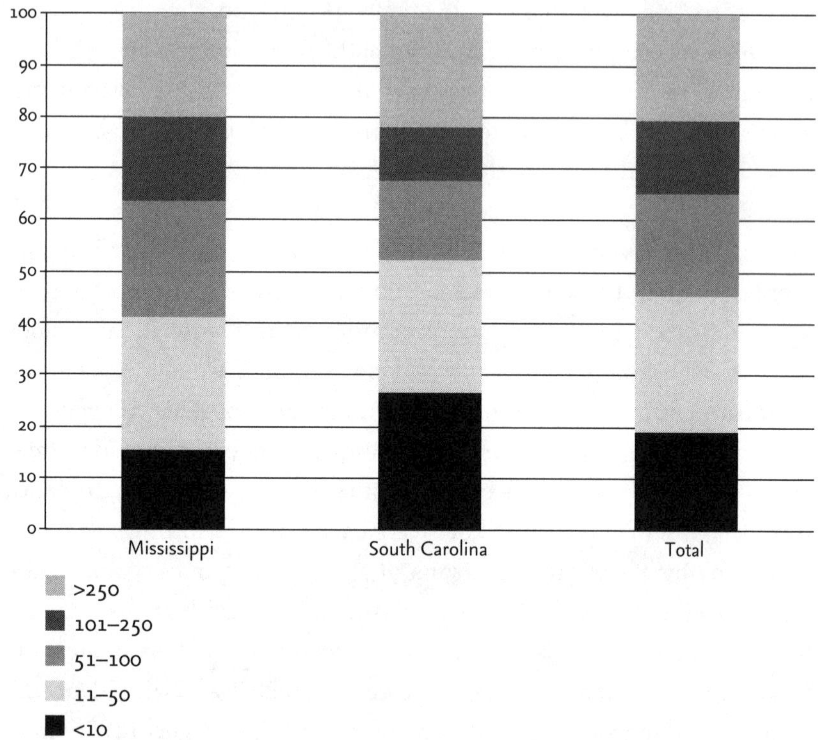

portant effect on the size and function of mobs. Most, but not all, alleged crime victims were white. South Carolina had only two lynching incidents that involved an African American alleged crime victim, but Mississippi had forty-four, most of which occurred in heavily African American regions such as the Bluff Hills, the Old Natchez, and the Yazoo Delta. African American mobs performed about 70 percent of these lynchings, while mixed-race mobs were responsible for about 13 percent of incidents that involved African American alleged crime victims. In the 1880s, about 20 percent of Mississippi lynchings occurred in retaliation for crimes against African Americans. After the turn of the century, however, black-on-black lynching declined sharply, with only three incidents occurring after 1908.

Almost all of the lynchings that African American mobs committed were against adult black males. Most of these men were accused of mur-

FIGURE 9. Mob size by category of alleged crime in Mississippi and South Carolina (percent)

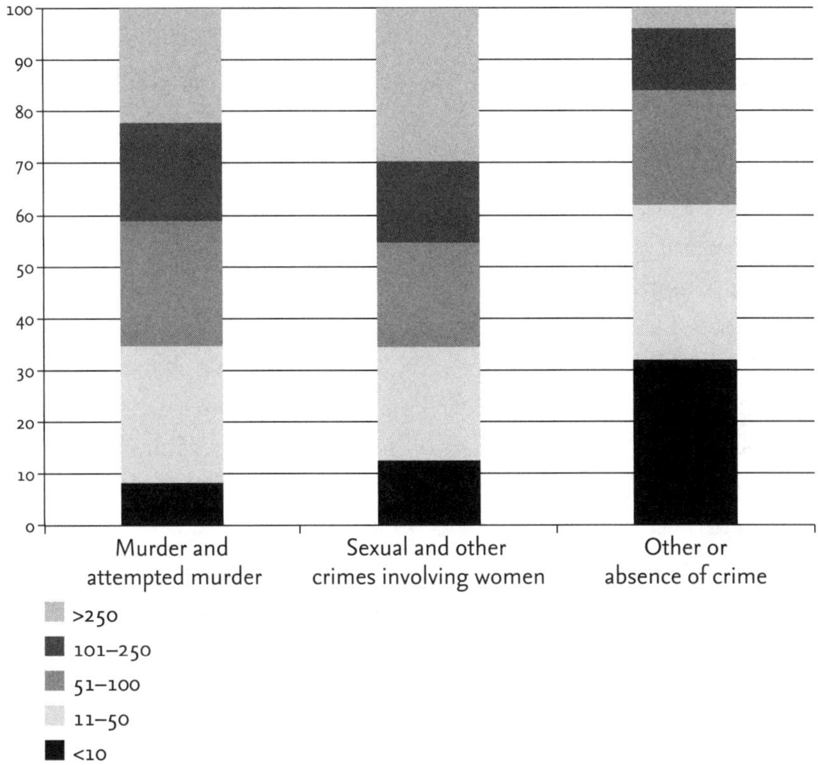

der or rape, usually of young females. Surprisingly, nearly 60 percent of African American mobs removed their victims from the custody of law officers. Almost all African American mobs operated at night and preferred hanging to shooting by a margin of two to one. Only three African American mobs were comprised of more than one hundred persons. A typical African American mob was small, spurned torture (only one African American mob burned its victim), and rarely displayed a corpse for public viewing.

The function of African American mobs, like that of white-on-white lynching, was punitive, not terroristic.[10] African American mobs usually reserved lynching for deviant individuals, such as child rapists and wife murderers. A black mob from the Bluff Hills region of Mississippi, for instance, hanged Emmanuel Munday for the brutal rape and murder of an eight-year-old black girl. Munday was arrested for the crime, but after his arraignment a mob of about eighty masked men tricked the jailer into letting them inside the jail, and the mob then hanged Munday on the outskirts of town. The lynching created a "profound sensation" among whites, who had previously regarded the formation of an African American mob as "hardly . . . a possibility."[11]

In 1885, a rather inept African American mob from Mississippi's Black Prairie region lynched Jacob Doss, who allegedly had murdered his wife. Doss apparently wanted to divorce his wife so that he could marry his mistress, but his wife refused to accept the arrangement. One day Doss took his wife on a ride in the country, killed her with a club to the head, and dumped her body in a creek. Two days later, Doss married his mistress and moved to nearby Starkville. Neighbors became suspicious, however, and eventually discovered the remains of Mrs. Doss. When Doss returned to stand trial, a mob of two hundred black men took him from the custody of officers. After holding a prayer service, the mob attempted to hang Doss from a railroad trestle, but discovered that the hanging rope was too long when Doss fell unhurt to the ground. Doss's reprieve was short-lived, however; the next day his body was found hanging from the trestle.[12] African American mobs rarely desecrated the corpse of a lynching victim, even for egregious offenses such as wife killing and child rape. The worse that African Americans would do was not bury a lynching victim, and the body of one man was devoured by hogs.[13]

Mobs of black "whitecappers" occasionally lynched for moral transgressions other than murder and rape. In 1894, for instance, a mob of African Americans beat and killed a black "voodoo doctor" against whom the mob apparently had numerous grievances. In this instance, however, one person was primarily responsible for the death, and he was arrested for the murder.[14] Mobs that lynched for moral reasons, whether they were black or white, often did so in the heat of the moment, without lynching having been the mob's stated intent. Sam Howard, for instance, was an older black man who was living in adultery in the Northern Pee Dee region of South Carolina. Neighbors had warned Howard that if his offensive behavior did not stop, he would have trouble. One night, while his paramour was away, a mob of about a dozen black men called Howard from his cabin. The men wanted to whip Howard so that he would either leave the area or stop living with his mistress, but Howard fought back with an iron rod. When Howard hit one of the mob members on the hand, the armed man shot Howard dead.

The lynching created unease in the white community, and eleven men were arrested quickly. The *Charleston News and Courier,* which described the incident as a "perfectly regular lynching" and "a comparatively merciful one," pointed out that the lynchers were being prosecuted only because they were black. "Why," the paper asked, "should any extraordinary ado be made over [this lynching]?" Those involved had merely "accepted and applied the lessons taught them by many of their white fellow citizens, and it was merely a negro that they lynched." After disfranchisement, whites found black mobs disquieting, and six of the lynchers were sentenced to a life of hard labor in the state penitentiary.[15]

When African Americans had been, at least in theory, politically equal with whites, whites had often been more circumspect in their lynching activity and were careful that lynching did not unnecessarily alienate the African American community. In July 1883, for instance, a mob of blacks and whites from the Yazoo Delta lynched Martin Jones for allegedly murdering a pregnant white woman. If a similar crime had occurred in the 1920s, it would have elicited paroxysms of outrage from the white community, but a reporter who covered this lynching commented that "great credit is to be given to the colored people in general for their fairness in seeing that a ruffian, although of their own color, should be served with such an appropriate penalty."[16] Before disfranchisement, lynching did not have an exclusively antiblack overtone, and whites sometimes regarded the participation of blacks in mobs as a sign of communal solidarity.[17]

Prior to disfranchisement, it was even possible for blacks to lynch an alleged white criminal, as happened when an African American mob from South Carolina's Upper Piedmont region lynched a white man named Manse Waldrop.[18] Waldrop was a "half-witted" farm laborer from Anderson County, who in late December 1887 allegedly had raped and murdered fourteen-year-old Lula Sherman, the daughter of a black sharecropper. Under the cover of darkness, the local constable and another white man who wanted to lynch Waldrop attempted to take Waldrop to a jail at Pickens, but a mob of fifteen or twenty blacks ambushed the trio and shot Waldrop several times. Waldrop was only slightly wounded, however, and as more whites arrived, including two local physicians, it appeared that a lynching might be averted. But the black men regrouped and charged past the unarmed whites and seized Waldrop. After ordering the white men to leave, the mob hanged Waldrop from a roadside tree. Waldrop's lynching evoked consternation among local whites, and six African Americans, including the rape victim's father, were eventually indicted for murder.

In July 1888, in the midst of unbearably hot weather, throngs of people attended the trial of the six accused lynchers. After a day of testimony, an all-white jury deliberated all night before returning a mistrial. Ten of the jurors reportedly wanted to convict two of the defendants, while two others wanted to convict all of the men. At a second trial, in March 1889, three of the accused, including the victim's father, were declared not guilty, another was granted a new trial, and two defendants were found guilty and sentenced to hang.[19]

Immediately after the verdict, African Americans started a petition drive requesting that Governor Richardson grant clemency to the lynchers. In a few weeks, nearly four thousand signatures, many of them from white people, had been obtained. Dr. T. W. Folger, who had done as much as anyone to prevent Waldrop's lynching, now condoned it and argued that the condemned men should be pardoned in order to silence northern critics and to demonstrate that "the negro can lynch the white perpetrator of crime with as much impunity as can his Caucasian brother lynch the negro."[20] Richardson eventually pardoned the men because he could not "in justice" allow these "ignorant colored men . . . [who] had seen lynchers go unpunished time and again" be the first to suffer the death penalty for lynching. In the future, however, Richardson warned that clemency would not be granted to lynchers, be they white or black. The *Charleston News and Courier* hoped that the Waldrop case might dampen the enthusiasm among whites for lynching. Now that the racial roles had been reversed and whites had been forced to acknowledge that "the colored men have equal right, in the presence of similar wrongs, to declare that their women 'must be protected,'" the paper predicted that whites might abandon extralegal violence because of the distressing prospect that "persons who are proposed to be regulated can and will hit back."[21] Whites recognized that African Americans regularly resisted white hegemony with violence, which made it difficult for many whites to condemn lynching, even when it involved a white man and a black mob.[22] Whites had sacrificed justice on the altar of racial antipathy, and as the lynching plague continued, it became clear that no quarter would be shown in defense of racial supremacy.

As whites struggled to justify the imposition of the color line, so-called "spectacle lynchings," which "conjured whiteness" through the ritualized participation of hundreds and sometimes thousands of residents (and the vicarious participation of many thousands more through newspaper accounts) occurred more frequently.[23] Large mobs formed most often during the first two decades of the 1900s and then declined sharply as African Americans and progressive whites became more vociferous in their opposition to lynching (see fig. 10).[24]

Large mobs formed often in the Piney Woods region of Mississippi, where a coalescence of social conditions fostered malignant outbreaks of racism. In addition to being a lumber-producing region that attracted itinerant black laborers, the three coastal counties of the Piney Woods were also an important tourist destination. Fifteen of the twenty-two lynching incidents that occurred in Mississippi's coastal counties, moreover, involved alleged crimes against white women. Consequently, the Piney Woods had the highest percentage of large mobs of any region in Mississippi. Eighteen mobs in the Piney Woods numbered more than one hundred people, and eleven of these formed in response to alleged rape or attempted rape and another gathered for a lesser charge involving a white woman.

A mob in Mississippi City, Harrison County, for instance, hanged and burned two men for the rape and murder of the teenage daughter of a prosperous local farmer. The attack occurred in early June 1900, when the villages and resorts in the area started filling up with summer guests.

FIGURE 10. Mob size by decade in Mississippi and South Carolina (percent)

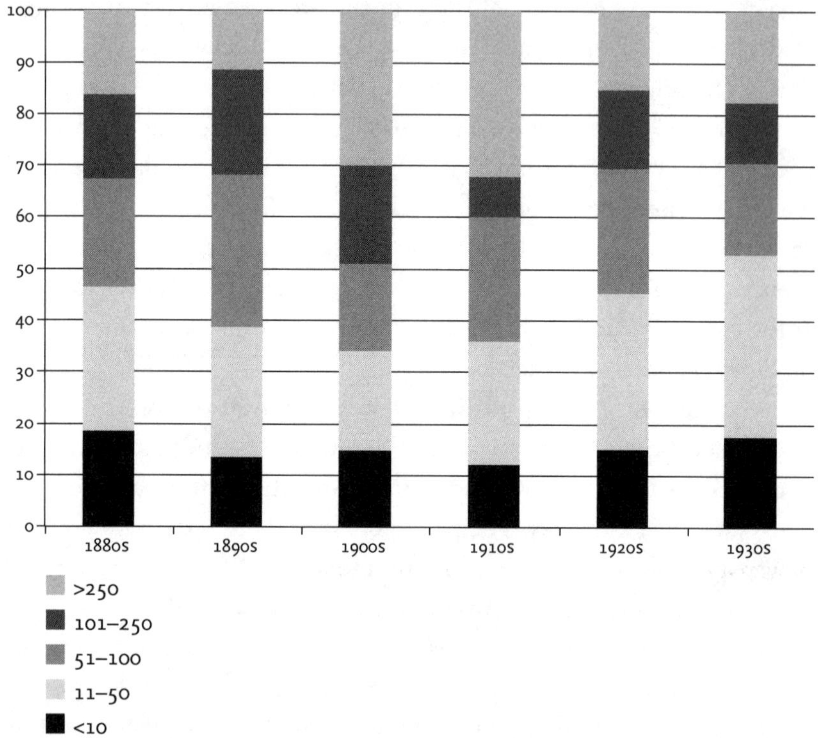

Despite a public pronouncement from the local district attorney that the suspects were probably innocent, a mob lynched the men anyway, fearing that "if it is not safe for the ladies and children to be in the woods alone, the advantages of this section as a summer resort are ruined."[25]

The personal characteristics of the lynching victims increased the mob's desire to kill the men. Henry Askew, for instance, was an unemployed laborer who had been visiting houses in the area and asking for work when the murder occurred. After his arrest, Askew was stripped naked and "minutely examined" for scratches, cuts, and bloodstains. While nude, Askew was cross-examined and admitted that he once had been arrested at Brookhaven, Mississippi, for assaulting a white woman but later was proven innocent and released. With a howling mob waiting outside the marshal's office, authorities considered Askew's admission as proof of "innocence or idiocy." To prevent a lynching, officials then decided to send Askew to Mississippi City for safekeeping.

Two other men arrested for the crime were lumber workers, one from Biloxi named Charles Jenkins and the other a stranger named Ed Russ. When law officers failed to link any of the suspects to the crime, a mob of thirty men took Askew from the Mississippi City jail to extract a confession from him. The mob first brought Askew to the rape victim's mother, who tearfully pleaded with Askew to tell the truth. When Askew managed to answer the woman's questions satisfactorily, however, the mob tied Askew to a pine tree and gathered wood to burn him. After twice demanding that Askew admit to the crime, the mob lit a fire and watched as Askew writhed in pain but still refused to confess. Wondering if Askew was guilty or not, the mob doused the flames and returned Askew to the Mississippi City jail.

But when another black man accused of the crime was cleared, whites again turned their attention toward Askew and Russ, who were being jailed together in Mississippi City. After more than a week of frustration in which authorities were unable to arrest any solid suspects, a mob took Askew and Russ from the custody of Mississippi City officers, tied them back to back, and hanged them from the same tree behind a rail depot. After the two corpses were riddled with bullets, the mob set the bodies ablaze and quietly dispersed. The white people of Biloxi reportedly felt that "to allow such a crime to pass without energetic action would be a disgrace upon the locality." As an additional warning to African Americans, local white businessman, who were concerned about a drop in tourism, purchased bloodhounds that could be used if similar outrages occurred again.

Just over three years later, Harrison County whites lynched another accused rapist, nineteen-year-old Sam Adams, who allegedly had raped the wife of a popular New York entertainer vacationing in the area.[26] Adams had a bad reputation around Pass Christian, where the lynching occurred, because whites claimed that Adams's father had delivered a "vicious address" to local African Americans after the July 1900 Robert Charles riot in New Orleans. While three officers waited with Adams to board a train to Mississippi City, where authorities planned to safely incarcerate Adams, a mob of one hundred white and black men took Adams from the officers and quickly hanged him in a nearby oak grove. After the lynching, some whites wanted to start a pogrom against other "objectionable" African Americans, but calmer heads "thought it better not to subject the place to any additional notoriety."

The participants in the lynching held a public meeting beforehand and appointed a ten-man committee, which supposedly included three African Americans, to carry out the grim task. The committee told the law officers, who had been assigned to escort Adams to Mississippi City, that it would be better to take Adams at night. Because the committee had the authority to "arrest" the first man who fired a shot at Adams, the corpse was not mutilated and the lynching was supposedly one of the most "orderly" in memory.

The mob leaders were well known to the public, and they made no attempt to conceal their involvement. When the requisite coroner's jury was impaneled, "for the first time in the history of lynchings in the South" a jury openly declared that the lynching was committed "at the hands of male citizens, both white and colored, of Pass Christian, who were organized and determined to finish the said Adams for the crime committed, which meets death wherever perpetrated."

Concerned that another attack on a white female would further diminish tourism, whites went to extraordinary lengths to convince outsiders that peace and harmony existed between the local black and white communities. Newspapers reported that a majority of African Americans "heartily approved" of the lynching. Several prominent black leaders allegedly condoned the lynching. Even Adams's father, who only a few years earlier had been inciting blacks to insurrection, supposedly said: "Blood is thicker than water, but that boy of mine did wrong, and he met the proper punishment. I have a wife and two daughters, and if anyone had assaulted them I shouldn't wait for the law to take its course, but I would kill the nigger myself." Less than four months after Adam's lynching ostensibly had solidified racial solidarity, however, two more African Americans were lynched in separate incidents in Harrison County. Unable to acknowledge, much less address, the racial tensions that divided the white and black communities, Gulf Coast whites buried their fears in terroristic violence.

Smaller mobs were common in regions where African Americans had greater independence from whites.[27] The South Carolina region with the largest percentage of small mobs, for instance, was the Outer Coastal Plain, which was an extremely poor region in which over 40 percent of lynching incidents stemmed from assaults or property disputes. Smaller mobs were more prevalent in the Outer Coastal Plain for another reason as well: African Americans in this region were more independent (the Outer Coastal Plain had the highest percentage of black landowners in the state) and better organized politically and socially than African Americans in other parts of South Carolina. African Americans from the Outer Coastal Plain also had a history of resisting white aggression.[28] When whites lynched a black sailor from Port Royal in Beaufort County, for example, local African Americans made an extensive search for the body, and whites feared that African Americans might attempt to kill "white crackers."[29] After the Willie Spain lynching in Dorchester County, local African Americans organized an economic boycott of the coroner S. E. Kizer, who blacks believed had not done enough to investigate the lynching.[30] Kizer's situation became so desperate that he filed a lawsuit against about a dozen African American leaders, which alleged that they had conspired to prevent black tenants from working for him. Pressure of this sort may not have prevented lynching, but it probably tempered the virulent racism of some whites.

In the southern regions of Mississippi, such as the Pine Hills and the Red Hills, mobs tended to be small because of deep divisions within the white community. During the 1890s and 1900s, small groups of whitecappers, who often worked at the behest of labor agents from the Yazoo Delta, routinely fired guns upon the homes of African American tenants and farmers in the hope of scaring them from their land. These white terrorists often worked closely with black informants, who singled out the largest and most industrious families for persecution. Some African Americans found the offer of twenty-five dollars for each family that moved to the Delta, plus extra compensation for any livestock left behind, too tempting to resist.[31]

Although whitecapper organizations sometimes had hundreds of members, a small cadre of men who enjoyed drinking, "coon hunting," secret signs and oaths, and the excitement of gunplay (the Pine Hills and Red Hills had the highest percentage of lynchings by shooting in Mississippi) apparently was responsible for most of the attacks. At particular risk were prosperous African American farmers who owned their own land and had worked hard to improve it, and black tenants who worked for absentee landlords. Many whites regarded both groups of African Americans as too independent from white control.

An African American farmer from Lincoln County, Mississippi, for instance, became the target of whitecappers shortly after he managed to clear much of his prime farmland of stumps. A white farmer first offered to buy the man's land for a price far less than it was worth, and when the black farmer refused, he received threatening notices from whitecappers. A short time later, one of the man's sons was nearly killed in a confrontation with whitecappers. About the same time, two African American landowners in the vicinity were killed for remaining on their farms. Henry List was killed in November 1903, when a mob of fifteen whitecappers riddled his cabin with bullets. List had received prior warnings to leave, and whitecappers had shot at his house at least once before. Personal animosities also may have played a role in List's death. A short time before his lynching, List refused to rent a horse to a local white man, who warned that List would be sorry for his intransigence. The mob that killed List, however, did not escape unscathed. List managed to fire several shots before he died, and he may have killed two white men. One of the men wounded in the raid apparently left the area for several months to recover from his injuries and to avoid arrest in connection with List's death.[32]

About three weeks later, another African American farmer, named Eli Hilson, was gunned down on his way home from Brookhaven, Mississippi. Hilson was a prosperous farmer with about 80 acres of land. Whitecappers had previously warned Hilson to leave, and a month before his death, several rounds of gunfire were aimed at his house. After Hilson was killed, his wife was told to leave the farm immediately or "be sent to hell a flying." Mrs. Hilson left without taking any of her livestock, but she eventually managed to rent half of her land on shares to a local farmer.[33]

Some whites, especially merchants, bitterly opposed the activities of whitecappers. A group of white merchants from the Red Hills region of Mississippi, for example, complained to Governor Vardaman that a "crowd of Lawless rough brutal men Has beaten and run off All the negroes in the cumnety [*sic*] with out cause, All we know as reason that it was did, is because they are negroes it was done in the night and we could not help it Our farms is vacated and merchants left in the hole." The merchants reported that whites who actively opposed the violence were also threatened and warned the governor that the situation would get worse if he did not immediately arrest those involved.[34]

Many white businessmen held Governor Vardaman personally responsible for the whitecapping. Lumber operators from Lincoln County, for example, blamed Vardaman's poisonous racial invective for encouraging "the lawless whites to misuse the negro and run them off." One mill owner complained that even though the price of lumber was high, whitecappers had so constricted the local labor supply that he had to operate his mill at a sharply reduced capacity.[35]

In the opinion of some whites, whitecapping resulted from the notion "that lynching for certain crimes is excusable." To merchants, bankers, and other businessmen, lynching was counterproductive because it "tended to turn away capital."[36] Although firmly supportive of white supremacy, white businessmen worried that whitecapping and lynching could lead to class warfare because "if one class could take the law into their own hands in regards to blacks[,] then another class could do the same in regards to any other class."[37]

Some white businessmen actively fought against whitecappers by forming "Law and Order" leagues and utilized Pinkerton detectives to uncover evidence against perpetrators. In general, 80 percent of lynching incidents in which arrests followed involved mobs of fewer than fifty persons, although few convictions resulted. A group of Lincoln County businessmen, however, successfully prosecuted some whitecappers. In late 1904, one man was sentenced to life imprisonment for the death of Eli Hilson, and five other men were sentenced to five years imprisonment in connection with the murder of Henry List. A few years after the violence dissipated, however, Governor Vardaman pardoned all the men involved.[38]

Demographic circumstances and traditional methods of imposing the color line made the Yazoo Delta a region of small to medium-sized mobs (two-thirds of Delta mobs had fewer than one hundred persons).[39] Most lynching victims in the Delta were never arrested for a crime but were killed quickly by a mob of friends or relatives of an alleged crime victim (typically a white male). Part of the reason why Delta mobs were smaller than those found in other regions was because a high concentration of African Americans lived in the area. In some parts of the Delta, one could "ride for miles along the Mississippi River . . . without seeing a white man."[40] The number of white men available to participate in mobs was not as large in the Delta as in other regions; consequently lynch mobs there tended to be smaller.

Another reason for the smaller size of Delta mobs was that for the most part Delta planters wanted to handle tenant problems without interference from outsiders. Unless requested by an overseer or planter, law officers usually did not come on plantations. Although violence on plantations occurred often, many whites considered the violent death of a black man as "just another worker gone."[41] The insular ways of Delta planters encouraged the formation of small to medium-sized mobs that were often composed of relatives or friends of a white crime victim.

A mob composed of family members of a white planter from near Yazoo City, for example, inflicted a typical treatment of Delta "justice" on a family of African American tenants.[42] Whites considered Abe Johnson a "peaceable negro" even though he had been a leader during Reconstruction. Johnson and three of his sons worked a farm for Ben Sandidge, who was the father-in-law of a well-known planter named T. D. Kirk. In early June 1907, the Johnson boys were working in a field when Alex Johnson had an argument with T. D. Kirk over a three-dollar debt. The Johnsons lived about a hundred yards from Kirk, and when Kirk's wife came outside to investigate the trouble, Alex Johnson supposedly cursed at her. Kirk became infuriated at this affront and returned from his house with a gun in hand. A gunfight then broke out between the Johnsons and

Kirk, the planter's brothers, and Kirk's brother-in-law. During the battle, one of the Johnsons was killed and some of the white men were wounded slightly. The Johnsons retreated to their cabin, which whites from the neighboring countryside quickly surrounded. After a long standoff, two of the Johnson brothers tried to escape, but the mob almost immediately shot and killed them. Afterward mob members whipped two other members of the Johnson family. The semi-private nature of many Delta mobs, which often formed in retaliation for an attack on a relative or friend, resulted in smaller mobs in the Yazoo Delta than in other regions that were less prone to lynching. The vindictive nature of Delta mobs, however, also led to more multiple lynchings, and about one-third of the multiple lynchings that happened in Mississippi occurred in the Yazoo Delta.

On the state level, Mississippi mobs were often more daring and tenacious than mobs in South Carolina. Mississippi mobs (57 percent) were more likely than mobs in South Carolina (51 percent) to lynch victims already in official custody, and Mississippi mobs (31 percent) more often lynched during daylight hours than mobs in South Carolina (23 percent). Mississippi mobs were also more brutal than their counterparts in South Carolina. Although shooting could be considered a more bloody method of lynching than hanging, a flurry of gunshots usually killed a victim instantaneously, but a victim who was hanged often struggled before succumbing to death. Hanging, moreover, afforded mobs the opportunity to torture their victim, as happened with John Henderson, who was lynched in Bolivar County, Mississippi, in April 1884.[43] Henderson allegedly raped the daughter of a wealthy planter and was captured after a short manhunt. The mob that lynched Henderson repeatedly hoisted him over a tree branch until he was almost dead, then let him down, revived him, and hanged him all over again. The differences in the size and methods of mobs in Mississippi and South Carolina reflect the more acrimonious racial climate that existed in Mississippi than in South Carolina.

The agricultural work conflict that was at the center of many lynchings caused some mob activity to follow a seasonal pattern.[44] Mobs most often lynched for murder and assault-related crimes during the harvest season and settling-up time, from October to December, and again when tenants considered moving to a different farm in February. Random lynching for no apparent crime occurred most frequently from November through April, perhaps because work-related conflict was less evident at this time of year. Rape and other alleged crimes that involved women, however, occurred most often during the warmer months from May through October.

Lynching in retaliation for alleged property crimes, such as arson and theft, occurred more often during the winter season, especially during the slack months from January through March. Many whites viewed lynching as a necessary remedy against "indolent, vagabond" black tenants who glided "through the miry blackness of the night as evil birds of prey to rob the thrifty white and even the thrifty black man of his field crops, his implements, his ox and his ass and everything that is his." More perceptive whites, however, realized that the exploitation fundamental to the tenant system spawned the insecurity that lynching was intended to prevent. Some tenants had no choice but to steal or starve, opined the *Charleston News and Courier,* because they had "to pay their rent in cotton, have to plant so much cotton and cultivate it, without regard to the certain demands of their families for food and clothing and shoes in the winter, and perhaps for medicines and other incidentals in times of sickness."[45] The economic exploitation of the cotton-based tenant system encouraged the racial antipathies that inspired lynchers.

Because the number of participants in a mob was closely related to the crime that allegedly had been committed, mob size also had an observable seasonal variation. With the notable exception of August, most large mobs occurred during the harvest season of October and November or during the slack months of January and February, when murder and property-related lynching were most frequent. Mid- to late winter was the time of year when contracts were signed and tenants thought about moving. Relations between landlords and tenants were often strained during this time of year, and violent disputes were common. The tenant Luther Holbert, for instance, allegedly killed the planter James Eastland after Eastland had ordered Holbert off his plantation.[46] Similarly, Sam Petty was a tenant who was shot and then burned by a mob of three hundred in February 1914 after Petty allegedly killed a deputy sheriff who had come to arrest Petty for a minor offense.[47]

Heightened hostility between landlords and tenants also occurred at the end of the harvest season. A mob of about one hundred farmers, for instance, lynched two tenants from the Black Prairie region of Mississippi in December 1886 for allegedly trying to burn the barn and residence of a local farmer.[48] One of the most infamous lynching incidents in South Carolina history, the so-called "Barnwell massacre," happened after a series of violent attacks against white landlords.[49] Race relations in Barnwell County had soured after the prominent planter James Heffernan was murdered by two of his tenants during a business argument near the end of October 1889. Two other white men supposedly were shot by black men before mid-December, when black tenants allegedly killed a young planter who had a reputation for being harsh with his employees. The following day, 19 December 1889, another prominent planter was killed by a longtime tenant in a dispute over a crop settlement.

When the trial of the two tenants accused of the Heffernan murder was continued to the next term, local whites became enraged that "negroes [were] shooting and killing whites without being punished by law."[50] A few days after Christmas, a mob of one hundred masked men took eight African American prisoners, who had been accused in the murders, from the Barnwell jail and tied them to trees just beyond the town limits, where the mob shot them dead. Many whites believed there was "quasi-justification" for the lynchings because someone had "to teach the negroes of Barnwell County that they cannot kill white men with impunity."[51] When black tenants considered relocating to more favorable circumstances or when landlords attempted to cheat tenants at settlement time, whites often found it necessary to resort to terroristic violence.

The status and personal characteristics of an aggrieved party in a lynching had an important effect on the composition and behavior of mobs, both white and black. Alleged white crime victims were typically adults who had a position of some standing in a community.[52] Although a precise classification of the social status of alleged crime victims was not possible, the agricultural basis of lynching was obvious in both states. In Mississippi and South Carolina, about 46 percent of all alleged crime victims were involved in agriculture in some way or another.

In the plantation regions of both states, well over half of all white alleged crime victims were either planter/managers or well-known residents. Outside of the plantation regions, in the Midlands of South Carolina or the Pine Hills of Mississippi for example, 50 percent or more of white alleged crime victims were also either farmers or tenants. South Carolina had only a few nonfarm alleged crime victims who could be identified, but in the more industrialized regions of the Mississippi, such as the Piney Woods and Red Hills in the south or the Pontotoc Tennessee Hills in the northeast, nonfarm alleged crime victims were more common.

The continued presence of agricultural conflict made the lynching plague last longer in Mississippi than in South Carolina. In Mississippi, the categories of farmer/tenant and planter/manager accounted for about 27 percent of white alleged crime victims during the 1880s and rose to 59 and 65 percent during the 1920s and 1930s respectively. In South Carolina, on the other hand, the farmer/tenant and planter/manager categories accounted for 50 percent or more of white alleged crime victims until the first years of the twentieth century, but declined dramatically to only 36 percent in the 1910s and to none in the 1930s.

Agricultural conflict lasted longer in Mississippi than in South Carolina partially because the African American population in Mississippi's plantation regions declined less dramatically than did the black population in South Carolina regions. From 1910 to 1940, for example, the black population of the Yazoo Delta declined about 12 percent, less than half as much as the nearly 28 percent drop that occurred in the Western Piedmont of South Carolina. And even with the decrease, the Yazoo Delta still was almost 73 percent African American, while the Western Piedmont had become a majority-white region. From 1880 to 1920, the average out-migration rate of African Americans in South Carolina was 57 percent greater than the average out-migration rate for African Americans in Mississippi, and the larger exodus from South Carolina tempered the need for racial violence in comparison to Mississippi.[53]

Although South Carolina endured less lynching than did Mississippi, especially after the Great Migration began in earnest, the resilient efforts of African Americans to protect themselves from racial oppression and seek judicial redress could prompt some appalling outbreaks of "depravity, barbarity, and terrorism" that shocked even a hardened investigator like Walter White. The October 1926 lynching of Bertha, Demon, and Clarence Lowman at Aiken, South Carolina, was, according to White, the "most startling" lynching that he had ever encountered.[54] About two years earlier, Sam Lowman had moved his family from Saluda County to work on a farm near Monetta, about thirteen miles from Aiken. The Lowman family consisted of Sam and his fifty-five-year-old wife, Annie; twenty-seven-year-old daughter, Bertha; twenty-two-year-old son, Demon; and Demon's wife, Rosa; another daughter named Bridle; and a teenage nephew named Clarence. The Lowmans worked for a white farmer named W. J. Hartley and generally were regarded as an "industrious, law-abiding and respected family."

The Lowmans had lived in the Horse Creek Valley but a year, however, when they became pawns in a game of violent intimidation directed against their landlord. Hartley apparently had repossessed two mules from a white man and had allowed the Lowmans to use the animals. Shortly thereafter, a mob of robed and hooded Klansman visited the Lowman farm and may have whipped Demon Lowman. To further embarrass Hartley, the disgruntled white man told Aiken County sheriff Henry Howard that the Lowmans were selling whiskey from their farm. At the time, the Horse Creek Valley had a flourishing bootleg liquor trade that reputedly was controlled by the Klan and a notorious gang known as the "famous seventeen." The "whiskey ring" consisted of local politicians, law-enforcement officers, and officials from the nearby Graniteville Manufacturing Company, who used liquor raids to eliminate competitors and to intimidate opponents.

In late April 1925, Sheriff Howard and three deputies, Nollie Robinson, A. D. Shepard, and R. L. McElheny, all of whom were Klan members, raided the Lowman house. The men were dressed in plain clothes and wore no badges. The officers apparently did not know the Lowman family because when they encountered Demon and Clarence Lowman in a field, they asked them where Sam Lowman lived. When Annie Lowman and her daughter Bertha saw the men running toward their house, the frightened women decided to go inside. The sheriff and his deputies surrounded the house, however, before the Lowman women could retreat safely inside.

When Annie and Bertha Lowman encountered Sheriff Howard in their backyard, they screamed, which brought Demon and Clarence Lowman running in from a field. Inside the house, Demon Lowman grabbed a revolver, but Deputy McElheny prevented him from leaving the house. As Demon Lowman struggled with McElheny, Rosa and Bridle Lowman fled out the back door. A shot sounded from the backyard, and seconds later Clarence Lowman came flying out the back door with a shotgun in hand. Deputy Shepard began to chase Clarence Lowman but stopped when he saw Sheriff Howard lying mortally wounded with a gunshot wound to the head. At the front of the house, more shooting ensued, and Bertha Lowman was shot in the breast and abdomen while fighting with Deputies Robinson and McElheny. In the confusion, Demon Lowman managed to escape. When Annie Lowman tried to attack Shepard with an ax, he shot her dead.

At the time of the raid, Sam Lowman had been at a nearby mill having meal ground, but after Howard's death he was immediately arrested. Two days later, officers allegedly found jugs of whiskey buried on Lowman's farm. The rest of the Lowman family was also arrested (Clarence Lowman was seriously wounded before being captured) and charged with murder. Sheriff Howard had been killed with a revolver, but Walter White claimed that Demon Lowman had never been close enough to the sheriff to have shot him. Rumors circulated around Aiken that Deputy Robinson had killed Howard because Howard had planned to fire Robinson.[55] After Howard's death, Nollie Robinson was appointed sheriff.

The Lowmans were arraigned in early May before Judge H. F. Rice, another prominent member of the South Carolina Ku Klux Klan. Rice appointed a fellow Klansman, John Edwin Stansfield, to head the defense and assured the public that the defense attorneys found their task "very disagreeable" and served only at the request of the court.[56] At trial, the state presented little hard evidence against any of the Lowmans and charged that Clarence Lowman had killed Howard with a shotgun. Despite a lack of credible evidence, Clarence and Demon Lowman were convicted and sentenced to death in the electric chair, and Bertha Lowman received life imprisonment. The two other Lowman women were acquitted and released, but Sam Lowman was later sentenced to two years hard labor on a trumped-up liquor charge.

Nathaniel J. Frederick, a courageous African American attorney from Columbia, took it upon himself to appeal the verdicts to the state supreme court in November 1925. In the interregnum before the court's decision, Aiken Klansmen made their sentiments known when they held a massive rally on the first anniversary of Howard's death. Some 1,500 people enjoyed free lunches and lemonade while they listened to eulogies of Howard. The following May, however, the court ruled in favor of the Lowmans and ordered that they be given a new trial. At the second trial, which was held in October 1926, Frederick secured the assistance of a flamboyant white attorney from Spartanburg named L. G. Southard.[57]

Local African Americans strongly supported Frederick's efforts and even raised money to pay for most of Frederick's and Southard's attorney fees. But some local whites resented the "Nigger lawyer . . . [who] took the case to the Supreme Court an' raised a lot o'holler about the warrant not bein' exactly right and such." One white lumberman complained that it was "kind of against the law in South Carolina" for an African American to address a white jury. During the proceedings, the "smart actin" Southard, moreover, "blustered, spluttered and shouted in a cock-of-the-walk manner," and Southard enraged whites when he brashly predicted that all the defendants would be freed. It was "a marvel," claimed one white reporter, that Southard "was not taken from his hotel and whipped by indignant citizens."[58]

The state did not introduce any new evidence at the second trial, and Frederick and Southard asked Judge S. L. Lanham (who, like Southard, was also from Spartanburg) to acquit Bertha and Demon Lowman, since the state supreme court had ruled that the evidence from the first trial had been insufficient to prove a conspiracy. The judge's decision that Demon Lowman should be freed was, according to Frederick, "the deciding point for mob violence. . . . [since] the man everyone thought would certainly be convicted, was to go clear."[59]

Immediately after Lanham's ruling, officials charged Demon Lowman with assault and battery to keep him in jail. Klan officers then met at the law offices of John Edwin Stansfield to plan the lynching. Within an hour of the verdict, news had reached Columbia that the Lowmans would be lynched that night. Longtime Aiken attorney "Colonel" Claude Sawyer, who had served on the staff of Governor Wade Hampton and was one of the last surviving "Red Shirts" from Reconstruction, warned Judge Lanham and the solicitor Bert Carter that a lynching was imminent. But the officials paid no heed, and nothing was done to protect the Lowmans from a mob. Carter later claimed that he understood Sawyer's admonition not as a warning but as a "personal opinion or casual remark."[60]

Around 3:00 a.m. on 8 October, Sheriff Robinson and his deputies roused the Lowmans out of bed and handed them over to a mob. A small group of twenty or so men talked and laughed in the jail foyer, while they waited for the Lowmans to be brought downstairs. When Bertha Lowman began to scream in terror, someone told her to "shut her God dammed mouth or they would kill her there on the spot" and two shots were fired in the air. Outside the jail, five touring cars waited to take the mob members and the Lowmans to the lynching scene.[61] When Clarence Lowman tried to escape from the car that carried him, he was shot and quickly recaptured. To avoid getting blood in the car, mob members tied Clarence Lowman to a bumper and dragged him two miles to a nearby campground, where the lynching occurred.

When the mob arrived at the campground, some two hundred cars and one thousand people were waiting, including the president of the Graniteville Manufacturing Company, two cousins of Governor Thomas McLeod, Sheriff Howard's first cousin, and the future "dean" of the South Carolina Senate Edgar Brown, and some women Klan members who had been driven to the scene by their African American chauffeurs. Before being killed, the Lowmans were forced to stand some fifty feet apart, and the spectators turned on their headlights so as to not miss any of the gruesome proceedings. Pierce Howard, brother of the deceased sheriff, was given the honor of executioner, but when "his nerve failed," in stepped Deputies McElheny and Shepard. Aiken law-enforcement officers apparently considered it an honor to kill African Americans. "Almost every petty official in Aiken has at least one dead Negro to his credit," claimed one reporter, "and there is an acquittal in almost every case." The murderers dispensed quickly with Demon and Clarence Lowman, but took more delight in killing Bertha, who begged and pleaded for her life as she crawled on the ground after being shot. Bertha Lowman died from a revolver shot to her head and a shotgun blast to the abdomen, which was delivered at such close range that it set her clothes on fire.[62]

Outside of Aiken, the brutal lynching of the Lowmans elicited widespread condemnation. Almost every major daily paper in South Carolina condemned the lynching and demanded that those responsible be brought to justice. Concerned that the lynching would have a negative impact on South Carolina's national reputation, the Columbia and Charleston chambers of commerce condemned the murders, which brought "shame and disgrace" to the state. Governor McLeod promised a member of the state interracial commission that he would do "everything possible . . . to bring to justice the members of the Aiken mob." The editor of the *Columbia Record,* R. Charlton Wright, pointed out that the Aiken lynching made it difficult for white southerners to credibly oppose a federal antilynching law, which many southern apologists argued was an unwarranted expansion of federal power. How could an "honest" newspaperman "stoutheartedly" defend states' rights, Wright wondered, "when the people for whom he undertakes to fight cut the ground from beneath his feet[?]" Unless Aiken was "purged of its rottenness," Wright warned, few would believe "that South Carolina can and will abolish lynch law."[63]

Many whites from around Aiken, however, staunchly defended the lynchers. The attorney Edgar Brown, for instance, who had been retained as defense counsel by two of the alleged lynchers, blasted the "investigation and hullabaloo" surrounding the lynching, which was nothing but "pure, unadulterated bunk." Brown ridiculed the governor and other "law and order citizens" who publicly condemned the lynching but who also knew that "nobody is going to be punished and [that] nobody wants anybody punished" for the murders. Brown howled that "the people of

South Carolina are still white, with red blood in their veins, chivalry and manhood in their hearts, and expect to keep our country clean and pure notwithstanding the ravings and rantings of a Negro-loving Northern press, when an occasional black brute is summarily dealt with." The Aiken Ku Klux Klan sponsored a Thanksgiving-night rally and cross burning on Graniteville Hill (where Howard was buried) in support of the lynchers, and Edgar Brown was one of the featured speakers.[64]

African Americans did not acquiesce to racial intimidation from whites. The day after the lynching, for instance, rumors abounded that the Klan planned to whip attorney Frederick, but African Americans escorted him from Aiken without incident. An imprisoned Sam Lowman retained "Colonel" Sawyer to sue Aiken County for two thousand dollars in damages for each of his murdered kin. Other African Americans disrupted the Thanksgiving-night Klan rally. The day of the rally, black men ominously walked the streets of Aiken, wearing heavy overcoats that concealed weapons, which they occasionally flashed to whites with whom they were friendly. The night of the rally, blacks gathered in the hollows around the cemetery in anticipation of the Klan's festivities. When Klan members lit the cross and the speeches began, African Americans fired their weapons and shouted and screamed, which infuriated the bewildered Klansmen. Other African Americans resorted to the time-honored tactic of leaving for other locales in protest of the lynching.[65]

The Aiken tragedy, like so many other post-1920 lynchings, became a commentary on the status of African Americans in southern society. The NAACP used the Aiken lynching as a vehicle to expose the injustices of southern white racism, which reactionary white southerners ignored with the old prattle about white chivalry, red blood, and black rapists. But the demands of African Americans for justice and equality could make even sympathetic whites like L. G. Southard uncomfortable. When the NAACP publicly denounced Governor McLeod for inaction in the Aiken case and asked President Coolidge to withdraw McLeod's appointment to the Federal Trade Commission, for example, Southard appealed to Walter White to have the NAACP rescind the condemnation. Southard maintained that the "best white people" would react negatively to the protest and that McLeod had always tried to treat African Americans fairly. McLeod resented the political pressure of the NAACP and complained to Nathaniel Frederick that the NAACP did not understand that he "could not get results and show his hands at the same time." The unwillingness of African Americans to endure the egregious injustices of white racism put many white southerners on the defensive, and consequently during the 1920s and 1930s some lynchings took on a more communal and carnival-like atmosphere. Thousands of whites came to see the barbaric burning of a "fiend" like Charley Sheppard or the brutal slaying of the cop-killing Lowmans to assure themselves that whites were the superior race and so always would remain.

The depraved nature of the Lowman lynching notwithstanding, an African American attorney who could overturn a capital case before the state supreme court was unfathomable in Mississippi. Two lynchings that occurred in 1933, one in the Yazoo Delta of Mississippi and the other in the Upper Piedmont of South Carolina, illustrated the different racial climates that existed in the two states. Richard Roscoe was a thirty-nine-year-old black Baptist deacon and tenant farmer from around Minter City in Leflore County, Mississippi.[66] The white plantation manager J. F. Matthews considered Roscoe "too damm smart for a darky," and started a fight with Roscoe while Roscoe picked cotton. Matthews first assaulted Roscoe, which prompted Roscoe to charge Matthews, who then shot Roscoe twice in the body. Despite his wounds, Roscoe managed to bite off Matthews's left index finger before Matthews shot Roscoe a third time. Roscoe apparently was not seriously wounded, however, because he grabbed Matthews's gun and beat him with it. After other tenants separated the men, Matthews vowed that he would have Roscoe lynched.

Less than an hour later, Matthews and one hundred white landowners took Roscoe from his tenant cabin and shot him more than thirty times. The mob then tied Roscoe's body to the rear of a sheriff's car and dragged it through the streets of Minter City. Afterward the mob dumped Roscoe's body on the steps of his home with a sign in red letters that warned, "Let this be a lesson to all darkies." The murder of Roscoe received scant attention from authorities, and no arrests were made in the case.

In South Carolina's Upper Piedmont, George Green was a seventy-three-year-old tenant who refused to move off his land after his landlord had ordered him to leave.[67] The landlord then enlisted the aid of the local Ku Klux Klan, twelve members of which visited Green's tenant cabin on the night of 16 November 1933. When the robed Klansmen ordered Green to come out of his cabin, Green grabbed an ax and threatened to attack the first man that came near him. The lynchers proceeded to beat down the door to Green's cabin and shot him three times. Green died a short time later.

Within a week, seven men were in jail in connection with Green's lynching. In late November, a state constable helped investigate the case, and four more men were then charged with the lynching. Former Republican National committeeman Joseph Tolbert, whose family had been the target of a mob during the Phoenix massacre, helped prosecute the case about a year later. Although four of the defendants turned state's evidence, the state was unable to secure a conviction. A civil jury, however, subsequently ordered Greenville County to pay a two-thousand-dollar indemnity to Green's relatives. Greenville County appealed the decision to the South Carolina Supreme Court, however, which ordered a new trial. The next jury decided that because Green was not accused of a crime at the time of his death, no lynching had occurred and the county was not liable under state law. Despite these setbacks, Green's death was not completely in vain because South Carolina experienced no additional lynching until 1941. Mississippi, conversely, suffered nineteen lynching incidents in the five years after Richard Roscoe's murder.

Although the large mob that brutalized Richard Roscoe for assaulting his plantation manager was not unusual by Mississippi standards, large mobs formed most often for alleged crimes against adolescent females. More than eight out of ten mobs that lynched for alleged crimes against adolescent females had one hundred or more participants. More than two-thirds of the mobs that lynched in retaliation for alleged crimes against adult females involved mobs of one hundred or more persons, but less than half of mobs that ostensibly lynched for crimes against adult males were this large. Sexual crimes against white females touched a raw nerve among southerners, who used lynching to solidify negative attitudes toward blacks. John Dennis, for example, was lynched in the Yazoo Delta for allegedly attempting to rape an unmarried, white telephone operator in June 1903.[68] A mob of seven hundred persons, which included men and women of "every class," hanged Dennis to a telephone pole on a prominent corner in Greenville. One witness remembered the lynching as "quite a gala occasion" with "much laughing and hilarious excitement." After the lynching, the corpse was left hanging in front of the telephone exchange as a reminder to African Americans that white men would protect "their women and homes." After the body was cut down, the white community capped off the activities with a game of baseball at a local park.[69]

The public display of a lynching victim's corpse heightened the terror that whites inflicted upon the African American community. The spectacle of a murdered and mutilated victim was a revolting and frightful sight that people never forgot. An African American man from Mississippi, for example, recounted the emotional and psychological scars that stemmed from his encounter with the mutilated remains of a lynching victim:

> When we got there in the woods, everyone started crying and turning their heads away in horror. I looked up at the man. I knew him, yet he was so messed up I could not tell who he was. He was naked, and they had put tar on him and burnt him. He smelled awful. Then I saw what they had done. Even though I was only nine, I knew what they had done was a sin. They had cut out his private and left it laying on the ground. The blood was caked all about his legs and thighs.[70]

Predictably, mobs in Mississippi were more likely to display a victim after a lynching than were mobs in South Carolina (69.4 to 46.1 percent).

Although large mobs (one hundred persons or more) were more likely than smaller mobs to mutilate a victim, victims accused of rape or other crimes involving women appear to have been no more likely to suffer mutilation than victims accused of murder or minor crimes.[71]

In all likelihood, however, the practice of mutilation was probably more common than is believed because this type of information often was not reported, at least not during the early years of the lynching era. Some lynchers apparently wanted to mutilate not only to torture and dehumanize a victim, but also to retain a macabre relic that would signify their power and masculinity. The wife of a Yazoo Delta lumberman, for instance, recalled attending to a wounded timber worker who had fainted in a "woman-like" manner from a foot injury. When the woman reached into the man's pocket for a piece of string to bandage his foot, however, she was startled to find that a "Negro's finger fell in my hand. I yelled, dropped that thing like it was a red-hot iron, and started to run," the woman remembered. "It was all I could do to get home, I was so sick and mad." Another lumberman later explained that the two men had recently committed a lynching and that the wounded man had cut off the victim's finger for a "souvenir." The lumberman defended the lynching because "women and children have to be protected," and "there is no law in this country yet." The woman replied that she understood about the lynching, but warned the lumberman that "if you have any fingers or toes about you don't bring them in the house." As for the injured lyncher, the woman decided against further contact with him and wondered if the man's conscience had caused him to hurt himself.[72]

As the lynching era wore on, the percentage of alleged crime victims who were female declined steadily from 58 percent in the 1880s to 32 percent in the 1930s. During the later years of the lynching plague, when some whites began to vigorously oppose lynching, a rape-related lynching could actually divide a white community more than unite it.[73] Allen Green, for instance, was a prominent "mulatto" from Walhalla, which was situated in the Upper Piedmont region of South Carolina.[74] Green reputedly was a grandson of John C. Calhoun and one of the most successful African Americans in Walhalla; he was also a skilled firefighter who had on two occasions saved the community from devastation. Upper-class whites liked Green and frequently employed him on the city payroll. Occasionally, Green even supervised white street and sanitation workers. Thanks to the largesse of white elites, Green managed to buy a truck, some livestock, and a tidy little home one block off the main street of Walhalla that was better than the homes of most of the white mill workers who lived in town.

Given his family history and economic status, Green considered himself the social equal of any white man. Green made no secret of his relationships with white women, and this repeatedly got him into trouble. On one occasion, a white employer threatened to kill Green because of Green's unacceptable behavior toward the man's wife. In 1915, Green was convicted of attempting to rape a twenty-six-year-old white mill worker who lived near Green's mother. Green served only three years of his thirteen-year sentence, however, before forty of his white patrons petitioned Governor Richard Manning for a pardon. The petitioners pointed out that Green had "a very much better reputation amongst the white people than the average negro." Green's accuser, according to one petitioner, had a notorious "reputation for illicit traffic with men, both white and black." The verdict in the case, moreover, "never had the approval of the white people of the town who knew both parties." Although Governor Manning denied the pardon, his successor, Richard Cooper, granted it. In 1919, Green was released from a chain gang near Walhalla, a moment that his lynchers would later commemorate.

Walhalla was a heavily white mill town, with two cotton mills that employed most of the town's white workforce. In 1930, however, the mills were only running at half time. Green's continued prosperity, which apparently resulted from his city job, became a political issue in the mayoral campaign of 1930.[75] To win the support of mill workers, a young lawyer named R. I. Ballentine promised that if he was elected mayor, he would fire Green from the city payroll. After Ballentine won the election, however, the astute Green resigned rather than suffer the humiliation of being fired.

On Easter Sunday morning 1930, a white tenant named Bert Ramey, along with his wife and sister, came to Green's house to trade for a mule. Bert Ramey had previously rented a mule from Green, and Carrie Ramey occasionally visited Green's wife, who sometimes gave Mrs. Ramey gifts. On this particular morning, Green gave Carrie Ramey a compact and some bows for her shoes, perhaps at the behest of his wife, who was not home during the visit. Green's beneficence did not please Bert Ramey, however, who that evening claimed that Green had strapped his wife to a chair and sexually assaulted her while Ramey had been outside talking with his sister. Green was arrested around 11:00 p.m. after Ramey's father told Sheriff John Thomas that Green had raped his daughter-in-law.

Few if any upper-class white people believed that the rape had actually occurred, but mill workers had a different attitude. They regarded Green as the "sort of Negro . . . [who] deserved to die on general principles." Mill workers resented Green's relationship with wealthy white people, whom they said would have lynched Green had he attacked a wealthy white woman but instead had him pardoned for assaulting a mill woman. "Green should have been killed long ago," said one working-class white woman after the lynching. "These big 'Petes' who had him waiting on them liked him but everybody else is glad he's gone."

For two nights after Green's arrest, scores of mill workers gathered at a local ball field to discuss how to proceed. Then on Wednesday night, with the active encouragement of Mayor Ballentine, a mob of 150 to 200 textile operators, working-class men, and farmers rushed the jail. Sheriff Thomas met the mob with a gun and was severely injured. The mob then took Green about two miles outside of Walhalla, near the spot where years earlier Green had been paroled. After Green said a few prayers, the mob tied him to a tree and riddled his body with bullets. Nailed to the tree was a sign that succinctly expressed the racial and class resentments of the mob: "On this spot Allen Green got his Parole and here he got his lynch." After the lynching, the tree attracted hundreds of white pilgrims and was occasionally decorated with American flags.

Governor John Richards assigned a special investigator to the case who was able to obtain about forty sworn statements concerning the lynching. On the basis of this evidence, seventeen men, including Mayor Ballentine, were indicted for Green's murder. At the trial, Sheriff Thomas positively identified two of the lynchers, but the state's case was hampered when witnesses claimed that their statements had been made under duress. In addition, Judge M. L. Bonham excluded a number of other statements, including that of a gas station attendant who admitted that he drove the truck that carried Green to the lynching scene. The jury deliberated less than a half hour before returning a verdict for acquittal. Two years later, one of the lynchers "got religion" and admitted to Sheriff Thomas that he had helped lead the mob. As a result of the lynching, Green's widow was awarded a two-thousand-dollar judgment against Oconee County, but the county delayed the matter so long in court that the judgment apparently was never paid. The former mayor and attorney Robert Ballentine emerged from the affair unscathed; in 1935, Ballentine was appointed counsel for the Atlanta office of the Securities and Exchange Commission.

The divisions that surfaced among whites as a result of Green's killing demonstrated that by the 1930s lynching could no longer unite the white community as it had in the past. Decades earlier, South Carolina's Ben Tillman and Mississippi's James Vardaman had politically dominated their respective states with the help of a vitriolic stand in favor of lynching. By 1930, however, incumbent U.S. senator Coleman Blease was defeated in part because of his outspoken support of lynching. Two weeks after a lynching in Union County, for instance, Blease delivered a race-baited speech in which he reminded his listeners of his long and vigilant support of the right of white men to lynch. "Whenever the Constitution comes between me and the virtue of the white woman of South Carolina," Blease exhorted, "I say to hell with the Constitution." Blease assured his Union County audience that he was not a cowardly progressive who would call out the state militia to protect a black rapist. "White supremacy and the protection of the virtue of white women of the South," Blease declared, "comes first with me."[76]

The response of the press to Blease's scurrilous racial invective was so overwhelmingly negative that Blease later complained that he was being persecuted. With the important prompting of southern white women, most of South Carolina's press rejected the tired old apology that lynching was a defense of white womanhood and realized, as did the *Greenville Enterprise,* that those thousand "members of Baptist and Methodist Churches did not surround a human [Dan Jenkins] and encourage those of the crowd that had firearms to go to it, because an accusation of an assault had been made. Those many bullets were fired into the head and body of that man because God made him colored."[77] Some whites in the South had begun to acknowledge that lynching was a pathological manifestation of white racism rather than a noble expression of vengeance from an outraged populace.

In a runoff with the former congressman James Byrnes, Blease polled significant support only in the relatively lynch-free Pee Dee regions in the southeastern portion of the state. In the heavily black Inner and Outer Coastal Plain regions, Byrnes trounced Blease. Byrnes also won in the Piedmont regions, even outpolling Blease in Oconee and Union Counties, which had lynchings in the same year.[78] Blease's defeat in 1930 made it clear that open support for lynching was no longer politically adroit in South Carolina.[79]

What had awakened the conscience of some white southerners to the evils of lynching? The federal antilynching campaign of the NAACP, the educational work of the Commission on Interracial Cooperation, and the efforts of the Association of Southern Women for the Prevention of Lynching to expose the hypocrisy of mobs that claimed to defend the virtue of white women all helped change the attitudes of some whites. In October 1904, for example, a South Carolina judge had declared that no matter how strong the sentiment for lynching, he would never hold court "under the guns of any militia."[80] The NAACP'S vigorous fifteen-year campaign for the passage of a federal antilynching bill, however, helped weaken such intransigence.[81] A Mississippi judge, for instance, requested that the National Guard be present during the trial of three black men accused of rape. In light of the antilynching bills that were pending in Congress, the judge felt justified in authorizing this affront to local sentiment. "The effect of these bills would be to destroy one of the South's most cherished possessions—the supremacy of the white race," the judge explained, "and I believe a lynching in this case would have effect inevitably in the passage of one of these laws by Congress."[82] The dynamics of national politics made it clear to whites that lynching could work against the best interests of a local white community.

The most important impetus for the end of lynching, however, came from African Americans who lived and worked in the South. The opposition to mob violence from African Americans in Mississippi and South

Carolina was vigorous and sustained.[83] On various occasions, African Americans responded to lynching with violent confrontation, work stoppages, economic boycotts, statewide conferences, increased voter registration, the building of a school, the collection of funds to help prosecute lynchers, the disruption of a Ku Klux Klan rally, the forced removal of a federal official who allegedly took part in a lynching, the initiation of lawsuits, and most importantly, the mass migration of hundreds and sometimes thousands of African Americans from places where lynching occurred.

Even during the most intense periods of lynching, African Americans openly confronted white mobs. In late July 1892, for instance, thirty black men armed with Winchester rifles rescued a black suspect accused of rape from the custody a white constable before a white mob could lynch the man. Before releasing the suspect to authorities, the black men made sure that the accused man would be sent to a safe and secure jail.[84] Similarly, during a whitecapping outbreak in the Piney Woods of Mississippi, African Americans routinely armed themselves in anticipation of white attacks, and on at least one occasion a black man drove off a white mob after he killed a white man in defense of his home.[85] When a white mob from the Piney Woods gathered around a ramshackle jail in Wiggins, Mississippi, to lynch a black man accused of shooting a deputy sheriff, African Americans gathered across a ravine at a turpentine camp and fired on the mob, killing one of the would-be lynchers.[86]

Lynching was a crude and ineffectual means of social oppression, and African Americans responded to lynching with tactics that agitated the racial anxieties of whites. In July 1903, for example, whites from Norway in Orangeburg County lynched Charlie Evans for shooting a planter who had ordered his sons to whip Evans. Whites may have hoped that the lynching of Evans would make African Americans more docile, but they could not have been more wrong. Three days after the lynching, a large crowd of "surly" blacks gathered in Norway and forced whites to request a contingent of troops from Columbia to calm the situation. The lynching did little to restore a sense of security in the white community, and one white resident claimed that only the militia "could produce such an effect that incendiary talk will cease and quiet will be fully restored."[87] Even after the militia had come and gone, many African Americans refused to work in the fields until whites arrested five other agitators in connection with the murder of the planter.[88]

Almost a decade later, another white mob from Norway lynched John Felder, who likely was one of the men who had encouraged African Americans to demonstrate against the Evans lynching. Felder was arrested on a trumped-up minor charge and then taken from the Norway guardhouse, severely beaten, and shot to death a short distance from town. The murder stemmed from "ugly threats" that Felder had issued against a white man some days earlier.

The Felder lynching severely strained race relations in the area, and even some whites realized as much. The *Charleston News and Courier* said that another lynching like Felder's "would be a calamity for whites." The paper recognized that African Americans were the chief labor supply in the area and said that further "criminal folly will . . . encourage a policy which insteady [*sic*] of stimulating them [blacks] to have greater confidence in and respect for the white man tends to breed fear and distrust."[89] The cause of lynching in Norway and elsewhere was the conflict that raged between whites and blacks over authority, respect, and how a person should conduct his or her daily activities.

In the aftermath of the 1903 Charlie Evans lynching, African Americans held a lynching conference in Columbia, South Carolina, which was at least the third of its kind. The conference featured several "fire-eating" speakers, who denounced the hypocrisy of whites in regard to lynching. Reverend G. C. Rowe of Charleston, for instance, declared that blacks were tired of whites claiming that lynching would cease when black men stopped raping white women. "Men are lynched . . . for murder, arson, burglary, attempt at murder, impertinence, and also on suspicion of having committed a murder, on suspicion of knowing where a criminal is concealed, and for being a United [S]tates postmaster," Rowe flared. "Yet the cry goes forth: 'Stop the crime and lynching will stop.'" Rowe insisted that lynching was "a miserable failure" that had no corrective purpose and did nothing except to degrade and to condemn a "so-called superior people."

The next speaker was George Washington Murray, one of only three

African Americans elected to Congress from South Carolina after Reconstruction. Murray claimed that 250 years of "wicked and damnable" slavery had created a fraudulent caste system that spawned lynching in the South. The economic and social disparities of caste, in Murray's opinion, had replaced a "peace-loving spirit of brotherhood, with its limitless and colorless standards of merit ... with the narrow, bigoted spirit of slavery, with its limited standard of color." As a result, "war and unpleasantness" plagued the South.[90]

Support for the notion that lynching was a legacy of slavery and the caste system at times came from unlikely voices in the South. W. P. Beard, for instance, was a former bodyguard of Coleman Blease and the publisher of the radical-populist and iconoclastic paper the *Abbeville (S.C.) Scimitar.* Shortly after the lynching of Anthony Crawford, Beard published an extended treatise on the "socio-economic-industrial and political features" of lynching. Beard, like George Washington Murray, found the roots of lynching in the evils of slavery, which he claimed "instilled into the poor white man a hatred for the negro." Blacks had their own contempt for "poor white trash," and this "mutual hatred" had finally matured into lynching. Lynching was frequent in agricultural areas, according to Beard, because the status of white farmworkers was "arbitrarily fixed, to a large extent, by what the negro is willing, or COMPELLED to work for.... Therefore he is in the poor white man's way to self advancement ... and it is extremely DANGEROUS for a negro to get in the way of ANY WHITE MAN." Racial demagogues like Benjamin Tillman and Coleman Blease, Beard asserted, capitalized upon the desire among lower-class whites to eliminate black competition both politically and economically. The lynching plague would never end, Beard insisted, until whites had found "a means to LEGALLY classify free negroes in their relation to white people, in a social industrial and political way."[91]

Lynching did decline, as Beard suggested it would, after whites had implemented de jure segregation, which perhaps lessened the need for African American scapegoats because the subordinate status of blacks was now enshrined in law. But it would be wrong to suggest that whites ended the practice of lynching because African Americans no longer protested their subjugated status.[92] To the contrary, the experiences of African Americans in the struggle against lynching were important precursors to the modern civil rights movement. The responses of African Americans to lynching, such as nonviolent protests, public pressure on elected officials, economic boycotts, and judicial redress, would all become integral tactics in the movement for social equality that began in earnest after World War II.[93] African Americans exploited the demographic changes that resulted from the Great Migration to apply federal pressure against lynching. George Koester, for instance, was forced to resign his federal patronage position because of his alleged participation in a lynching.[94] Koester complained that many Republicans on the Senate Finance Committee had told him in private that they were satisfied that he was innocent but that they nevertheless refused to support him because he was "regarded throughout the North as the type and representative of Southern lynchers and for a Republican Senate to confirm me would do the Republican party harm, especially in those Northern Congressional districts where the negro vote is a factor." In the 1950s and 1960s, the influence of African Americans who lived in the North would help accomplish even greater things—the dismantling of de jure segregation and the restoration of political equality in the South.

Hundreds of thousands of African Americans left the South during the Great Migration, and out-migration was perhaps the most effective weapon against lynching. Scholars have established a statistical relationship between out-migration and the decline in lynching, but one only needs to read a few accounts of the aftermath of some brutal lynchings to realize that such a pattern existed.[95] After the burning of Willie Minnifield in 1923, for instance, ten thousand blacks reportedly fled from the Yazoo Delta.[96] After the lynching of the preacher W. T. Sims in York County, South Carolina, blacks left the area in droves, land values plummeted, and nearly four years later whites were desperately searching for black laborers to resettle the area.[97] In the opinion of the NAACP antilynching activist Walter White, nothing was more important to the decline of lynching "than [the] realization by the more intelligent South that mobbing Negroes was not the best method of retaining Negro labour."[98]

The terror of lynching emanated from the daily conflict and oppression that enveloped parts of the South. In the fields of the South, where blacks and whites met on a daily basis, conflict occurred that frequently spawned lynching. Lynch mobs, of course, did not spontaneously generate from racial antagonisms but resulted from the thoughts and actions of the men who led and participated in them.[99] Different circumstances, however, affected the size, purpose, and behavior of lynch mobs. The historical, demographic, and economic characteristics of a region had a significant influence on the formation and actions of mobs as did the crime that allegedly prompted a lynching. Mob characteristics were also influenced by the status, gender, age, and race of an alleged crime victim. More mundane factors, such as the time of year and the time of day, also had an effect on the formation of mobs. The incessant conflict that racial oppression generated in the daily lives of blacks and whites inspired fear among whites and motivated mobs to lynch African Americans "for anything or [for] nothing" at all.[100]

Conclusion

In January 1938, as the lynching era drew to a close, the U.S. Senate debated a federal antilynching bill that would have given federal courts jurisdiction in lynchings that were committed by three or more people. At the time, the senior senator from Mississippi was Pat Harrison, a former prosecutor from Gulfport who first had been elected to Congress with the support of James Vardaman's allies. Harrison became an ardent ally of Woodrow Wilson, however, and was considered a moderate during the Roosevelt era. A key supporter of the New Deal, Harrison fell out of favor with President Roosevelt because Harrison wanted to reduce the tax on capital gains to help stimulate the economy.[1] Throughout his long congressional career, however, what mattered most to Harrison was the Democratic Party, and Harrison believed that the passage of a federal antilynching bill would be disastrous for the future of the party in the South.

Harrison and several other influential senators, including Harrison's close friend James Byrnes from South Carolina, organized a filibuster against the antilynching bill, which the Senate debated from early January until the last week of February 1938.[2] Harrison began his two-hour speech against the bill by claiming that the prospects of a federal antilynching statute put fear "into the hearts of the womanhood of the South."[3] Harrison acknowledged that northern Democrats were feeling pressure from African American voters to support the legislation, but he pleaded with his colleagues not to "ravish" the Constitution and not to "tear down the pillars upon which the white civilization of this country was builded" in order to retain the vote of fickle African Americans.

Recent history, Harrison claimed, proved that a federal statute was unnecessary because lynching was on the wane in the South. Lynching had only developed in the first place, moreover, because northern "carpetbaggers" and agitators had put the South through "the fires of hell" during Reconstruction, when white government was dismantled and "every state office was filled by a Negro." With "no law to protect them," Harrison declared, whites had been "compelled to take the law in their own hands, not only to inflict punishment upon the guilty but to put fear into the minds of others." Harrison acknowledged that during Reconstruction lynching had "increased tremendously," but he offered no apology for the actions of his forbears and admitted that if he had faced the "situation that confronted them, I have no doubt that I would have attended their daily councils and been present at their nightly meetings."

But times had changed, and Harrison claimed that African Americans were not "maltreated, unprotected and discriminated against" in the South. In fact, he and other white southerners were "the best friends that the Negro ever had." Harrison defiantly declared that no member of the Senate had "a greater interest in the welfare of the American Negro" than he did. The issue raised by the antilynching bill, however, was not the protection and progress of blacks, which Harrison claimed was "a matter of pride" to him, but rather the preservation of constitutional government and white civilization.

If Congress passed an antilynching bill, Harrison warned, the NAACP and other activists would soon want to dismantle Jim Crow laws and public segregation. Next would come the demand to end miscegenation, and that would be followed by worse: the triumph of radicals who would "no doubt seek to have the Federal Government, perhaps under the cover of bayonets, compel every State to permit Negroes to vote in white Democratic primaries of the South."

Harrison reminded his Democratic colleagues that the South was now "wildly Democratic" because southern whites believed in local self-government and "that the Democratic Party would stand on guard and seek at all times to protect and preserve the white civilization of the South." If Democrats continued down the road to "usurp the rights of their States and destroy the fundamental principles of government," then Harrison saw no future for the Democratic Party in the South.

Ten months after Harrison made his impassioned plea on behalf of white civilization in the South, a mob of whites from Wiggins, Mississippi, just thirty-five miles north of Harrison's home of Gulfport, lynched a courageous young man named Wilder McGowan. Whites accused McGowan of raping and robbing a seventy-four-year-old white woman, but Thurgood Marshall later claimed that McGowan's innocence was well known throughout Wiggins and that "the alleged crime was merely used as an excuse to lynch McGowan because he . . . 'did not know his place.'"[4]

The twenty-four-year-old McGowan owned a prosperous moving and hauling business and lived with his aged grandmother. McGowan apparently became a marked man in Wiggins because he had repeatedly resisted the violent intimidation of local whites. On one occasion, a mob of drunken whites attacked McGowan after he stood his ground when a white mob tried to run some blacks down with a car. McGowan fought off the mob and took a revolver from one white man, whereupon the mob decided to disperse. On another occasion, when a white mob in search of some "good looking nigger women" tried to enter an African American dance hall, McGowan used a knife to fight off and wound a white man.[5]

A lynch mob, which reportedly included the Stone County sheriff and his deputies, finally took its revenge on McGowan one morning as he worked on his truck. The armed mob forced McGowan into a woods and "hanged him without any investigation or consideration."[6] A merchant then took McGowan's body back to Wiggins, where white onlookers greeted the corpse with glee while McGowan's friends and relatives wept. Whites then cordoned off the black section of Wiggins, and mobs severely beat a black woman and a young black man in separate incidents, which brought the day's violence to a conclusion.[7] The NAACP attributed the terror to the "pent-up anger" of the white community over McGowan's refusal "to accommodate himself to the attempt of white ruffians to frighten colored citizens."[8]

After nearly seventy-five years of unrelenting violence, southern whites continued to declaim that lynching was necessary to protect white women from black rapists but at the same time acknowledged that the bloody business resulted from the upheaval of Reconstruction and the desire of African Americans for social and political equality.[9]

Predictably, Harrison and his allies succeeded in fending off the anti-lynching bill. Harrison died of cancer in June 1941, but before his death, Harrison reconciled with President Roosevelt, and he was elected president pro tempore of the Senate.[10]

Mississippi governor Paul Johnson decided to appoint James Eastland, the son of his friend Woods Caperton Eastland, to serve the remainder of Harrison's term. Eastland and his son, whom he had named James after his slain brother, were "as close as a father and son could be." In fact, James Eastland made his home at Doddsville, on a 5,000-acre cotton plantation where the elder Eastland had heinously lynched Luther and Annie Holbert some thirty-seven years previously.[11] During his long Senate career, which spanned nearly four decades, Eastland was an intransigent opponent of civil rights legislation. Eastland characterized the 1954 *Brown* decision as a "monstrous crime" that he ominously predicted would lead to the "destruction of the American government, and the mongrelization of the white race."[12]

The vision of race relations that Eastland received from his father and espoused throughout his Senate career made the Yazoo Delta an "American Congo," where whites resorted to violence to thwart the social aspirations of blacks. Although lynching was an integral part of the arsenal of white supremacy, it never vanquished the desire of blacks for equality. Whites regularly lynched African American men for self-assertion or for being "uppity," and yet African Americans continued to vigorously resist the efforts of whites to deprive them of their dignity.

In some ways, African Americans defined the course that lynching took in regions throughout the South. In the coastal regions of South Carolina, for example, whites seldom used the rope and faggot. African Americans in these regions avoided some of the brutality that plagued other regions because of their economic and social independence and their well-known proclivity for resisting white aggression. In other places, like the river regions of Mississippi or parts of the Piedmont in South Carolina, African Americans suffered intensely from the inequities of the white caste system. In cotton fields, white men continually tried to demonstrate their superiority over African Americans in countless conflicts and confrontations that were part of the ebb and flow of life. Most of these confrontations did not lead to violence, but when a white man pulled the chains of caste too hard, they occasionally broke violently in his face. Other whites would then respond with a lynching but to little avail because inevitably another black tenant or black laborer would refuse to accept similar indignities.[13] The Delta was the home of James Eastland, but not twelve miles down the road from the Eastland plantation lived Fannie Lou Hamer.

Humans have an almost instinctual attraction to collective solidarity, which frequently causes them to regard outsiders with suspicion and hostility. In the white South, African Americans were outsiders, and some southerners considered this the root cause of lynching. In a sermon before an Episcopal parish in Greenville, Mississippi, for instance, Reverend Quincy Ewing claimed that whites did not lynch to maintain white supremacy, because no white man could possibly fear black ascendancy. Whites lynched blacks rather "for the very simple reason that in race he is alien to the people who lynch him." Ewing suggested that if any other "race of aliens" replaced African Americans, "as certain as the sun shines they would be lynched just as the negro is."[14] The tragedy of lynching was that thousands of victims were brutally killed simply because African Americans refused to accept that the color of their skin made them an alien people. But out of this bloody calamity came a spirit of resistance and dignity that would first bring an end to lynching and would later help soothe some of the deep scars that blemished the South.

NOTES

Introduction

1. Patricia A. Schecter, *Ida B. Wells-Barnett and American Reform, 1880–1930* (Chapel Hill: University of North Carolina Press, 2001), 86.

2. Ida B. Wells-Barnett, "The Case Stated" (1895), reprinted in *Lynching in America: A History in Documents,* ed. Christopher Waldrep (New York: New York University Press, 2006), 4. The sociologists Stewart Tolnay and E. M. Beck agree with Wells-Barnett that the "key to the beginning of the lynching era rests with the collapse of slavery" (see Stewart Tolnay and E. M. Beck, *A Festival of Violence: An Analysis of Southern Lynchings, 1882–1930* [Urbana: University of Illinois Press, 1995], 246). William Fitzhugh Brundage also identifies "the refusal of most whites to accept the emancipated slaves' quest for economic and political power" as the underlying cause of lynching (see William Fitzhugh Brundage, *Lynching in the New South: Georgia and Virginia, 1880–1930* [Urbana: University of Illinois Press, 1993], 6).

3. Nancy Bercaw, *Gendered Freedoms: Race, Rights, and the Politics of Household in the Delta, 1861–1975* (Gainesville: University Press of Florida, 2003), 85–91, 118. The journalist Wilbur J. Cash also connects the fear that whites had of African American equality with the rape complex that whites concocted to justify lynching. Whites lynched blacks, according to Cash, because "any assertion of any kind on the part of the Negro constituted in a perfectly real manner an attack on the Southern woman" (see Wilbur J. Cash, *The Mind of the South* [New York: Knopf, 1941], 117–19).

4. Christopher Waldrep, *The Many Faces of Judge Lynch: Extralegal Violence and Punishment in America* (New York: Palgrave, 2002), 67–84.

5. See Steven Hahn, *A Nation under Our Feet: Black Political Struggles in the Rural South from Slavery to the Great Migration* (Cambridge: Harvard University Press, 2003), 426.

6. Joel Williamson argues that "whites began the practice of lynching as a reaction against the presumed threat of the black beast to white womanhood." For Williamson, the primary cause of lynching was the psychological need of south-

ern white males to compensate for their inability "to play the role of protector-as-breadwinner with the satisfaction to which they always aspired and had sometimes achieved." Thus, white men seized the role of "protector-as-defender of the purity of their women" as a means of satisfying their craving for power. Because this new role was necessarily directed against African Americans, Williamson claims that lynching started and was most prevalent in the "black belt" counties of the South (see Joel Williamson, *The Crucible of Race: Black/White Relations in the American South since Emancipation* [New York: Oxford University Press, 1984], 184). William Pinar takes the psychosexual interpretation of lynching to its logical conclusion and argues that lynching was "primarily, a gendered form of racial politics and violence" in which the "repressed, racialized homosexual desire [of white men] expressed itself in the mutilation and sexual torture of thousands of young black men." "Lynching," according to Pinar, "was in no small measure a mangled form of queer sex" (see William F. Pinar, *The Gender of Racial Politics and Violence in America: Lynching, Prison Rape, and the Crisis of Masculinity* [New York: Peter Lang, 2001], 11).

7. Walter White, *Rope and Faggot* (1929; repr., New York: Arno Press and New York Times, 1969), 10.

8. In his study of violence in late nineteenth-century and early twentieth-century South Carolina, John Hammond Moore concludes that lynching was both random and sporadic and was ineffective as a mechanism of racial intimidation (see Moore, *Carnival of Blood: Dueling, Lynching, and Murder in South Carolina, 1880–1920* [Columbia: University of South Carolina Press, 2006], 1).

9. Christopher Waldrep, *Roots of Disorder: Race and Criminal Justice in the American South, 1817–80* (Urbana: University of Illinois Press, 1998), 174.

10. Grace Elizabeth Hale, *Making Whiteness: The Culture of Segregation in the South, 1890–1940* (New York: Pantheon, 1998), 229–30.

11. Walter White claims that lynching resulted from the economic advances that African Americans had made since the Civil War and the resentment that poorer whites felt toward the same (see White, *Rope and Faggot,* 12).

12. Adam Fairclough argues that the fact that lynching varied "*within* the South is less significant than the fact that lynchings occurred *throughout* the South." One can agree readily with this point and still find it necessary to discern why lynching varied across time and place (see Adam Fairclough, ed., *The Star Creek Papers* [Athens: University of Georgia Press, 1997], xxix).

13. The best biography of Vardaman remains William F. Holmes, *The White Chief: James Kimble Vardaman* (Baton Rouge: Louisiana State University Press, 1970). Bilbo's career was ably chronicled in Chester M. Morgan, *Redneck Liberal: Theodore G. Bilbo and the New Deal* (Baton Rouge: Louisiana State University Press, 1985). On Tillman, see Stephen Kantrovitz, *Ben Tillman and the Recon-*

struction of White Supremacy (Chapel Hill: University of North Carolina Press, 2000); and the older but still useful Francis Butler Simkins, *Pitchfork Ben Tillman, South Carolinian* (Baton Rouge: Louisiana State University Press, 1944). Although a published biography of Blease has yet to appear, valuable information can be found in Ronald D. Burnside, "The Governorship of Coleman Livingston Blease of South Carolina, 1911–1915" (Ph.D. diss., Indiana University, 1963); and Bryant Simon, *A Fabric of Defeat: The Politics of South Carolina Millhands, 1910–1948* (Chapel Hill: University of North Carolina Press, 1998).

14. Lynching incidents do not necessarily equal the number of persons lynched. For example, a lynching in which one person was killed and a lynching in which five persons were killed are both treated as a single lynching incident. From 1881 to 1940, 705 persons were killed in 572 lynching incidents in Mississippi, and in South Carolina 213 persons were killed in 178 lynching incidents. Included in this total are some race riots, which not all scholars consider lynching. Contemporaries often described them as such, however, and a credible argument can be made for doing so. See, for instance, *New Orleans Daily-Picayune*, 19 September 1913. In a recent work on the literary response to lynching, Anne Rice argues that race riots were not distinct from lynching, but rather "magnified mass lynching" (see Anne Rice, *Witnessing Lynching: American Writers Respond* [New Brunswick, N.J.: Rutgers University Press, 2003], 3).

15. The main sources for the lynching necrology used in this study were the *Chicago Tribune* inventory, published from 1882 to 1918; the National Association for the Advancement of Colored People (hereafter referred to as NAACP); *Thirty Years of Lynching in the United States, 1889–1918* (New York: Arno Press, 1969); Daniel Williams, "Amid the Gathering Multitude: The Story of Lynching in America," manuscript, Tuskegee University, 1968; and the lynching inventory compiled by Stewart Tolnay and E. M. Beck in *A Festival of Violence*. Qualitative information about the lynchings in Mississippi and South Carolina was obtained from the investigative files of the NAACP, the Tuskegee Institute, and the Association of Southern Women for the Prevention of Lynching (hereafter referred to as ASWPL). Some lynchings were also the subject of state and local investigations, the records of which can be consulted in the Mississippi Department of Archives and History (MDAH), Jackson, and the South Carolina Department of Archives and History (SCDAH), Columbia. In addition, every extant issue of newspapers such as the *New Orleans Times-Picayune* and the *Charleston News and Courier* were searched for additional information about lynching incidents.

16. Tolnay and Beck, *A Festival of Violence*, 262. John Hammond Moore doubts the validity of studies that utilized quantitative data in conjunction with extant lynching necrologies, claiming that such lists were of questionable accuracy.

After concluding that a regional analysis of lynching in South Carolina was "statistically meaningless," however, Moore finds that from 1880 to 1947 the western half of South Carolina had more than three times as many lynching incidents than did eastern South Carolina (see Moore, *Carnival of Blood,* 5–6, 56–60). Christopher Waldrep has written incisively about the quixotic quest of activists and scholars to arrive at a workable definition of lynching. Waldrep, himself, could arrive at no definitive definition of lynching and concluded that the inscrutable decisions of small-town newspaper editors often determined whether a particular killing was identified as a lynching or a murder (see Waldrep, *The Many Faces of Judge Lynch,* 2–3).

17. From 1880 to 1940, Mississippi had an average African American population of 904,262, and during these same years Mississippi had 538 lynching incidents involving African American victims, which translates to a lynching rate of 5.9 incidents per 10,000 black population. The comparable figures for South Carolina are 769,103 and 163, which equals 2.2 incidents per 10,000 black population. Although useful for comparative purposes, lynching rates have some theoretical problems. Lynching per capita, for instance, does not reflect that whites lynched blacks. A per-capita white rate, on the other hand, ignores the theoretical dependence of lynching on the number of blacks available to be lynched. Finally, a per-capita black rate suffers from the natural tendency to decrease as the percentage of blacks increases. Hence, the number of lynching incidents is generally the best indication of how severe the problem was in a particular region or state (see John Shelton Reed, "Percent Black and Lynching: A Test of Blalock's Theory," *Social Forces* 50 [March 1972]: 356–67).

18. George Wright's research on Kentucky suggests that lynching was an entrenched part of southern culture from the end of the Civil War onward. Hence, one cannot say with confidence that the 1890s was the worst decade for lynching but only that it was the worst decade for which lynching records are readily available (see Wright, *Racial Violence in Kentucky, 1865–1940: Lynchings, Mob Rule, and "Legal Lynchings"* [Baton Rouge: Louisiana State University Press, 1990]).

19. On these themes, see James Cutler, *Lynch-Law: An Investigation into the History of Lynching in the United States* (1905, repr., Montclair, N.J.: Patterson Smith, 1969); John Dollard, *Caste and Class in a Southern Town,* 2nd ed. (New York: Harper and Brothers, 1949); Jacquelyn Dowd Hall, *Revolt Against Chivalry: Jessie Daniel Ames and the Women's Campaign Against Lynching* (New York: Columbia University Press, 1979); Bertram Wyatt-Brown, *Southern Honor: Ethics and Behavior in the Old South* (New York: Oxford University Press, 1982); Williamson, *The Crucible of Race;* White, *Rope and Faggot;* and Southern Commission on the Study of Lynching, *Lynchings and What They Mean* (Atlanta: The Commission, 1931).

20. During the period 1882–1930, Tolnay and Beck ranked Mississippi as the worst of ten southern states in terms of the number of black lynching victims and as the second-worst (behind Florida) if the measure was black victims per 100,000. South Carolina, on the other hand, was eighth of ten states in terms of both the number of victims and on a per-capita basis. Given that most of both states lay within the "cotton-dominant" areas of the South, Tolnay and Beck could provide no explanation as to why the two states would have such different lynching records (see Tolnay and Beck, *A Festival of Violence*, 37–38, 120).

21. Belton O'Neal Townsend, "The Political Condition of South Carolina," *Atlantic Monthly*, February 1877, 192.

22. See Thomas W. Kremm and Diane Neal, "Challenges to Subordination: Organized Black Agricultural Protest in South Carolina, 1886–1895," *South Atlantic Quarterly* 77 (Winter 1978): 98–112; and Brian Kelly, "Black Laborers, the Republican Party, and the Crisis of Reconstruction in Lowcountry South Carolina," *International Review of Social History* 51 (2006): 375–414.

23. Brundage utilizes a regional framework to explain when, where, and why lynching was most evident in Georgia and Virginia. Noting that "the tone of race relations and the status of blacks" varied significantly from region to region, Brundage identifies "the refusal of most whites to accept the emancipated slaves' quest for economic and political power" as the underlying cause of lynching. Because white mobs that lynched blacks were no threat to the state, however, Brundage downplays the political significance of lynching. In "hard-core" regions with significant black populations and an economy that was dependent on plantation-based cotton cultivation, lynching became "integral to the ongoing struggle between whites intent on preserving their control and blacks desperately trying to escape white exploitation." In coastal regions and much of Virginia, on the other hand, lynching occurred less often because African Americans had more economic and social opportunity than in other regions and because white paternalism was more benevolent than in mono-agricultural regions where the need to coerce black laborers was more urgent. Brundage concludes that lynching was most common in "those regions where plantation agriculture and the racial line separating white landlords and black laborers were most pronounced" (see Brundage, *Lynching in the New South*, 6, 105–8, 138, 141–43).

24. The historian Michael Pfeifer claims that lynching resulted from a cultural war between rural and working-class advocates of "rough justice" and middle-class supporters of "due process." A typical lynching in the Louisiana cotton belt, according to Pfeifer, involved a black male challenging the authority of a planter or overseer, which often led to physical violence and then lynching. "Law," wrote Pfeifer, "was too capricious, too unpredictable, too formal, too abstract, and too concerned with process and at least the procedures of fairness to

regulate the crucial social distinctions of the color line" (see Michael J. Pfeifer, *Rough Justice: Lynching and American Society, 1874–1947* [Urbana: University of Illinois Press, 2004], 22, 67–69).

25. Lynching, according to Tolnay and Beck, had three related functions: to control the black population through terrorism; to eliminate black competition for social, economic, and political rewards; and to reinforce white racial solidarity. Tolnay and Beck find "little regional variation in the reasons given for mob violence," and claim that lynching occurred most often in places where "southern whites felt threatened in some way by their African-American neighbors." Throughout the South, whites resorted to lynching instead of legal execution to "terrorize specific blacks" and to "engender generalized terror" among the African American community. Until the advent of the boll weevil, however, cotton-producing regions were more prone to lynching than other places because unfavorable economic conditions in these regions exacerbated social tensions between whites and blacks. Although Tolnay and Beck find that disfranchisement did not have an "appreciable effect on black lynchings in the South as a whole," they conclude that in regions where the Republican Party was relatively strong, lynching occurred less often (see Tolnay and Beck, *A Festival of Violence,* 18–19, 48, 81, 113, 119, 133–41, 186, 193–94).

26. J. William Harris argues that deep-rooted conflicts over the control of labor, the protection of white women, and the meaning of citizenship resulted in widespread lynching in some parts of the South. The Delta was a more dangerous place for African Americans than was the Piedmont, which, in turn, was more dangerous than coastal regions because Delta whites were obsessed with racial etiquette and social inequality. Hence, "the levee of race had to be constantly patrolled for possible breaches, and when these occurred, the white community had to respond, unified, to meet the threat." Racial resentment that stemmed from the bitter memory of Reconstruction made it difficult, according to Harris, for many whites to distinguish between political equality and the more sexually charged social equality, and lynching frequently emanated from "the accumulated humiliations of day-to-day racism" (see J. William Harris, *Deep Souths: Delta, Piedmont, and Sea Island Society in the Age of Segregation* [Baltimore: Johns Hopkins University Press, 2001], 57, 74, 77–78, 82).

27. The regions that demarcate the two states are based on geographic, demographic, cultural, agricultural, economic, and political characteristics. The most important source for the construction of these regions was the statistical summaries and maps found in the U.S. Census from 1880 to 1940. The relevant data and reports can be consulted in the following: Tenth Decennial Census of the United States, 1880: *Report on the Production of Agriculture* (Washington, D.C.: 1883); Eleventh Decennial Census of the United States, 1890: vol. 5, *Report*

on the Statistics of Agriculture (Washington, D.C.: 1895–97); Twelfth Decennial Census of the United States, 1900: vol. 5, *Agriculture of the United States* (Washington, D.C.: 1908); Thirteenth Decennial Census of the United States, 1910: vols. 5, 6, and 7, *Report on the Statistics of Agriculture in the United States* (Washington, D.C.: 1915); Fourteenth Decennial Census of the United States, 1920: vol. 6, *Agriculture* (Washington, D.C.: 1922); Fifteenth Decennial Census of the United States, 1930: vol. 2, *Agriculture* (Washington, D.C.: 1932); Sixteenth Decennial Census of the United States, 1940: vols. 1 and 2, *Agriculture* (Washington, D.C.: 1942). In their classic study of the post-emancipation South, Roger Ransom and Richard Sutch divide the "cotton South" into sixty-one economic regions, including eleven in Mississippi and seven in South Carolina (see Roger Ransom and Richard Sutch, *One Kind of Freedom: The Economic Consequences of Emancipation* 2nd ed. [Cambridge: Cambridge University Press, 2001], 273–81). Building upon the work of Ransom and Sutch, Edward Ayers identifies five subregions in Mississippi, including the Gulf Coastal Plain, the River Counties, the Cotton Uplands, the Black Belt, and the Central Plateau; Ayers divides South Carolina into four regions, including the Atlantic Coastal Plain, the Black Belt, the Piedmont, and the Mountains and Valleys. Ayers acknowledges, however, that "many more subregions" were possible (see Edward Ayers, *The Promise of the New South: Life after Reconstruction* [New York: Oxford University Press, 1992], 5, 443).

28. William Carrigan argues that white perceptions of Reconstruction along with conceptions of law played a crucial role in the manifestation of lynching in central Texas, which "rose and fell according to the degree which constituted authorities, especially the courts, condemned or tolerated it." Black resistance to white supremacy was the precipitating cause of lynching, according to Carrigan, and whites resorted to mob violence because the historical memory of eighty years of extralegal violence made participation in a lynch mob "a rite of passage, a public duty, and a source of prestige" for many whites (see William D. Carrigan, *The Making of a Lynching Culture: Violence and Vigilantism in Central Texas, 1836–1916* [Urbana: University of Illinois Press, 2004], 13, 154–60, 187).

29. The number of lynching incidents per 10,000 black population was 5.6 in the Yazoo Delta and Old Natchez regions respectively (these figures include white lynching victims). The same figure for the Western Piedmont was 3.8, the Upper Piedmont 2.8, and the Eastern Piedmont 2.1.

30. See J. C. A. Stagg, "The Problem of Klan Violence: The South Carolina Up-Country, 1868–1871," *Journal of American Studies* 8 (December 1974): 303–18.

31. From 1801 to 1865 the State (Territory) of Mississippi executed twenty-six persons, twelve of whom were white. In the same period, the State of South Carolina executed 125 persons, 44 of whom were white.

1. "Strictly a White Man's Country, with a White Man's Civilization"

1. For accounts and details concerning the lynching of Hartfield, see NAACP, *Papers of the NAACP: Part 7, The Anti-Lynching Campaign, 1912–1955,* ed. August Meier and John H. Bracey (Frederick, Md.: University Publications of America, 1987) (hereafter referred to as *NAACP Papers*), series a, reel 13, frames 820–82.

2. James Howell Street, *Look Away! A Dixie Notebook* (New York, 1936), 37.

3. Victoria Bynum, *The Free State of Jones: Mississippi's Longest Civil War* (Chapel Hill: University of North Carolina Press, 2001), 150–51.

4. C. J. Adams, Demobilization Group, Camp Shelby, Miss., to *Crisis,* 20 July 1919, *NAACP Papers,* series a, reel 13, frames 820–821. The 1920 census listed Ruth Meeks as single and twenty-four years old (see U.S. Bureau of the Census, *Manuscript Census, 1920,* Census Place: 4th Ward, Laurel, Mississippi, series T625, roll 881, page 212).

5. *Jackson Clarion-Ledger,* 1 July 1919.

6. Nicholas Lemann, *The Promised Land: The Great Black Migration and How It Changed America* (New York: Knopf, 1991), 10–11.

7. *Charleston News and Courier,* 4 March 1890.

8. Ibid.

9. Ibid.

10. See John C. Willis, "Closing the Plantation Frontier: Small Farmers in the Yazoo-Mississippi Delta, 1865–1920," paper delivered at the Southern Historical Association meeting, New Orleans, 1 November 1990. See also John C. Willis, *Forgotten Time: The Yazoo-Mississippi Delta after the Civil War* (Charlottesville: University Press of Virginia, 2000), 164–73.

11. Willis, "Closing the Plantation Frontier"; *New Orleans Daily-Picayune,* 6 August 1889.

12. U.S. Bureau of the Census, *Manuscript Census, 1900,* Census Place: Beat 1, Scott, Mississippi; series T623; roll 827; page 13A.

13. Marie M. Hemphill, *Fevers, Floods, and Faith: A History of Sunflower County, Mississippi, 1844–1976* (Indianola, Miss.: Sunflower County Historical Society, 1980), 343–44.

14. This account is drawn from *Chicago Tribune,* 8 February 1904; *Los Angeles Times,* 7–8 February 1904; *New Orleans Daily-Picayune,* 4, 5, 8 February 1904; *Wichita Searchlight,* 1 October 1904; Ralph Ginzburg, *One Hundred Years of Lynching* (New York: Lancer Books, 1962), 62–63; NAACP, *Thirty Years of Lynching,* 15; and Kay Mills, *This Little Light of Mine: The Life of Fannie Lou Hamer* (New York: Dutton, 1993), 29–31.

15. Annie Holbert almost certainly was lynched with her husband, even though an Annie "Halbert" was listed as the head of the Holbert family in the

1910 census. Halbert's age was listed as forty, however, when she should have been fifty-eight based on the record in the 1900 census. The accounts of Eastland's trial mention that Holbert was lynched with his wife, and it seems unlikely that reporters would have made this mistake seven months after the lynching occurred. In addition, Holbert had a sixteen-year-old son who was not listed in either the 1900 or the 1910 census schedule. This son may have been the child of Holbert and his paramour. The Eastland family returned to Scott County shortly after the lynching, and what remained of the Holbert family went with them (see U.S. Bureau of the Census, *Manuscript Census, 1910,* Census Place: Beat 1, Scott, Mississippi; series T624; roll 757; page 149B).

16. *Chicago Broadax,* 13 February 1904.

17. *Vicksburg Herald,* 17 February 1904.

18. See *New York Times,* 11, 18, 23 September 1904; *Jackson Clarion Ledger,* 19, 24 September 1904; *Memphis Commercial Appeal,* 22 September 1904.

19. Mills, *This Little Light of Mine,* 29.

20. For accounts concerning Coleman's trial and lynching, see *New York Times,* 21 December 1925; *New York World,* 22–23 December 1925; *New York Amsterdam News,* 13 January 1926; *New York Times,* 14 January 1926, *NAACP Papers,* series a, reel 13, frames 664–669; and *Memphis Commercial-Appeal,* 18 October 1925; 23, 31 December 1925; 2, 7, 8 January 1926; 21 March 1926; *Knoxville East Tennessee News,* 24 December 1925; *St. Louis Argus,* 25 December 1925; 19 February 1926; *Montgomery Advertiser,* 8, 14 January 1926; *Tuskegee Institute News Clipping File,* ed. John W. Kitchens (Tuskegee Institute, Ala.: Carver Research Foundation, 1976) (hereafter referred to as *Tuskegee Files*), roll 224, frames 224, 400–405, 445, 823–825, 853.

21. The sheriff also was indicted for failure to return an offender in connection with the torture of John Fisher, who was legally executed in May 1928.

22. *St. Louis Argus,* 25 December 1925, *Tuskegee Files,* roll 224, frame 400; *Crisis* 31 (February 1926): 163–64.

23. *Memphis Commercial Appeal,* 21 March 1926; *Tuskegee Files,* roll 224, frames 823–824.

24. The record of lynching in the Yazoo Delta, which was the center of the New South cotton economy, runs contrary to Tolnay and Beck's assertion that an increase in the constant dollar price of cotton was associated with less white-on-black lynching. Lynching activity in the Delta peaked during the first decade of the twentieth century, when wholesale cotton prices were also on the rise. Tolnay and Beck admit, however, that this relationship was "weakened considerably after 1900" and had all but disappeared a decade later (see Tolnay and Beck, *A Festival of Violence,* 133, 141). For a sociologist who finds that as the price of cotton decreased so too did lynching, see Doug McAdam, *Political Process and*

the Development of Black Insurgency, 1930–1970 (Chicago: University of Chicago Press, 1982), 114–15.

25. Neil McMillen, *Dark Journey: Black Mississippians in the Age of Jim Crow* (Urbana: University of Illinois Press, 1989), 268–69.

26. This pattern contradicts the findings of Brundage, who argues that the effects of urbanization and industrialization weakened the mystique of the white male code of honor and that "the fear of the black rapist lost its power to mobilize mobs with each decade" (see Brundage, *Lynching in the New South,* 70).

27. See Ronald L. F. Davis, *Good and Faithful Labor: From Slavery to Sharecropping in the Natchez District, 1860–1890* (Westport, Ct.: Greenwood Press, 1982), esp. chaps. 4 and 7.

28. Davis, *Good and Faithful Labor,* 113–15.

29. This situation apparently contrasted with that of Georgia's most lynch-prone region, the cotton belt, where white landlords exerted vast powers over the day-to-day lives of black sharecroppers and tenants (see Brundage, *Lynching in the New South,* 108–10).

30. William Cohen, *At Freedom's Edge: Black Mobility and the Southern White Quest for Racial Control* (Baton Rouge: Louisiana State University Press, 1991), 271–73.

31. Works Progress Administration, *Mississippi: A Guide to the Magnolia State* (New York: Hastings House, 1938), 230; see also Michael and Judy Ann Newton, *Racial and Religious Violence in America: A Chronology* (New York: Garland, 1991), 215–16.

32. William Carrigan has made a similar argument for lynching activity in central Texas (see Carrigan, *The Making of Lynching Culture,* 169).

33. Mississippi had twenty-six lynching incidents that only involved white victims; the Red Hills had nine.

34. *New Orleans Daily-Picayune,* 26 July 1890.

35. Quoted in Vernon Wharton, *The Negro in Mississippi 1865–1890* (Chapel Hill: University of North Carolina Press, 1947), 210–11.

36. *New Orleans Daily-Picayune,* 7, 15 November 1892; 1, 15, 20 December 1892.

37. McAlpin had been tried and acquitted of the murder (see *New Orleans Daily-Picayune,* 27 October 1903).

38. Ibid., 29 January 1903.

39. Ibid., 25 December 1906.

40. Ibid., 25, 27, 29 December 1906.

41. Seth Cagin and Philip Dray, *We Are Not Afraid: The Story of Goodman, Schwerner, and Chaney and the Civil Rights Campaign in Mississippi* (New York: Macmillan, 1988).

42. WPA, *Mississippi,* 100–101.

43. Ibid., 100.

44. McMillen, *Dark Journey,* 114.

45. William F. Holmes, "Whitecapping: Agrarian Violence in Mississippi, 1902–1906," *Journal of Southern History* 35 (May 1969): 167–68.

46. Mackie Odom, "The Introduction and Expansion of Railroad Lines in Mississippi, 1830–1973," *Mississippi Geographer* 2 (Spring 1974): 55–56. See also WPA, *Mississippi,* 109.

47. Nollie Hickman, *Mississippi Harvest: Lumbering in the Long-leaf Pine Belt, 1840–1915* (Oxford: University of Mississippi Press, 1962), 144.

48. Ibid., 144–45.

49. *Tuskegee Files,* roll 223, frame 308, *Memphis Commercial-Appeal,* 19 September 1923; frame 311, *Chicago Defender,* 29 October 1923.

50. The sociologist Arthur Raper claims that blacks had been statistically safest in "black belt" counties where "the variant economic and cultural levels of the mass of whites and the mass of Negroes are well defined, and far removed." The "purely statistical logic" that the more blacks the fewer the whites ensured, according to Raper, a lower incidence of lynching in black belt counties (see Raper, *The Tragedy of Lynching,* 27). The fact that the Pontotoc Tennessee Hills had a higher per-capita lynching rate (6.3 per 10,000 black population) than either the Yazoo Delta or the Old Natchez region (5.6 per 10,000 black population in both) is a good example of why scholars must use such calculations with caution. In fairness to Raper, however, it should be noted that the Pontotoc Tennessee Hills was the only region in Mississippi to experience a noticeable resurgence in lynching activity during this time.

51. The account of Ivy's lynching is taken from *New York Times,* 21 September 1925, *NAACP Papers,* series a, reel 13, frame 1075; *Memphis Commercial-Appeal,* 21 September 1925; *St. Louis Argus,* 25 September 1925, *Tuskegee Files,* roll 224, frames 232–234; *Baltimore Afro-American,* 3 October 1925, *Tuskegee Files,* roll 224, frame 400.

52. In his study of the Jim Crow era in Mississippi, Neil McMillen notes that "lynching rates, unlike other forms of race oppression, rise as black population decreases and fall as it increases." Nevertheless, McMillen considers the Yazoo Delta the worst lynching region in Mississippi and argues that Delta blacks took "cold comfort" in being statistically safer than their hill-country counterparts (see McMillen, *Dark Journey,* 231–32). Brundage reaches a similar conclusion about lynching in Georgia (see Brundage, *Lynching in the New South,* 129–30).

53. Harris, *Deep Souths,* 77. Brundage also finds that the leading alleged cause of lynching in Georgia's worst lynching region, the cotton belt, was murder (or violent assault) as opposed to rape (Brundage, *Lynching in the New South,* 111).

54. *Vicksburg Herald,* 17 February 1904.

2. "To Hell with the Constitution"

1. *Charleston News and Courier,* 6, 10 December 1912. The Governors Association eventually passed a resolution, which the southern governors opposed, that called upon states to protect alleged criminals from mob violence.

2. Diane Miller Sommerville, *Rape and Race in the Nineteenth-Century South* (Chapel Hill: University of North Carolina Press, 2004), 209.

3. *Charleston News and Courier,* 15 January 1896.

4. Kantrowitz, *Ben Tillman,* 207–8. George Frederickson has argued that "the Negro's overpowering desire for white women was often described as the central fact legitimizing the whole program of legalized segregation and disfranchisement" (see George Frederickson, *The Black Image in the White Mind: The Debate on Afro-American Character and Destiny, 1817–1914* [New York: Harper and Row, 1971], 282).

5. In Virginia, where race relations were presumably less acrimonious than in either Mississippi or South Carolina, Brundage finds that lynching for minor offenses ended prior to 1910, but alleged sexual crimes grew in importance after 1910. Given that Georgia and South Carolina shared a common border, it is not surprising that the states experienced similar patterns of alleged causes of lynching, although Georgia had a smaller percentage of lynching for "minor offenses" than did South Carolina probably for the same reasons as Mississippi (see Brundage, *Lynching in the New South,* 51).

6. Brundage did not explore the relationship between lynching and legal execution in either Georgia or Virginia. He attributed the relatively benign lynching record of Virginia to its northern outlook and orientation, the modernizing influence of industrial development, and the relative lack of racial conflict that resulted from a diversified agricultural sector that was not heavily dependent upon long-term tenant labor (see Brundage, *Lynching in the New South,* 140–43).

7. This was the view of James Cutler, who argued that abolishing the death penalty would lead to an increase in lynching (see Cutler, *Lynch Law,* 626).

8. One might question a number of assumptions that inform the conclusions of Tolnay and Beck. The first would be whether or not counties, the boundaries of which changed frequently over time, are the most appropriate unit of analysis. More important, the model that Tolnay and Beck devise to test the relationship between execution and lynching apparently assumes that legal executions could only influence lynching and not vice versa (see Tolnay and Beck, *A Festival of Violence,* 104–8).

9. Tolnay and Beck, *A Festival of Violence,* 111; David Oshinsky, *"Worse Than Slavery": Parchman Farm and the Ordeal of Jim Crow Justice* (New York: Free Press, 1996), 209; Pfeifer, *Rough Justice,* 152.

10. The data on legal executions were derived from M. Watt Espy and John Ortiz Smykla, *Executions in the United States, 1608–1987: The ESPY File* (Ann Arbor, Mich.: Inter-University Consortium for Political and Social Research, 1987).

11. Information on national trends concerning lynching and the death penalty can be found in Adalberto Aguirre Jr. and David V. Baker, *Race, Racism and the Death Penalty in the United States* (Berrien Spring, Miss.: Vande Vere, 1991), chap. 4. Aguirre and Baker claim that the number of legal executions first surpassed the number of lynchings in 1921 and that this shift was essentially a "transfer" of authority from the community to the state.

12. Oshinsky, *"Worse Than Slavery,"* 4, 124–25.

13. Ibid., 124–28.

14. Eighty percent of the people executed in Mississippi were black; in South Carolina, the figure was 85 percent. On conviction rates in South Carolina, see J. Clay Smith Jr., *Emancipation: The Making of the Black Lawyer, 1844–1944* (Philadelphia: University of Pennsylvania Press, 1993), 223.

15. In South Carolina, about 16.4 percent of lynching incidents resulted in arrests; the same figure for Mississippi was 5.4 percent. John Hammond Moore claims that mob members from South Carolina exposed themselves to the tangible risk of legal prosecution and that this "overlooked" fact had a discernible negative effect on lynching activity in the state (see Moore, *Carnival of Blood,* 81).

16. Smith, *Emancipation,* 297–98; Irvin C. Mollison, "Negro Lawyers in Mississippi," *Journal of Negro History* 15 (1930): 59. Neil McMillen notes the "lily-white" nature of the Mississippi Bar and argues that a black attorney before a white jury did "more harm than good" for a black defendant (see McMillen, *Dark Journey,* 214–15). The long-standing hostility toward black attorneys was a precipitating cause of the 1959 lynching of alleged rapist Mack Charles Parker, whose counsel was R. Jess Brown, an African American attorney who also filed the first federal lawsuit in regard to voting rights in Mississippi (see Dray, *At the Hands of Parties Unknown,* 435–36).

17. Smith, *Emancipation,* 224.

18. This incident is discussed in detail in chapter 4.

19. Peter A. Coclanis and Lacy K. Ford, "The South Carolina Economy Reconstructed and Reconsidered: Structure, Output, and Performance, 1670–1985," in *Developing Dixie: Modernization in a Traditional Society,* ed. Winfred B. Moore Jr., Joseph F. Tripp, and Lyon G. Tyler Jr. (New York: Greenwood Press, 1988), 102.

20. David L. Carlton, "Unbalanced Growth and Industrialization: The Case of South Carolina," in *Developing Dixie,* ed. Moore and Tripp, 115–16.

21. See the definitive study of this region by Orville Vernon Burton, *In My*

Father's House Are Many Mansions: Family and Community in Edgefield, South Carolina (Chapel Hill: University of North Carolina Press, 1985).

22. *Charleston News and Courier,* 20 April 1904.

23. See, for example, *Charleston News and Courier,* 4, 12 June 1882; and 2 April 1884.

24. *Charleston News and Courier,* 6 April 1887.

25. On Goode's role in the militia, see Federal Writers' Project Collection, South Caroliniana Library, University of South Carolina, B-1-16, "Chester County History: The K.K.K. at Mt. Pleasant."

26. Unknown female teacher (Bissie) to W. L. McKeown, 15 April 1887, uncatalogued, South Caroliniana Library, University of South Carolina.

27. *Tuskegee Files,* roll 222, frame 730.

28. "The K.K.K. at Mt. Pleasant," 3.

29. Brown, *Strain of Violence,* 67–90; George C. Rable, *But There Was No Peace: The Role of Violence in the Politics of Reconstruction* (Athens: University of Georgia Press, 1984), 165–72.

30. H. Leon Prather Sr., "The Origins of the Phoenix Racial Massacre of 1898," in *Developing Dixie,* ed. Moore and Tripp, 65–66.

31. Ibid., 60–61. The massacre is discussed in further detail in chapter 3.

32. Ibid., 68.

33. Pfeifer identifies similar patterns in Louisiana (see Pfeifer, *Rough Justice,* 141–42).

34. Brundage, *Lynching in the New South,* 138.

35. Coclanis and Ford, "The South Carolina Economy," 101–2.

36. See *Charleston News and Courier,* 24 July 1901; and Jack Simpson Mullins, "Lynching in South Carolina, 1900–1914" (master's thesis, University of South Carolina, 1961), 133.

37. *Charleston News and Courier,* 6, 8 June 1902; Mullins, "Lynching in South Carolina," 101.

38. *Washington Bee,* 19 July 1902.

39. Louis Harlan and Raymond Smock, eds., *Booker T. Washington Papers,* vol. 6, *1901–1902* (Urbana: University of Illinois Press, 1977), 414–15.

40. The Gaston lynching is discussed at length below.

41. *Charleston News and Courier,* 29 June 1902. Details concerning the infamous lynching at Gaston, which African Americans accused Koester of being involved in, can be found in *Charleston News and Courier,* 27–31 July 1893; and 1–3 August 1893.

42. Harland and Smock, *Booker T. Washington Papers,* 6: 289.

43. For details concerning the antilynching conference, see *Charleston News*

and Courier, 26, 27 August 1903; and Mullins, "Lynchings in South Carolina," 105–6.

44. Murray, incidentally, had been Koester's choice as deputy collector of internal revenue (see Harland and Smock, *Booker T. Washington Papers,* 6: 310–11).

45. Tillman, not coincidentally, was deeply fearful about the educational prospects of African Americans and considered the advocacy of compulsory education for blacks to be "criminal" (see Kantrowitz, *Ben Tillman,* 219–20).

46. See *Charleston News and Courier,* 29–30 November 1903; and 16, 17, 20, 21 January 1904.

47. Ibid., 3 March 1904; Mullins, "Lynching in South Carolina," 49–50.

48. The details concerning the Bookard lynching can be found in *Charleston News and Courier,* 18, 21, 22, 23, 25 July 1904; 5, 8 August 1904; 20 October 1904; 3, 9 December 1904; 10, 11 May 1905; and Mullins, "Lynching in South Carolina," 24–33.

49. *Charleston News and Courier,* 5, 8 August 1904.

50. For details of the Spain lynching and its aftermath, see *Charleston News and Courier,* 24, 25, 26, 31 August 1906; 5, 12 September 1906; 18, 21 October 1906; see also Mullins, "Lynching in South Carolina," 55–57.

51. Limehouse's conduct met with some scorn even among whites. Local ruffians apparently took delight in chiding Limehouse for his cowardice. One Thomas Harley, for instance, who had been tried and convicted in absentia for assault because Limehouse had refused to arrest him, informed the *Dorchester (S.C.) Eagle* that he would have surrendered but was afraid "that I would have been lynched by a mob as others have been while in the custody of Limehouse" (see Mullins, "Lynching in South Carolina," 55–57).

52. *Charleston News and Courier,* 25, 30 October 1906; 22 November 1906.

53. WPA, *South Carolina: A Guide to the Palmetto State* (New York: Oxford, 1941), 320.

54. *Charleston News and Courier,* 25, 26 October 1921; *Columbia Record,* 26 June 1924; *Atlanta Constitution,* 25 October 1921.

55. The seventeen executions include persons executed for crimes in Richland County but not persons tried in other counties and executed at the state prison in Columbia.

56. The summary of these lynching incidents is derived from *Charleston News and Courier,* 27, 28, 29, 30, 31 July 1893; 1, 2 August 1893.

57. Ibid., 1 August 1893.

58. Ibid., 5 August 1893; Francis Butler Simkins, *The Tillman Movement in South Carolina* (Durham: Duke University Press, 1926), 179–80.

59. *Charleston News and Courier,* 3 October 1893.

60. Ibid., 29 June 1902; Mullins, "Lynching in South Carolina," 101–2.

61. See, for example, the discussion of the Frazier Baker lynching in chapter 3.

62. Eldred E. Prince Jr., *Long Green: The Rise and Fall of Tobacco in South Carolina* (Athens: University of Georgia Press, 2000), 51–63.

63. Pfeifer, *Rough Justice*, 123.

64. Bryant Simon attributes the proclivity toward lynching in this region to the deteriorating economic prospects of "plain folks" that provided "a new sense of urgency [to] the privileges of whiteness and the virtues of patriarchy" (see Simon, *A Fabric of Defeat*, 22).

3. "No Rights for the Negro Which a White Man Is Bound to Respect"

1. Philip S. Foner, *The Life and Writings of Frederick Douglass* (New York: International, 1955), 491–524; see also Herbert Shapiro, *White Violence and Black Response: From Reconstruction to Montgomery* (Amherst: University of Massachusetts Press, 1988), 37–38.

2. D. Augustus Straker, *Negro Suffrage in the South* (Detroit: self-published, 1906), 35. Straker was an immigrant from Barbados who came to Charleston in 1875 and was dean at Allen University from 1882 to 1887. He went on to have a distinguished career in Detroit (see J. R. Oldfield, "A High and Honorable Calling: Black Lawyers in South Carolina, 1868–1915," *Journal of American Studies* 23, no. 3 [December 1989]: 396, 398). On Straker's accomplishments in South Carolina, see George Brown Tindall, *South Carolina Negroes, 1877–1900* (Columbia: University of South Carolina Press, 1952), 43, 48, 145–47, 232; see also Smith, *Emancipation*, 218.

3. Quoted in Wright, *Racial Violence in Kentucky*, 67. For a similar interpretation, see Oliver C. Cox, *Caste, Class and Race* (New York: Modern Reader Press, 1970), 559–60. In 1887, Robert Charles O'Hara Benjamin was the first black admitted to the bar in California, and he reportedly had practiced law in twelve other states, including Virginia and Alabama. In San Francisco, Benjamin was editor of the *Sentinel*, a black paper that advocated "political conciliation" with whites (see Smith, *Emancipation*, 232, 272, 485, 522 n. 15).

4. Cox, *Caste, Class and Race*, 555. See, for example, Frederick D. Wright, "The History of Black Political Participation to 1965," and David C. Colby, "White Violence and the Civil Rights Movement," both in *Blacks in Southern Politics*, ed. Laurence W. Moreland, Robert P. Steed, and Tod A. Baker (New York: Praeger, 1987), 9–30 and 31–48, respectively.

5. Wiegman, *American Anatomies*, 83, 90–91, 96, 102.

6. Henderson M. Somerville, "Some Cooperating Causes of Negro Lynching," *North American Review* (October 1903): 509–10. Somerville was a Democrat who served on the Alabama State Supreme Court from 1880 to 1890. In 1873, he

founded the law school at the University of Alabama (see *National Cyclopedia of American Biography* [New York: James T. White, 1922], 18: 220).

7. Quoted in John L. Love, "The Disfranchisement of the Negro," in The American Negro Academy, *Occasional Papers No. 6* (Washington, D.C.: American Negro Academy, 1899), 23.

8. George Wright has written about the debilitating effect of lynching on black political activity in Reconstruction Kentucky (see Wright, *Racial Violence in Kentucky,* 48–52).

9. See the comments of the Charleston minister G. C. Rowe in *Charleston News and Courier,* 26 November 1903.

10. For an able summary of the power-threat hypothesis and the problems associated with it, see Tolnay and Beck, *Festival of Violence,* chap. 3. Tolnay and Beck conclude that a "political threat model of black lynchings" could not be accepted or rejected (ibid., 69).

11. *Saluda (S.C.) Advocate,* 2 November 1898.

12. Ignoring this possibility, Tolnay and Beck assert that disfranchisement did not have an "appreciable effect on black lynchings in the South as a whole" because there was not "a marked decline in lynching after the widespread disfranchisement of African-Americans." However, during the 1880s, Tolnay and Beck find, Republican Party strength had "a strong negative effect on black lynchings" (see Tolnay and Beck, *Festival of Violence,* 186, 193–94).

13. Part of the argument advanced in this study is that the relationship between lynching and political power must be considered from a regional perspective. To replicate this analysis for the other southern states, one would have to construct sociopolitical regions for each state and then analyze a given state's lynching record in accord with those regions.

14. Because complete records of black voter registration during the period do not exist, the election of blacks to the state legislature was used as a substitute measure for black political participation. The record of African American service in the state legislatures of Mississippi and South Carolina during the post-Reconstruction period can be found in Mrs. Charles C. Mosely, *The Negro in Mississippi History* (Jackson, Miss.: Hederman Bros., 1969), 65–69; and Tindall, *South Carolina Negroes,* appendix.

15. From 1881 to 1890, Republican regions in Mississippi had approximately 61.5 percent of the state's black population and 64.1 percent of black lynching incidents. From 1891 to 1900, the same regions had approximately 63 percent of the black population but only 49 percent of black lynching incidents. From 1881 to 1895 in South Carolina, Republican regions comprised about 43.5 percent of the state's black population but had only 26.8 percent of black lynching incidents. From 1896 to 1910, the Republican regions had about the same percentage of the

black population, but black lynching incidents increased to 34.3 percent of the state's total.

16. John Ray Skates, *Mississippi: A Bicentennial History* (New York: Norton, 1979), 122.

17. William J. Cooper Jr., *The Conservative Regime: South Carolina, 1877–1890*, 2nd ed. (Baton Rouge: Louisiana State University Press, 1991), 105–15.

18. In one instance, a black mob lynched a white convict guard, which was a particularly unsettling precedent for Delta whites (see *New Orleans Daily-Picayune*, 29 April 1884). On black-on-black mob violence in the Mississippi Delta region, see also E. M. Beck and Stewart E. Tolnay, "When Race Didn't Matter: Black and White Mob Violence against Their Own Color," in *Under Sentence of Death*, ed. Brundage.

19. William F. Holmes, "The Leflore County Massacre and the Demise of the Colored Farmers' Alliance," *Phylon* 34 (September 1973): 273.

20. Ibid., 271.

21. Willis, *Forgotten Time*, 130.

22. *New Orleans Daily-Picayune*, 2 September 1889.

23. Holmes, "The Leflore County Massacre," 270–73.

24. *New Orleans Daily-Picayune*, 5, 6 September 1889.

25. Holmes, "The Leflore County Massacre," 274.

26. *New Orleans Daily-Picayune*, 8, 10 December 1890.

27. Willis, *Forgotten Time*, 136–37.

28. Brundage, *Lynching in the New South*, 132, 153.

29. Shapiro, *White Violence and Black Response*, 13, 21–22; W. McKee Evans, *Ballots and Fence Rails* (Chapel Hill: University of North Carolina Press, 1969), 101–2; Joel Williamson, *After Slavery* (Chapel Hill: University of North Carolina Press, 1965), 265–66; for a similar argument about coastal Georgia, see Brundage, *Lynching in the New South*, 133–35.

30. *Charleston News and Courier*, 6 November 1883.

31. Ibid., 29 December 1889; see also Tindall, *South Carolina Negroes*, 239–40.

32. Ibid., 29 December 1889.

33. Ibid., 31 December 1889.

34. Ibid., 3 January 1890; see also Tindall, *South Carolina Negroes*, 248–49.

35. *Charleston News and Courier*, 15, 19, 21, 22 April 1893.

36. Ibid., 11 July 1892, quoted in Tindall, *South Carolina Negroes*, 251–52. The Peterson lynching is also analyzed in Kantrowitz, *Ben Tillman*, 174–79.

37. *Charleston News and Courier*, 25–27 April 1893.

38. Ibid., 27 April 1893.

39. Ibid., 8 June 1894.

40. Ibid., 26–27 June 1895.

41. On the nature of the Jim Crow court system in Mississippi, see McMillen, *Dark Journey,* 201–4.

42. Information on the Willie Leaphart case can be found in Lexington County coroner inquisition book, 1890–1897, 22–44, SCDAH; and *Charleston News and Courier,* 6, 7, 8, 9, 10, 11, 14 May 1890; 14 June 1890. See also Tindall, *South Carolina Negroes,* 240–44.

43. Details on the Williams lynching can be found in *Charleston News and Courier,* 27 February 1904, 1, 2, 5 July 1904; and Mullins, "Lynching in South Carolina," 84–85.

44. General Records of the Department of Justice, record group 60 (hereafter referred to as DOJ), year file 17743-1898, box 1047a, folder 3, National Archives, College Park, Md.

45. J. Morgan Kousser, *The Shaping of Southern Politics: Suffrage Restriction and the Establishment of the One-Party South, 1880–1910* (New Haven: Yale University Press, 1974), 144.

46. *New Orleans Daily-Picayune,* 7 July 1894.

47. Ibid., 29 November 1895.

48. Ibid., 22 March 1897.

49. William F. Holmes, "Whitecapping in Mississippi: Agrarian Violence in the Populist Era," *Mid America* 55 (April 1973): 134.

50. U.S. Census, schedule of population, 1890 and 1900; information on land values was obtained from Thomas J. Pressly and William H. Scofield, eds., *Farm Real Estate Values in the United States by Counties, 1850–1959* (Seattle: University of Washington Press, 1965).

51. *New Orleans Daily-Picayune,* 6 May 1893.

52. See Philip Foner, "Black-Jewish Relations in the Opening Years of the Twentieth Century," *Phylon* 36 (Winter 1975): 369–70.

53. Ibid.

54. Holmes, "Whitecapping in Mississippi," 136.

55. *New Orleans Daily-Picayune,* 12 January 1893.

56. Ibid., 5, 6, 12 May 1894; 16 June 1894.

57. Holmes, "Whitecapping in Mississippi," 147–48. Holmes has also written on the reappearance of whitecappers (see William F. Holmes, "Whitecapping: Agrarian Violence in Mississippi, 1902–1906," *Journal of Southern History* 35 [May 1969]: 165–85).

58. On the organization of whitecappers, see *New Orleans Daily-Picayune,* 6 May 1893; and Holmes, "Whitecapping in Mississippi," 136–37.

59. Roger Ransom and Richard Sutch note that whites routinely targeted

black schools and teachers for violence in order to circumscribe the economic opportunities available to black laborers (see Ransom and Sutch, *One Kind of Freedom*, 27–31).

60. *New Orleans Daily-Picayune*, 3, 4, 5, 14, 16 July 1894.

61. A "no-crime" lynching occurred when whites killed a black person for no alleged crime or an affront against racial etiquette. Such incidents are distinct from "unknown" lynchings, in which the alleged cause could not be determined. Brundage notes that less than 10 percent of lynching incidents in Virginia were committed in response to minor or trivial infractions, but in Georgia it was around 25 percent. Brundage attributed such lynchings to the "impulsiveness" of some mobs, but did not explain why Georgia would have so many more impulsive mobs than Virginia (see Brundage, *Lynching in the New South*, 53–54).

62. *Charleston News and Courier*, 22, 23, 24, 25, 26, 27, 28 February 1898; 12 April 1899.

63. Ibid., 14 April 1899.

64. Ibid., 27 February 1898; 2 July 1898.

65. Tillman quote reported in the *Omaha (Neb.) Afro-American Sentinel*, 3 March 1898; Ellerbe quoted in the *Charleston News and Courier*, 24 February 1898; Elliot quoted in *Charleston News and Courier*, 23 February 1898.

66. *Charleston News and Courier*, 22 and 26 February 1898; *Louisville Courier Journal*, 23 February 1898.

67. Editorial reprinted in *New York Post*, 25 February 1898.

68. *New York Tribune*, 24, 25 February 1898.

69. *New York Post*, 26 February 1898.

70. *Chicago Tribune*, 24 February 1898; *New York Times*, 6 March 1898.

71. *Indianapolis (Ind.) Freeman*, 19, 26 March 1898.

72. *Omaha (Neb.) Afro-American Sentinel*, 5 March 1898.

73. *Washington Bee*, 26 February 1898.

74. *Springfield Illinois Record*, 26 February 1898; 26 March 1898.

75. *Salt Lake City (Utah) Broad-Ax*, 26 February 1898; 19 March 1898.

76. *Kansas City (Kans.) American Citizen*, 24 February 1898.

77. *Charleston News and Courier*, 5 March 1898.

78. Ibid., 8 March 1898.

79. Abial Lathrop to Attorney General, 24 April 1899, DOJ, year file 17743-1898, box 1047 A, file 3463198, folder 172.

80. Abial Lathrop to Attorney General, 18 April 1898, ibid.

81. Abial Lathrop to Attorney General, 25 June 1898, ibid.

82. *Charleston News and Courier*, 8 April 1899.

83. Abial Lathrop to Attorney General, 2 July 1898, DOJ, year file 17743-1898, box 1047 A, file 3463198, folder 172.

84. *Charleston News and Courier,* 11 April 1899; Lathrop to Attorney General, 24 April 1899, DOJ, year file 17743-1898, box 1047 A, file 3463198, folder 172.

85. *Charleston News and Courier,* 2 July 1898; 13 April 1899.

86. Ibid., 2 July 1898; 13 April 1899.

87. M. B. Springs to Department of Justice, 27 July 1899, DOJ, year file 17743-1898, box 1047 A, file 3463198, folder 222.

88. M. B. Springs to Department of Justice, 27 July 1899; Abial Lathrop to Attorney General, 5 August 1899, ibid.

89. *Charleston News and Courier,* 14 April 1899.

90. Ibid., 23 April 1899; 3 March 1900.

91. Abial Lathrop to Attorney General, 24 April 1899, DOJ, year file 17743-1898, box 1047 A, file 3463198, folder 172.

92. Ernest F. Cochran to Attorney General, 25 June 1908, DOJ, year file 17743-1898, box 1047 A, file 3463198, folder 222.

93. *Charleston News and Courier,* 24 April 1899.

94. *Indianapolis (Ind.) Freeman,* 8, 22 April 1899.

95. *St. Paul (Minn.) Appeal,* 15, 22 April 1899.

96. *Washington, D.C., Colored American,* 15 April 1899.

97. *Cleveland (Ohio) Gazette,* 15 April 1899.

98. *Washington, D.C., Colored American,* 27 May 1899.

99. Ibid., 15 April 1899; *St. Paul (Minn.) Appeal,* 27 May 1899.

100. *Cleveland (Ohio) Gazette,* 17 June 1899; *Indianapolis (Ind.) Freeman,* 3 June 1899.

101. *Charleston News and Courier,* 1 March 1898; *Parsons (Kans.) Weekly Blade,* 26 March 1898.

102. *Saluda (S.C.) Advocate,* 11 April 1900.

103. *Abbeville (S.C.) Scimitar,* 1 February 1917.

104. The account of the Phoenix massacre is drawn from H. Leon Prather Sr., "The Origins of the Phoenix Racial Massacre of 1898," in *Developing Dixie,* 62–93; Tindall, *South Carolina Negroes,* 256–58; and *Charleston News and Courier,* 9, 10, 11, 12, 13, 14, 15, 16, 17, 18, 22, 24, 26, 28 November 1898; 23, 25, 29 April 1899; 2 May 1899.

105. *Charleston News and Courier,* 28 November 1898.

106. Ibid., 11 November 1898.

107. Stephen Kantrowitz argues that Tillman never resolved the "conflicting imperatives" of forging a sense of white identity, which lynching promoted, with his desire to strengthen the authority of the state (see Kantrowitz, *Ben Tillman,* 180–81).

108. *Charleston News and Courier,* 14 November 1898.

109. McMillen, *Dark Journey,* 297.

110. Ibid., 43.

111. Quoted in Shapiro, *White Violence Black Response,* 121. Other African Americans shared the sentiments of Wells-Barnett. In December 1919, for example, Neval Thomas, a resident of Washington, D.C., wrote Attorney General A. Mitchell Palmer and complained that African Americans were "weary of lynching, jim crowism, peonage, disfranchisement, wholesale robbery of educational opportunity, exploitation of labor, the rape of the defenseless element of their womanhood by white vultures claiming culture and station and advocates of segregation, and the thousand other burning wrongs that they suffer daily." Given these outrages, Thomas wondered why Palmer did not "use your great office to stop lynching. . . . to use it to enforce the 14th and 15th amendments to the constitution, the fundamental law of the land, for which your department was created and still exists." Thomas warned Palmer that African Americans wanted "to get the freedom which we were told to die" for in World War I. "So, my dear sir, get ready for democracy," said Thomas. "We have fought for it, and now we are going to get it or the world will know the reason why" (see DOJ, numerical file 158260, box 1275, section 2, folder 1).

4. "The Equal of Some White Men and the Superior of Others"

1. *Abbeville (S.C.) Scimitar,* 1 February 1917.

2. The information on Anthony Crawford and his lynching is taken from many sources, the two most important being Roy Nash, "The Lynching of Anthony Crawford: South Carolina Declares an End to Mob Rule," *New York Independent,* 11 December 1916; and a series of investigative files from detective J. B. Eagan to Governor Richard Manning, Governor Richard I. Manning Papers, 1915–1919, box 15, miscellaneous—lynching, SCDAH. Other sources consulted include Lowry Ware, "A History of Abbeyville," manuscript; *NAACP Papers,* series a, reel 15, frames 360–404; *Tuskegee Files,* roll 221, frames 376–403; *Charleston News and Courier,* 10 December 1905; 13 September 1906; Page Garris, "The Decline of Lynching in South Carolina," 14–24; and George A. Devlin, *South Carolina and Black Migration, 1865–1940: In Search of the Promised Land* (New York: Garland, 1989), 171–88. The story of Crawford's lynching is also told in Loren Schweninger, *Black Property Owners in the South, 1790–1915* (Urbana: University of Illinois Press, 1990), 233–35.

3. Nash, "The Lynching of Anthony Crawford"; Ware, "A History of Abbeyville," 186.

4. W. C. Crawford to R. I. Manning, 25 November 1916, SCDAH.

5. Ware, "A History of Abbeyville," 184.

6. Eagan, Report of 11 November 1916, SCDAH.

7. Ware, "A History of Abbeyville," 185.

8. Nash, "The Lynching of Anthony Crawford"; Eagan, Report of 11 November 1916, SCDAH.

9. Nash, "The Lynching of Anthony Crawford."

10. *Charleston News and Courier,* 10 December 1905, 13 September 1906; Ware, "A History of Abbeyville," 185.

11. Eagan, Report of 19 November 1916, SCDAH.

12. Alexia Jones Helsley, "Harbison College: Metamorphosis of a Dream," *Proceedings of the South Carolina Historical Association* (1988): 14–26.

13. Eagan, Report of 20 November 1916, SCDAH.

14. *Charleston News and Courier,* 15 July 1915.

15. Eagan, Report of 11 November 1916, SCDAH; Nash, "The Lynching of Anthony Crawford."

16. Eagan, Report of 28 November 1916, SCDAH; Nash, "The Lynching of Anthony Crawford."

17. Eagan, Report of 11 November 1916, SCDAH.

18. Eagan, Report of 9 November 1916, SCDAH.

19. Eagan, Reports of 18, 23 November 1916; J. Howard Moore to R. I. Manning, 1 November 1916, SCDAH.

20. Nash, "The Lynching of Anthony Crawford"; *Columbia State,* 9 November 1916.

21. Eagan, Report of 23 November 1916, SCDAH.

22. Nash, "The Lynching of Anthony Crawford."

23. Ibid.

24. Eagan, Report of 11 November 1916, SCDAH.

25. Nash, "The Lynching of Anthony Crawford."

26. *Abbeville Medium,* no date, *Tuskegee Files,* roll 221, frame 835.

27. McMillen, *Dark Journey,* 236–37.

28. Edward Ayers asserts that lynchings were infrequent in places where blacks and whites lived in close proximity to one another but rampant in parts of the South where whites encountered "strange niggers" who had no roots in a community, were transient, and had little appreciation for the niceties of southern race relations (see Ayers, *The Promise of the New South,* 156–57).

29. For the majority of lynching victims, no information about their societal status is available. Consequently, these conclusions must be interpreted with caution. The societal status of about 38 percent of all lynching victims in Mississippi and South Carolina could be identified.

30. Brundage, *Lynching in the New South,* 81–82; Ayers, *Vengeance and Justice,* 236–43; Hickman, *Mississippi Harvest,* 139.

31. Loren Schweninger found that in 1890, for example, 21 percent of black farmers in South Carolina were landowners, while only 13 percent of black

farmers in Mississippi were the same (Schweninger, *Black Property Owners in the South,* 164).

32. Brundage, *Lynching in the New South,* 122.

33. *New Orleans Daily-Picayune,* 7–8 July 1903.

34. *Charleston News and Courier,* 27–29 December 1905; 3–5, 8 February 1906.

35. The sordid details surrounding the Howze-Clark lynching can be found in *NAACP Papers,* series a, reel 13, frames 1128–1163. The famed Walter White was the NAACP's primary investigator in the case.

36. Among the lynching incidents that grew out of strained landlord-tenant relations, at least forty-eight involved the murder or attempted murder of a landlord or overseer (or a relative of the same) by a tenant.

37. James Weldon Johnson, "The Practice of Lynching," *Century Magazine,* November 1927, 65–70; White, *Rope and Faggot,* chap. 5; William Pickens, *Lynching and Debt Slavery* (New York: American Civil Liberties Union, 1921); Shapiro, *White Violence and Black Response,* 198–99.

38. The information on labor requirements is taken from Warren C. Whatley, "Southern Agrarian Labor Contracts as Impediments to Cotton mechanization," *Journal of Economic History* 47 (March 1987): 68–69. The major-cotton producing regions included were the Black Prairie, Old Natchez, and Yazoo Delta regions from Mississippi and the three Piedmont regions (Eastern, Upper, and Western) along with the Inner Coastal Plain from South Carolina. For further information on these regions, see Terence Finnegan, "'At the Hands of Parties Unknown': Lynching in Mississippi and South Carolina, 1881–1940" (Ph.D. diss., University of Illinois, 1993), chap. 1.

39. The correlation was .35. If lynching incidents were not related to labor demand, then the correlation would have been 0; if, on the other hand, lynching incidents had varied exactly with labor demand, then the correlation would have been 1. The correlation was obtained by computing the Pearson's r between the average number of black lynching incidents (perpetrated by white mobs) per month with the average labor requirements per month to cultivate an acre of cotton.

40. Long ago James Elbert Cutler noted the relationship between fieldwork and lynching in his classic study *Lynch-Law.* Cutler hypothesized that the decline in lynching during August resulted from the black custom of attending religious-revivals during that month, while the increase in December was possibly related to the "indulgence in excesses" among African Americans celebrating Christmas (see Cutler, *Lynch-Law,* 165).

41. Willis claimed that lynching in the Delta occurred most often in the colder months, which is not accurate, and that black lynchings "corresponded to the rhythms of the crop cycle" (see Willis, *Forgotten Time,* 154). Tolnay and Beck

point out that in cotton-producing regions the need to lynch was less evident during the fall because tenants had a strong motivation to harvest the crop (see Tolnay and Beck, *A Festival of Violence,* 147–49).

42. Information on this lynching can be found in *NAACP Papers,* series a, reel 13, frames 1000–1001.

43. This was, of course, the same reason that whites had hanged slaves in the antebellum South. On slave hangings and honor-related violence among blacks, see Ayers, *Vengeance and Justice,* 136, 234. On blacks being lynched for rejecting the constraints of the white caste system, see Wright, *Racial Violence in Kentucky,* 10; and White, *Rope and Faggot,* 103–5.

44. Information on the Pullen lynching can be found in *Chicago Tribune,* 15, 17 December 1923; Nan Elizabeth Woodruff, *American Congo: The African American Freedom Struggle in the Delta* (Cambridge: Harvard University Press, 2003), 138–39; Mills, *This Little Light of Mine,* 11–12. Pullen's martyrdom, which was recounted in dozens of different versions throughout the years, apparently inspired many African American men in the Delta to routinely carry a firearm with them for personal protection (see Kim Lacy Rogers, *Life and Death in the Delta: African American Narratives of Violence, Resilience, and Social Change* [New York: Palgrave Macmillan, 2006], 34–36).

45. Ayers, *Vengeance and Justice,* 236–41. Ayers is correct in pointing out the social distance that existed between many whites and blacks. But this chasm was not as apparent among agricultural workers as it was in more segregated occupations. After whites lynched Dan Jenkins in Union, South Carolina, in 1930, for example, the *Greenville (S.C.) Enterprise* commented that most of those in the mob considered blacks their friends: "You take them [mob members] ordinarily—they live and work near colored people, sometimes on the same plantation, if farming, getting on all right. Why, they get along so well that when they want a chew of tobacco they will take out an old dirty-looking piece, bite or cut off a chunk, throw it into one side of their mouths and begin to chew and spit together, like blood kin" (*Greenville [S.C.] Enterprise,* 28 June 1930).

46. Ayers, *Vengeance and Justice,* 243; Brundage, *Lynching in the New South,* 114–15; Hickman, *Mississippi Harvest,* 148–50.

47. *Memphis Commercial-Appeal,* 19 June 1901; *New Orleans Daily-Picayune,* 19, 20 June 1901.

48. Accounts of Parker's life and lynching can be found in *New Orleans Daily-Picayune,* 28–29 December 1884.

49. Information on the lynching of Pink Willis can be found in *New Orleans Daily-Picayune,* 11–12 January 1909. Claude Singleton's lynching is described in *NAACP Papers,* series a, reel 13, frame 1059; and *Tuskegee Files,* roll 221, frame 643. An excellent account of the tragic lynching of Mack Charles Parker

can be found in Howard Smead, *Blood Justice: The Lynching of Mack Charles Parker* (New York: Oxford University Press, 1986); see also Patricia Older, "FBI Re-Opens Mack Charles Parker Lynching," *Picayune (Miss.) Item*, 9 May 2009.

50. *NAACP Papers*, series a, reel 13, frames 944–948.

51. Ibid., series a, reel 17, frame 612; *Charleston News and Courier*, 2–3 November 1932; Page-Garris, "The Decline of Lynching in South Carolina," 59–60.

52. Information on the strike and the lynching can be found in *New Orleans Daily-Picayune*, 18, 20, 22, 30 January 1912; 1, 16 February 1912; 1 March 1912; see also U.S. Congress, Senate, *Commission on Industrial Relations Report and Testimony*, 64th Cong, 1st sess., 1915–16, S.Doc. 28, 9714–9715.

53. See report of Walter White to Attorney General, 31 May 1921, DOJ, numerical file 158260, box 1230xh, sub 7.

54. Dowd Hall, *Revolt against Chivalry*, 133. On the late nineteenth-century crime wave, see Ayers, *Vengeance and Justice*, 169–84.

55. Unknown female teacher (Bissie) to W. L. McKeown, 15 April 1887, uncatalogued, South Caroliniana Library, University of South Carolina, Columbia.

56. In the early years of the twentieth century, the Piney Woods region of Mississippi experienced a similar outbreak in which five convicts (one was an ex-convict) were lynched in slightly less than forty months from October 1904 to December 1907. For details, see *New Orleans Daily-Picayune*, 9 October 1904; 5 August 1905; 22 October 1906; 16 December 1907.

57. *New Orleans Daily-Picayune*, 6 July 1892.

58. Wells-Barnett, *On Lynchings*, 24.

59. *New Orleans Daily-Picayune*, 5–6 October 1892.

60. The account of Patton's lynching is drawn from *New Orleans Daily-Picayune*, 9–10 September 1908; *New York Times*, 9–10 September 1908; and W. A. Roane to E. F. Noel, 13 September 1908, record group 27, vol. 209, folder 158, MDAH.

61. Lafayette County was, of course, William Faulkner's home. He undoubtedly knew of the Patton lynching, especially since a brother of one of his classmates participated in the mob. Faulkner's famous character Joe Christmas is at least partially based on Lawson Patton (see Jean Mullin Yonke, "William Faulkner as a Moralist and Cultural Critic: A Comparison of His Views with Those of Historians and Social Scientists" [Ph.D. diss., University of Kansas 1981], 194).

62. Despite the protestations of Reverend Spruggins, Amy Wood emphasizes the religious sensibilities that may have inspired some in the mob; she argues that evangelical fears of moral decay played a prominent role in the 1885 Oxford lynching of Harris Tunstal (see Wood, *Lynching and Spectacle*, 46–47).

63. *New York Times,* 10 September 1908.

64. Information on the Sheppard lynching can be found in *NAACP Papers,* series a, reel 13, frames 740–749; 1038–1039; see also Harris, *Deep Souths,* 290–91.

65. Quoted in Shapiro, *White Violence and Black Response,* 83.

66. *New Orleans Daily-Picayune,* 31 January 1886; 1 February 1886; Wells-Barnett, *On Lynchings,* 10–11.

67. Dollard, *Caste and Class in a Southern Town,* 289–90; Brundage, *Lynching in the New South,* 80–81.

68. *New York Times,* 18 April 1881.

69. *New Orleans Daily-Picayune,* 25 July 1894.

70. *NAACP Papers,* series a, reel 13, frames 371–401.

71. *Chicago Defender,* 18 December 1915.

72. *Charleston News and Courier,* 7 December 1895; 18 December 1895; 26 December 1895.

73. *Charleston News and Courier,* 9 January 1896.

74. Pfeiffer, *Rough Justice,* 3.

75. *Charleston News and Courier,* 9, 24 January 1896.

76. An account of the trial can be found in *Charleston News and Courier,* 18, 21–23, 25–27 February 1896.

77. *Charleston News and Courier,* 24 January 1896.

78. *New York Times,* 3 January 1927.

79. See chapter 1 for further details on white lynchings in this region.

80. Brundage found a similar pattern among white lynchings in Georgia and Virginia (see Brundage, *Lynching in the New South,* 87).

81. Details on the Culbreath lynching can be found in the *Edgefield (S.C.) Chronicle,* 16, 21, 23, 30 September 1885; 7, 14, 21, 28 October 1885; 11, 18, 25 November 1885; *Charleston News and Courier,* 23 September 1885; 10 August 1887. The census-related information is from Orville Vernon Burton, *Edgefield Database.* Brundage found a similar case of wife abuse that resulted in a lynching in Georgia (Brundage, *Lynching in the New South,* 88–89).

82. Interestingly, Jenny Culbreath subsequently married a distant cousin of William, Lewis Hammond, who eventually purchased the Culbreath farm.

83. On the relationship between honor and family integrity, see Wyatt-Brown, *Southern Honor,* 436–37. A Mississippi lynching that involved an upper-class white man who killed his son-in-law is described in *New Orleans Daily-Picayune,* 20 July 1898.

84. For the story of Knox's lynching, see *New Orleans Daily-Picayune,* 27–28 February 1901; 1–2, 7, 9–11, 15–17, 19, 24, 26 March 1901; 3, 23, 24 April 1901.

85. On Morrison's lynching, see *Charleston News and Courier,* 2–7, 10, 15, 20–21,

30 October 1904; 3–4 November 1904; 26–27, 29 April 1905; Mullins, "Lynching in South Carolina," 33–38. For a similar case in Virginia, see Brundage, *Lynching in the New South,* 90.

86. Brundage found a similar tendency to describe the mobs that lynched white men as more orderly than those that lynched blacks (Brundage, *Lynching in the New South,* 91–92).

87. McMillen, *Dark Journey,* 240; Brundage, *Lynching in the New South,* 101.

88. Brundage reached a similar conclusion in his chapter on white lynchings (see Brundage, *Lynching in the New South,* 92).

5. "An Example Must Be Made"

1. Cox, *Caste, Class, and Race,* 555; Williamson, *Crucible of Race,* 302; Hall, *Revolt Against Chivalry,* 141–42; Harris, *Exorcising Blackness,* 19–20.

2. Hall, *Revolt Against Chivalry,* 139.

3. *Charleston News and Courier,* 8 January 1897.

4. Governor E. F. Noel to Sheriff E. Carr, 14 September 1908, record group 27, vol. 309, folder 158, MDAH.

5. *Charleston News and Courier,* 19 September 1905.

6. Information on the Bob Davis lynching is found in *Charleston News and Courier,* 15, 16, 17, 18 August 1906; and Mullins, "Lynching in South Carolina," 38–47.

7. On the lynching of Jake Davis, see *Charleston News and Courier,* 22–23 August 1893.

8. For an extended discussion on the tensions between social justice and social caste, see McMillen, *Dark Journey,* 201–6.

9. *Memphis Daily Appeal,* 2 September 1884.

10. Tolnay and Beck argue that same-race lynchings were more likely to follow a "popular justice" model than were interracial lynchings (see Tolnay and Beck, *A Festival of Violence,* 98).

11. *New Orleans Daily-Picayune,* 17 July 1892.

12. Ibid., 22 March 1885.

13. Ibid., 11 March 1900.

14. *Memphis Commercial-Appeal,* 21 July 1894; *New Orleans Daily-Picayune,* 21 July 1894.

15. *Charleston News and Courier,* 16, 17, 18, 23 November 1898; 11 February 1899.

16. *New Orleans Daily-Picayune,* 4 July 1883.

17. Waldrep, *The Many Faces of Judge Lynch,* 101.

18. *Charleston News and Courier,* 3, 5, 6 January 1888; 10, 12 July 1888; 16 April 1889; 16 October 1904. For an excellent analysis of this lynching, see Bruce E. Baker, "Lynch Law Reversed: The Rape of Lula Sherman, the Lynching of

Manse Waldrop, and the Debate over Lynching in the 1880s," *American Nineteenth Century History* 6 (September 2005): 273–93.

19. Baker, "Lynch Law Reversed," 282.

20. Quoted ibid., 283.

21. *Charleston News and Courier,* 6 January 1888.

22. Baker, "Lynch Law Reversed," 283–84.

23. Hale, *Making Whiteness,* 201–3.

24. Brundage, who considers mob size a barometer of community sanction, also finds that larger mobs occurred less frequently after 1900 but were oddly more evident in Virginia in the 1910s and 1920s than in Georgia (Brundage, *Lynching in the New South,* 21, 37).

25. Details on this lynching are found in *New Orleans Daily-Picayune,* 3, 4, 5, 6, 7, 8, 9, 10, 11, 14 June 1900; and *New York Times,* 11 June 1900.

26. *New Orleans Daily-Picayune,* 6, 9, 10 November 1903; McMillen, *Dark Journey,* 242.

27. Steven Hahn, *A Nation under Our Feet: Black Political Struggles in the Rural South from Slavery to the Great Migration* (Cambridge: Harvard University Press, 2003), 428.

28. In 1883, for example, a mob of one thousand blacks succeeded in having a white store clerk charged with murder for the death of an "insolent" and drunken black man whom the clerk had killed in an argument (see *Charleston News and Courier,* 6 November 1883). For an analysis of the remarkable mobilization of lowcountry rice workers during Reconstruction, see Brian Kelly, "Black Laborers, the Republican Party, and the Crisis of Reconstruction in Lowcountry South Carolina," *International Review of Social History* 51 (2006): 375–414.

29. *Charleston News and Courier,* 24 July 1901; Mullins, "Lynching in South Carolina," 133.

30. The Spain lynching and its aftermath are discussed in chapter 2.

31. Most of the information in this section comes from a series of investigative reports on whitecapping in Lincoln County written by the Pinkerton detective A. J. Hoyt and sent to Governor James Vardaman (see MDAH, record group 27, vol. 286, folders 2, 3, 4, 6, 7). Information in record group 27, vol. 287, folder 34 indicates that the State of Mississippi spent about $2,500 on investigations of whitecappers from 1904 to 1907.

32. Details concerning whitecapping in Lincoln County and the lynchings of List and Hilson can be found in *New Orleans Daily-Picayune,* 23 May 1904; 11 September 1904; 23, 28 November 1904; 7, 9, 12, 13, 14, 15, 16, 17, 20, 21, 23, 25 December 1904; and 8 March 1905.

33. *Memphis Commercial Appeal,* 22 December 1903.

34. J. C. Stribling, postmaster and merchant; Samuel Hustan, justice of peace;

T. H. Hays, merchant; James Ray, farmer; and G. W. Silkes, farmer, to James K. Vardaman, 17 August 1907, record group 27, vol. 288, folder 62, MDAH.

35. Report of A. J. Hoyt, 12 April 1904, record group 27, vol. 286, folder 3, MDAH.

36. Pfeiffer, *Rough Justice,* 139.

37. *New Orleans Daily-Picayune,* 23 May 1904.

38. McMillen, *Dark Journey,* 121.

39. In Georgia, Brundage claims, mass mobs were most common in the cotton-belt region (Brundage, *Lynching in the New South,* 111).

40. "Rosedale, Bolivar County, Mississippi," 7–8, subject file lynching 1930–33, box 88, George Fort Milton Papers, Manuscripts Division, Library of Congress, Washington, D.C.

41. "Rosedale, Bolivar County, Mississippi," 17.

42. *New Orleans Daily-Picayune,* 9, 10 June 1907.

43. Ibid., 28 April 1884.

44. See chapter 4.

45. *Charleston News and Courier,* 24 January 1896.

46. The Holbert lynching is discussed in chapter 1.

47. *New York Times,* 25 February 1914,

48. *New Orleans Daily-Picayune,* 1 January 1886.

49. This incident is also discussed in chapter 3.

50. *Charleston News and Courier,* 29 December 1889.

51. Ibid., 30 December 1889.

52. The social status of alleged crime victims could be determined in about 46 percent of the 743 lynching incidents that occurred in the two states. Most female and child victims were assigned the status of their spouse or parent(s).

53. U.S. Bureau of the Census, *Historical Statistics of the United States, Colonial Times to 1970, Bicentennial Edition, Part 1* (Washington D.C.: U.S. Government Printing Office, 1975), 30, 34, 95.

54. Walter White to Herbert Swope, executive director of the *New York World,* 26 October 1926, *NAACP Papers,* series a, reel 16, frames 508–509; NAACP press release, 29 October 1926, *NAACP Papers,* series a, reel 16, frame 516. The account of the Lowman lynching is drawn primarily from the investigative files of Walter White, which can be found in *NAACP Papers,* series a, reel 16, frames 440–742; another important source was a series of investigative articles by Oliver H. P. Garrett that originally appeared in the *New York World* from 4 November 1926 to 18 November 1926 and can be found in *NAACP Papers,* series a, reel 16, frames 763–828.

55. James Quinby, Graniteville, South Carolina, to Walter White, 22 November 1926, *NAACP Papers,* series a, reel 16, frames 690–693.

56. Stansfield was elected to the South Carolina legislature in 1926 and later opposed a house resolution condemning the lynching (see *Charleston News and Courier,* 2 February 1927).

57. Statement of N. J. Frederick, Columbia, South Carolina, *NAACP Papers,* series a, reel 16, frame 462.

58. On Frederick's legal expenses, see *NAACP Papers,* series a, reel 16, frame 592; the comments of the Bleasite lumberman can be found ibid., frames 799–801; the observations concerning Southard came from *Augusta Chronicle* correspondent James Edwin Kerr, ibid., frames 627–628.

59. Statement of N. J. Frederick, *NAACP Papers,* series a, reel 16, frame 462.

60. *Columbia State,* 10 November 1926.

61. See affidavits of Lucy Mooney and Charles Lee, 2 November 1926, *NAACP Papers,* series a, reel 16, frames 440–442.

62. Information on the lynching itself can be found in Walter White to Herbert Swope, 26 October 1926, *NAACP Papers,* series a, reel 16, frames 508–509; James Quinby to Walter White, 24 November 1926, ibid., frames 739–741; and the series of articles by Oliver Garrett in the *New York World.*

63. *NAACP Papers,* series a, reel 16, frames 483, 789–790; *Columbia Record,* 28 November 1926, ibid., frames 1014–1015.

64. *NAACP Papers,* series a, reel 16, frames 991, 1013, 1079.

65. *New York Age,* 16 October 1926, *NAACP Papers,* series a, reel 16, frame 662; *New York World,* ibid., frames 779–780; James Quinby to Walter White, 1 December 1926, ibid., frames 729–732; *Columbia State,* no date, ibid., frame 1017.

66. Details on this lynching are found in *Tuskegee Files,* roll 227, frame 636; roll 228, frame 713.

67. *Charleston News and Courier,* 18, 24, 25, 28 November 1933; *NAACP Papers,* series a, reel 17, frames 554–556, 578; Association of Southern Women for the Prevention of Lynching, *Association of Southern Women for the Prevention of Lynching Papers, 1930–1942,* ed. Mitchell F. Ducey, microform (Ann Arbor, Mich.: University Microfilms International, 1983) (hereafter referred to as *ASWPL Papers*), reel 2, frame 1720.

68. *New Orleans Daily-Picayune,* 3, 4, 5 June 1903; *New York Times,* 5 June 1903.

69. Diary entry for June 5, 1903, pp. 83–84, Henry Waring Ball Diaries, series 1, box 1, folder 5, no. Z 1841.00 S, MDAH.

70. Quoted in Calvin C. Hernton, *Sex and Racism in America* (New York: Grove Press, 1965), 111.

71. Mobs of more than one hundred persons accounted for about 35 percent of all mobs in Mississippi and South Carolina, but large mobs performed more than 46 percent of all known cases of mutilation. An accusation of rape, attempted rape, or other crimes involving women occurred in about one-third of all lynch-

ing incidents and one-third of the mutilations were associated with this category of crime.

72. Helen Dick Davis, *Trials of the Earth: The Autobiography of Mary Hamilton* (Jackson: University of Mississippi Press, 1992), 98–99.

73. In the aftermath of the grisly 1919 lynching of Lloyd Clay, for instance, who was wrongfully accused of assaulting a young white woman, influential whites from Vicksburg denounced the lynching, saying it had "cast an ineffaceable black shadow upon the fair name of our city." Although nearly 10 percent of the adult white male population signed a petition condemning the lynching, no one was indicted for the crime, and the signatures of blue-collar whites were notably absent from the petition (see Harris, *Deep Souths,* 265–68).

74. The most useful source of information on the Green lynching is the investigative report of R. B. Eleazar that Arthur Raper used for his book *The Tragedy of Lynching;* the report is found in series 3, folder 750 of the Howard H. Odum Papers, Southern Historical Collection, University of North Carolina, Chapel Hill; for other useful information, see part II, 14(4): 823–25, Arthur Raper Papers, Southern Historical Collection, University of North Carolina, Chapel Hill. Additional information is found in *NAACP Papers,* series a, reel 17, frames 305, 644–653, 665; *Tuskegee Files,* reel 226, frames 142, 426–431.

75. Bryant Simon has ably identified the class and sexual tensions that informed lynching in this region (see Bryant, *A Fabric of Defeat,* 32–34).

76. Quoted in "Union, Union County, South Carolina," series 3, folder 751, page 23, Howard W. Odum Papers, Southern Historical Collection, University of North Carolina, Chapel Hill.

77. *Greenville (S.C.) Enterprise,* 28 June 1930.

78. The election results are from Frank E. Jordan Jr., *The Primary State: A History of the Democratic Party in South Carolina, 1896–1962* (Columbia: State Democratic Party of South Carolina, 1968), 71–72.

79. On the 1930 election, see Robert Everett, "Race Relations in South Carolina, 1900–1932" (Ph.D diss., University of Georgia, 1969), 212–16. Bryant Simon claimed that Blease lost because many whites were more concerned about their material well-being and "fulfillment through consumption" than "the privileges of whiteness and masculinity" (see Simon, *A Fabric of Defeat,* 44).

80. *Charleston News and Courier,* 20 October 1904.

81. The antilynching efforts of the NAACP are chronicled in Robert Zangrando, *The NAACP Crusade Against Lynching, 1909–1950* (Philadelphia: Temple University Press, 1980). Zangrando notes that the NAACP secured House passage of an antilynching bill on three occasions in 1922, 1937, and 1940.

82. Quoted in NAACP, *25th Annual Report for 1934* (New York: NAACP, 1935), 25.

83. This theme is also found in Wright, *Racial Violence in Kentucky.*

84. *New Orleans Daily-Picayune,* 26 July 1892.

85. Ibid., 4 December 1894.

86. Ibid., 6 November 1906.

87. *Charleston News and Courier,* 2, 3, 5, 6 July 1903; Orangeburg county coroner's inquisition book 6, 412–14, SCDAH.

88. Mullins, "Lynching in South Carolina," 93–95.

89. *Charleston News and Courier,* 22, 23 December 1912; *Atlanta Constitution,* 22 December 1912.

90. *Charleston News and Courier,* 26 August 1903. The same conference is also discussed in chapter 1.

91. *Abbeville (S.C.) Scimitar,* 1 February 1917, *NAACP Papers,* series a, reel 16, frames 399–404.

92. Michal Belknap, *Federal Law and Southern Order: Racial Violence and Constitutional Conflict in the Post-Brown South* (Athens: University of Georgia Press, 1987), 8.

93. Under the provisions of the 1895 South Carolina constitution, the survivors of lynching victims sued South Carolina counties no fewer than nine times for monetary compensation for a lynching. The first recorded suit involved the lynching of Elbert Harris in 1898. George Brown Tindall claims that African American delegates "forcefully and repeatedly" reminded their white counterparts of the need for an antilynching provision in the new constitution (see Tindall, *South Carolina Negroes,* 253).

94. *Charleston News and Courier,* 29 June 1902. This incident is also discussed in chapter 1.

95. Stewart E. Tolnay and E. M. Beck, "Racial Violence and Black Migration in the American South, 1910 to 1930," *American Sociological Review* 57 (February 1992): 103–16. See also Tolnay and Beck, *A Festival of Violence,* 230.

96. *NAACP Papers,* series a, reel 14, frame 337; *Tuskegee Files.*

97. *Charleston News and Courier,* 21 June 1921.

98. White, *Rope and Faggot,* 112.

99. Shay, *Judge Lynch,* 86.

100. Wells-Barnett, *On Lynchings,* 43.

Conclusion

1. Harrison's involvement in the New Deal is chronicled in Martha Swain, *Pat Harrison: the New Deal Years* (Jackson: University Press of Mississippi, 1978).

2. Ibid., 203–5.

3. *Congressional Record,* 75th Cong., 3rd sess., 253–57 (10 January 1938).

4. Thurgood Marshall, assistant special counsel for the NAACP, to U.S. attor-

ney general Frank Murphy, 15 April 1939, DOJ, numerical file 158260, box 1230xg, section 45.

5. Ibid.; *St. Louis Argus,* 16 December 1938.

6. George Baldwin, Wiggins, Miss., to Joseph Gelders, chairman of the National Committee for Peoples Rights, Birmingham, Ala., 21 November 1938, DOJ, numerical file 158260, box 1230xg, section 45.

7. Marshall to Murphy, 15 April 1939.

8. Ginzburg, *One Hundred Years of Lynching,* 234.

9. Victoria Bynum has shown that as early as the late 1860s, whites from the Piney Woods, Harrison's home region, were engaging in a "rhetoric of rape" intended to discredit Unionists and interracial political coalitions (Bynum, *The Free State of Jones,* 150–51).

10. Swain, *Pat Harrison,* 241–46.

11. *Washington Post,* 30 December 1973.

12. *Los Angeles Times,* 18 November 1977; Mills, *This Little Light of Mine,* 32.

13. Woodruff, *American Congo,* 5.

14. *New Orleans Daily-Picayune,* 2 September 1901.

INDEX

THE AMERICAN SOUTH SERIES

Anne Goodwyn Jones and Susan V. Donaldson, editors
Haunted Bodies: Gender and Southern Texts

M. M. Manring
Slave in a Box: The Strange Career of Aunt Jemima

Stephen Cushman
Bloody Promenade: Reflections on a Civil War Battle

John C. Willis
Forgotten Time: The Yazoo-Mississippi Delta after the Civil War

Charlene M. Boyer Lewis
Ladies and Gentlemen on Display: Planter Society at the Virginia Springs, 1790–1860

Christopher Metress, editor
The Lynching of Emmett Till: A Documentary Narrative

Dianne Swann-Wright
A Way out of No Way: Claiming Family and Freedom in the New South

James David Miller
South by Southwest: Planter Emigration and Identity in the Slave South

Richard F. Hamm
Murder, Honor, and Law: Four Virginia Homicides from Reconstruction to the Great Depression

Andrew H. Myers
Black, White, and Olive Drab: Racial Integration at Fort Jackson, South Carolina, and the Civil Rights Movement

Bruce E. Baker
What Reconstruction Meant: Historical Memory in the American South

Stephen A. West
From Yeoman to Redneck in the South Carolina Upcountry, 1850–1915

Randolph Ferguson Scully
Religion and the Making of Nat Turner's Virginia: Baptist Community and Conflict in the Old Dominion, 1740–1840

Deborah Beckel
Radical Reform: Interracial Politics in Post-Emancipation North Carolina

Terence Finnegan
A Deed So Accursed: Lynching in Mississippi and South Carolina, 1881–1940